"A wise, much needed book offered to Western Chr̲i̲s̲t̲.̲.̲.̲ for complex reasons, have become unable and/or unwilling to speak openly about the God of the gospel. Sara Wenger Shenk speaks clearly about the steps to take in order that the church may faithfully, honestly, and persuasively speak about the God in whom it trusts. She suggests, in lyrical cadence, that we must again be 'subject to the mystery' and then may speak 'from storied holy ground.' This book is a gentle and significant contribution to the recovery of nerve by the faithful church."

—WALTER BRUEGGEMANN, Columbia Theological Seminary

"*Tongue-Tied* is energetic, inspirited, inspiring, and passionate. Reading it opens possibilities for deeper, life-giving relationships with God, other persons, and creation. Sara Wenger Shenk is a reliable guide for everyday mystics and contemplative kindred spirits who seek to live with intention and talk with ease about the faith that grounds us."

—REBECCA SLOUGH, former dean at Anabaptist Mennonite Biblical Seminary

"In poetic and prophetic prose, Sara Wenger Shenk reawakens readers to the possibilities and power of authentically talking about faith. She reckons honestly with myriad challenges that keep believers tongue-tied. Weaving together the curated wisdom of theologians, public figures, and her diverse network of friends, Shenk evokes anew an imagination for articulating faith that wells up from the depths of soul, body, heart, and mind."

—SARAH ANN BIXLER, instructor in formation and practical theology at Eastern Mennonite Seminary

"Releasing our tongues for witness is not about accessing the latest, glitzy gospel brochure or adopting the slickest strategy for evangelizing our neighbors. Rather, it is about doing the hard work of facing the personal, social, and cultural obstacles that tied our tongues in the first place. Sara Wenger Shenk is a trustworthy guide leading us into the mess and—step by step—back out again."

—**JAMES R. KRABILL**, core adjunct faculty at Anabaptist Mennonite Biblical Seminary and general editor of Worship and Mission for the Global Church

"Sara Wenger Shenk's assessment of the reasons for the lack of 'faith talk' in many parts of the church brings fresh, new thinking to a pervasive problem, and resonates with my own observations. Her wise reflections, paired with her particular gift for making scenes, experiences, and feelings come alive, makes the book both a sage analysis and enjoyable to read."

—**JEWEL GINGERICH LONGENECKER**, dean of lifelong learning at Anabaptist Mennonite Biblical Seminary

"In this book, Sara Wenger Shenk urges Christians to let their love—of God, and of narratives of faith—be known. Wenger Shenk conducts a compelling analysis to explain why many contemporary Christians struggle to talk about their faith. It is significant that the author acknowledges Christianity's historical legacy of complicity with colonization and enslavement, discrimination and state-sponsored violence as part of being 'tongue-tied' about faith. The author does not offer easy platitudes, but convincingly asserts that faith stories—which are ultimately love stories—are worth talking about."

—**REGINA SHANDS STOLTZFUS**, professor of peace, justice & conflict studies at Goshen College

Tongue-Tied

Tongue-Tied

Learning the **LOST ART**
of Talking about Faith

SARA WENGER SHENK

HERALD
P R E S S

Harrisonburg, Virginia

Herald Press
PO Box 866, Harrisonburg, Virginia 22803
www.HeraldPress.com

Library of Congress Cataloging-in-Publication Data
Names: Shenk, Sara Wenger, 1953- author.
Title: Tongue-tied : learning the lost art of talking about faith / Sara
    Wenger Shenk.
Description: Harrisonburg, Virinia : Herald Press, 2021. | Includes
    bibliographical references.
Identifiers: LCCN 2020052706 (print) | LCCN 2020052707 (ebook) | ISBN
    9781513807782 (paperback) | ISBN 9781513807799 (hardcover) | ISBN
    9781513807805 (ebook)
Subjects: LCSH: Witness bearing (Christianity) | Conversation--Religious
    aspects--Christianity.
Classification: LCC BV4520 .S4525 2021 (print) | LCC BV4520 (ebook) | DDC
    248.5--dc23
LC record available at https://lccn.loc.gov/2020052706
LC ebook record available at https://lccn.loc.gov/2020052707

Study guides are available for many Herald Press titles at www.HeraldPress.com.

TONGUE-TIED
© 2021 by Herald Press, Harrisonburg, Virginia 22803. 800-245-7894.
    All rights reserved.
Library of Congress Control Number: 2020052706
International Standard Book Number: 978-1-5138-0778-2 (paperback); 978-1-5138-0779-9
(hardcover); 978-1-5138-0780-5 (ebook)
Printed in United States of America
Cover and interior design by Reuben Graham

Unless otherwise noted, Scripture text is quoted, with permission, from the *New Revised
Standard Version*, © 1989, Division of Christian Education of the National Council of
Churches of Christ in the United States of America.

Scripture quotations marked (NIV) are taken from the *Holy Bible, New International Version*®, NIV®. Copyright © 1973, 1978, 1984, 2011 by Biblica, Inc.™ Used by permission
of Zondervan. All rights reserved worldwide. www.zondervan.com. The "NIV" and "New
International Version" are trademarks registered in the United States Patent and Trademark
Office by Biblica, Inc.™

Scripture quotations marked (NLT) are taken from the *Holy Bible, New Living Translation*,
copyright © 1996, 2004, 2015 by Tyndale House Foundation. Used by permission of Tyndale
House Publishers, Inc., Carol Stream, Illinois 60188. All rights reserved.

Scripture quoted by permission. Quotations designated (NET) are from the *NET Bible*®
copyright © 1996, 2019 by Biblical Studies Press, L.L.C. All rights reserved. http://netbible.
com.

Scripture quotations marked (KJV) are taken from the *King James Version*.

25 24 23 22 21   10 9 8 7 6 5 4 3 2 1

To Gerald
whose lighthearted talk about faith
feels like the most natural thing in the world

Contents

Foreword

During the eleven years I served as the McCreless Professor of Evangelism at Perkins School of Theology, I rarely told strangers who asked what I did for a living that I was an evangelism professor. To do so would have been tantamount to saying something like "I have an active case of tuberculosis" while coughing. What I said instead was that I taught a form of theology that has to do with the practices of ministry, and with relating the Christian faith to a rapidly changing world. I knew from having been a pastor and having planted new churches that the word evangelism had been so hijacked by violence, exploitation, colonization, money-grubbing hucksters, and gimmickry that the word itself could not be used, either in practicing evangelism or in talking about evangelism. Like Lord Voldemort in the Harry Potter series, evangelism is That Which Must Not Be Named.

But it wasn't just people outside of the church who had experienced bad evangelism and were allergic to the word. Every semester when I started a new class on the theory and practice of evangelism, I invited students to write on index cards something they wanted to learn, and something they thought might be a challenge. Without fail, over half the cards had some version of "I am opposed to cramming religion down people's throats. I'm only taking this class because it's required for ordination."

Evangelism, in other words, ran with the wrong crowd, broke a whole lot of laws, lost all credibility, and now nobody wants anything to do with it. The tragedy of this entire sorry development is that real evangelism is at the heart of who Jesus is and what Jesus does. Evangelism is the initiation of persons into the reign of God, revealed in Jesus the Christ, empowered by the Holy Spirit, for the healing and transformation of the world. The point of Bible study, theology, and ministry of all kinds ought to be evangelistic at its core, to enable us to companion one another and our neighbors into a life of profound love and meaning, a life that truly matters.

That is why Sara Wenger Shenk's book, *Tongue-Tied*, is so timely for people who struggle to talk honestly about faith, for the church, and for those of us for those of us who equip others to be leaders in the church. While Shenk doesn't use the word *evangelism* in her book, she is being thoroughly evangelistic. In these pages we find winsome and practical guidance for how to think about, talk about, and practice sharing our faith with others. Shenk deftly points us to the way of compassion and humility, ways of living and speaking evangelistically that are true to the God who, as *The Message* puts it, "became flesh and blood and moved into the neighborhood" (John 1:14).

The jury is still out about whether we will be able to reha-
bilitate the word *evangelism*. But the practice is alive and well,
everywhere that people embody, speak, and act in the ways of
Jesus. This book is sure to become a dog-eared, trusted companion for God's people in the future who want to share their
faith within and beyond the church.

Elaine A. Heath, PhD
President of Neighborhood Seminary
www.elaineaheath.org
www.neighborhoodseminary.org

Introduction

For a lot of us, it's awkward to talk about God. Or whether we believe in God, and if so, what kind of God we believe in. Many of us who call ourselves Christian talk effortlessly about sports, movies, politics, fashion, cool gadgets, pop music, our jobs, and how we're feeling. But when it comes to describing our faith or whether we relate to God in our daily lives, we clam up. We rarely talk with each other about whether we pray or engage in spiritual practices. We're not very tuned in to how God may be active in our world and how we might watch for evidence of an animating force for good in our circles of connection.

I have worked for two and a half decades in theological schools, where we thrive on conversations about faith and where faith language is alive and well. I have lived among faith-oriented church folk for close to seven decades of my life, in Africa, Europe, and North America. Yet in many circles I relate to, faith talk rarely shows up unless we're at church.

And even at church, talk about faith seldom becomes personal. There are countless topics we eagerly talk about: the major league playoffs, how much we hate or love our jobs, political shenanigans, the latest kitchen design, amazing vegan recipes, the wildly erratic weather, late-night comedy, our workout regimen, and what Netflix show has us currently enthralled. So why are a lot of us, particularly educated professionals, reluctant to talk about our personal experience of God—even with other Christians? Or with our children? What is rendering us incapable, embarrassed, or hesitant to talk about God? What tangled threads are tying our tongues in knots? Is a heartfelt, intelligible language of faith in danger of going extinct?

There are numerous contributing factors to why we would rather go silent than give voice to our spiritual yearnings or our loss of whatever faith we might have once had. The factors vary along with our personal stories. But no doubt, we also share many in common. Some of us lack experiences of mystery or awe and rarely hear others describe their "God" encounters. Or we hear language in sermons, from acquaintances, in the news, or from TV preachers that sounds like pious nonsense and makes a mockery of any real experience of God. Or we've seen so little real faith and are ashamed of all the harm done in the name of religion, even in our own church. Or we recoil from biblical insider language used by some religious leaders to manipulate fear and separate out who is and who isn't "one of us." Or we're mute because we lack the modeling or community space that might free us to describe our spiritual wonderings about God honestly and vulnerably.

The existential dread of the end of the world as we know it constantly lurks on the edges of our awareness. Political, professional, church, environmental, and family crises often debilitate our daily ability to function. Hardly a day goes by when there isn't another headline-grabbing report about our "planet in peril" or a world-upending pandemic or the dysfunctionality of our government or some new threat of violence. Many of us are finding life harder and harder to manage. Countless persons are acutely lonely and longing for genuine connection with a just and loving God—and either not inclined to look for it in Christian churches or not finding it there when they do show up.

The disquieting irony is that at a time in our North American history when we seem least able or willing to talk about faith, it is massively urgent that we learn to do so. Whether it is because of embarrassment, apathy, busyness, disillusionment, or ignorance about faith, our loss of fluency is seriously undermining the moral fabric of our national discourse, disabling faith communities, exacerbating personal loneliness, and contributing to the breakdown of neighborhood networks. To make matters worse, many publicly visible Christians align themselves with governing powers who undermine a faith that reflects the true character of the Scriptures: compassion, justice, truth-telling, peacemaking, and the well-being of all creation.

In *Tongue-Tied: Learning the Lost Art of Talking about Faith*, I excavate layers of reasons why people who usually consider ourselves Christian have become less attentive to God's presence in our lives and find it hard to talk about faith. I offer a rallying cry for us to wake up to the devastation that our loss of attentiveness to God's activity and declining fluency in language about God has led us into, and examine why it is imperative that we learn to pay attention and speak again, or for the first time, in trustworthy and brave ways.

This book isn't about correct dogma-speak, or a rhetoric of right belief. Nor is it about a technique for recovering fluency in a prescribed Christianese. At its heart, it is about how we might learn to tell a love story and describe a vision that can magnetize our deepest human longings and desires in relation to God.[1] It is about how we might learn to talk about falling in love with something larger than ourselves; some *One* whose unfathomable largeness encompasses all that is good, true, and beautiful. Some *being* as vastly magnificent and infinitely infinitesimal as our blue green world. Some *ones* so multi-splendored, diversely gifted, and infuriatingly complicated as our fellow human beings. When one is swept up into a love story, it's hard to keep quiet. Love, more than any state of being, compels us to find words, brings us to stammering speech; even on occasion to poetic eloquence. When we're in love, we grow animated. We take risks and say foolish things in the hope that love will carry the day.

The language of faith is giving voice to a story of love. It's not just what one stutters in the initial flush of starstruck love—though that first embrace can become a "strangely warmed" touchstone to which we return. It's not a superficial lovey gloss of sentimentality we paint on when it's time to play church. It is instead a story of love that is born like a baby in vulnerability, dumbstruck by beauty, mellowed through suffering, outraged at the harm inflicted on fellow human beings; a love story that knows grief for our languishing rivers, trees, and birds, and is both in awe of and horrified by what humans have wrought throughout our history. It is a story of love whose powerful wings provide lift that can travel the distance because their feathers, muscles, and bones hold passion *together with* reason, intuition, and spirit in the embodied ways needed to fulfill the responsibilities of daily life. It's a story of love so enthralled by the beauty and terror of that-of-God in everyone and everything that it can't easily be reduced to pious "insider" language or formulaic Christianese. It's a story about a love that "is not glad about injustice, but rejoices in the truth." That "bears all things, believes all things, hopes all things, endures all things." A story of love that "never ends" (1 Corinthians 13:6-8a NET).

Learning to be alert to how God shows up in the world and to speak about what we see doesn't require us to spiritualize and sanitize our language. It is rather learning to talk honestly about what we desire, what we love, what we trust or don't trust, and the happy and hard stuff in a daily labor of love. When we are honestly vulnerable about what we grieve, what we long for, and what we're elated about, vital faith is awakened and we find ourselves in need of a language that will free us to speak truthfully, humbly, and sometimes with moral authority about a God who *so* loves the world that God became one-with-us—in Jesus Christ.

This book is in part addressed to my peers—moderately progressive and relatively comfortable North Americans—who grew up with faith language that we largely jettisoned upon becoming educated professionals. Many of us remained nominally Christian and even go to church. But we rarely talk vulnerably about heartfelt faith to each other or with our children or pray with genuine affection or watch for evidence of the Spirit at work in the world. It's not too late to change our ways. One of our greatest gifts to the next generations, including our children and grandchildren, will be learning to talk more freely about what we've discovered of God's ways in the world, how we've found ways to follow Jesus in daily life, and how we anchor our lives in the love of God amid all manner of disappointments, tragedies, and hard times.

I'm also writing for my peers in religiously conservative circles for whom faith language comes more easily. *Tongue-Tied* is an invitation to members of my own family, Mennonite church family, and larger so-called evangelical family, on how we might expand beyond tribal assumptions about who we are as church, the dogmatic certainties we bring to some bib-lical texts, and the criteria we use to decide who's right and who's wrong, who's in and who's out. We are all in danger of making God in our own image and can benefit from thinking about faith in more hospitable and humble ways.

Above all, I've written *Tongue-Tied* for a new generation of parents and community leaders. I invite everyone who longs to find ways to flourish as human beings, as parents, activists, professionals, and leaders to consider how a heart-felt, biblically enriched, and morally grounded faith is worth intentionally cultivating with their own children at home and in community with other people of faith on a journey of dis-covery about God's ways in the world.

In part 1 (chapters 1–6), I reflect on several of the many factors that tie us up in knots about faith—what faith is and why we find it so hard to talk freely and honestly about faith. I use repeated topical subheadings to examine the contours of this reluctance:

- Full of ourselves
- Out of tune
- Disappointed in love
- Pulling the world apart
- Silencing stories

In part 2 (chapters 7–17), I reflect on how we can learn freedom and honesty when talking about faith. I describe the qualities that will help us become fluent in these ways:

- First listen!
- Submit to mystery
- It's all about being in love

- Hold the world together
- Speak from storied, holy ground

What I offer are convictions that grow out of many years as a daughter, wife, mother, grandmother, sister, Mennonite church member, teacher, practical theologian, seminary president, and global citizen. I seek to emulate what renowned Old Testament theologian Walter Brueggemann calls "the counsel of the wise," or wisdom literature.[2] It is Woman Wisdom[3] personified in Jesus who, I believe, will free us to talk in everyday, down-to-earth ways about what we believe to be true. What we find trustworthy. What we love. It is the work of wisdom to show how God is most fully present when we allow daily experiences, our bodies, scientific discoveries, suffering neighbors, and the "fear of the Lord" to teach us.

It is the sages or wise ones who were "interested in words and proverbs for teaching proper, God-fearing ways of speaking to others," writes biblical scholar Glenn Pemberton. "It is wise to speak cautiously and truthfully and not to gossip, slander, insult, or belittle others," because, as we've learned at our own peril, and for "generation after generation, *words matter*. . . . And so does the thought behind the words."[4]

And along with the sages are the prophets. The prophets, Brueggemann has said, were able to imagine the world other than the way it was in front of them. What they believed deeply "is that God is a lively character, and a real agent who acts in the world, who causes endings and who causes new beginnings." This way of thinking about God is out of step with what many of us think is ordinary, Brueggemann says. "If you consider most conservative evangelicals, they do not believe that God is a lively character and a real agent, because they've got God all packaged up into sustained systematic explanations. And if you consider most theological progressives, they don't believe that God is a real character and a lively agent, either, because they really believe that God has no hands but our hands." What we are called to do, Brueggemann asserts, is "articulate the alternative world that God has promised, and that God is birthing before our very eyes. If we have eyes to see it."[5]

This is a frontline urgent task for followers of Jesus today—believing that God is "a lively character and a real agent." Learning from the wise ones and the prophets. Holding together the eye-popping discoveries of science with biblical wisdom. Learning to notice what it is we most love and how that opens us to what is holy, drops us to our knees, and awakens a faith that unleashes our tongues.

We can relearn or learn for the first time the winsome language of Christian faith so important for human flourishing in these grave times. As we open ourselves to the mystery of God-with-us, we will learn to recognize that-of-God in everybody, in everything, and everywhere. We will discover how to orient our faith toward the North Star of God's vision for the world, best described as shalom—a word that encompasses full-orbed wholeness, peace, fairness, tranquility, and interdependent harmony. And we will reach for words to give voice to Isaiah's stunning shalom vision: "They will not hurt or destroy on all my holy mountain; for the earth will be full of the knowledge of the Lord as the waters cover the sea (Isaiah 11:9).

PART 1

LOSING FLUENCY

Why Is It So Hard for Many of Us to Talk about Our Christian Faith?

A couple of years ago I noticed a story from the *New York Times* about an elderly man named Amadeo García García in Peru who is said to be "the last person on earth to speak his native language, Taushiro." Nicholas Casey reported in the *Times* that a combination of disease and exploitation has forced the Taushiro tribe in the Amazon to the verge of extinction.[1]

I can't imagine not having anyone else to talk to in the language I know best. Or the loss of the familiar family and community stories that make me who I am; that make us who we are—a community who shares many values, history, and assumptions about who God is and how God is active in the world. Linguists give widely varying answers about the number of languages spoken by peoples of our world, ranging from four thousand to seven thousand. But all linguists agree that the number of languages is declining rapidly, with at least twenty-five disappearing each year.[2]

In part 1 of this book, I describe my appraisal as a practical theologian and cultural observer about why many of us who call ourselves Christian or who grew up in Christian families are losing our ability to identify God's presence in our lives or to talk meaningfully about faith with others. And why children growing up in our homes aren't learning how to connect with God or the basic vocabulary necessary to name what we believe about God. The factors that have contributed are many and complex.

In part, much of our confusion revolves around what we mean by *faith*—which to begin with, means many different things to different people. Faith can be a triggering word, evoking painful memories about authoritarian leaders or sectarian communities that saw faith as a set of nonnegotiable, toe-the-line propositions. Talking about faith can feel like tiptoeing through a minefield so as not to set off explosive outbursts about what is right and wrong, who's in and who's out. Since *faith* is such a slippery word, it is often used as a cover for all kinds of harmful beliefs and practices. People who claim to have faith seem prone to gullibility—becoming easy prey for fabrications unhinged from facts. To suggest that faith may provide an important perspective in a university classroom discussion, for example, is often to be considered partisan, quaint, unenlightened, or given to "magical thinking."

Throughout this book, I won't be referring to *faith* as if it had one tidy, pure, precise meaning. I prefer to think of faith as a multivalent word—a multifaceted gem with light sparkling from many different angles depending on how it's held. Faith, as I use it, will occasionally refer to the wisdom accumulated by a specific Christian tradition that has been tested and found storm-worthy by communities of faith over many centuries. Faith, as I use it, will refer to my confidence and that of countless persons over the centuries that thoughtfully and prayerfully engaging the Bible will open us for an encounter with the Word of God—whose name is Love. Faith, as I use it, will suggest that listening, with the guidance of the Spirit of God, will help us discern new meanings for our time and place by bringing biblical wisdom into conversation with the messy stories of our lives. Faith, as I use it, will refer to the ways our bodies, relationships and the natural world prompt us to listen for God, seek out meaning for life, and daily compose the love song we are each intended to sing.

Former colleague and theologian of worship and the arts Rebecca Slough pondered with me about the relationship of faith and trust. In large part, faith is about learning to trust God and learning to trust that-of-God in each other and in the natural world. Learning the art of talking about faith will involve speaking openly about what we trust, whom we trust, how we express that trust, and the limits of trust. "If we are not able to say what we trust," Slough said, "it is very possible that we won't be able to say what we love or in what we place our faith."

In the introduction, I spoke about how the language of faith is giving voice to a story of love. Learning to love God is all about learning to trust God, and about learning to comprehend that "God's love is a profound expression of God's trust in us," said Slough. Yet there is no end to the ways that human expressions of love are distorted and unworthy of trust, and the many ways we question the reliability of God's love. Even if we have faith that ultimately the love of God will win over all that is loveless, inhumane, life-destroying, and fouled up, any honest talk about God will need to contend with betrayal, failure, disappointment, and defeat. Faith, and the language we use to describe faith, will be worth learning only if it is forged in a fire that burns out all that is false and dehumanizing; a fire that requires honest reckoning with suffering, sin, and evil.

The sad, sad reality is that much of what people pass off as faith and the language of faith is a masquerade of the real thing. Or, as the apostle Paul wrote about faith without love, it is nothing more than noisy gongs and clanging cymbals. And anyone knows that counterfeits and quackery—while not the real thing—certainly put people on their guard about whether the real thing is trustworthy.

Analyses about what contributes to our loss of faith and fluency in faith language are popping up more and more frequently. "Deep into the 20th century," writes journalist Derek Thompson, "more than nine in 10 Americans said they believed in God and belonged to an organized religion, with the great majority of them calling themselves Christian. That number held steady through the sexual-revolution '60s, through the rootless and anxious '70s, and through the 'greed is good' '80s." He continues, "But in the early 1990s, the historical tether between American identity and faith snapped. Religious non-affiliation in the U.S. started to rise—and rise, and rise." By the early 2000s, the number of Americans who said they didn't associate with any established religion had doubled. By the 2010s, they had tripled.

Thompson asks the obvious question: "What happened around 1990?" He cites University of Notre Dame sociologist Christian Smith, who claims that "America's nonreligious lurch has mostly been the result of three historical events: the association of the Republican Party with the Christian right, the end of the Cold War, and 9/11." Reflecting on Smith's research, Thompson observes that rather than science driving God from the public square, politics did. "In a twist of fate," writes Thompson, "the Christian right entered politics to save religion" and instead made "religion unacceptable to millions of young people—thus accelerating the country's turn against religion."

Thompson further reflects on why many persons found it important to distinguish themselves from the conservative, evangelical right. He notes the sexual abuse scandals of the Roman Catholic Church, which contributed to a loss of public trust and moral stature; the Internet, which makes it easier for individuals "to build their own spiritualities"; and most importantly, dramatic changes in the American family, with the spike in divorce rates in the 1970s through the 1990s, and the implications of family instability on how faith is practiced and communicated.[3]

In *Learning to Speak God from Scratch: Why Sacred Words Are Vanishing—and How We Can Revive Them*, religion writer Jonathan Merritt observes, "In the Western world, religious and moral terms have significantly declined over the course of the twentieth century." He cites a study in the *Journal of Positive Psychology* that analyzed fifty terms associated with moral virtue and found that a startling 74 percent of these words were used less frequently over the last century. Not only hefty theological terms like *atonement* or *sanctification* declined, but basic religious words are also falling out of use, he says—words like *grace, mercy, wisdom, faith, sacrifice, honesty, righteousness,* and *evil.* "I don't know about you," he laments, "but I miss these words and the virtues they express."[4]

Merritt writes persuasively about how "the language we *speak* and *hear* forms the lens through which we *see* the world," observing that "if we do not use sacred words, then our minds will be less attuned to transcendence. . . . And if moral language is vanishing—with the decline of words like *grace*, *mercy*, *honesty*, *courage*, and *wisdom*—then we can expect our communities and culture will reflect this shift."[5]

Michael S. Roth, president of Wesleyan University, writes frankly about how threatening it feels for students who are persons of faith to be "outed" in the classroom because their experience has taught them that if they are known as people of faith, they will be regarded as intellectually deficient or morally compromised. Roth describes his disappointment that students seem to "check their faith at the door" rather than honestly wrestling with questions of "love and judgment, justice and violence, grace and forgiveness." While these are historical questions, they are also immensely important to students' lives right now, and their ability to engage with what sustains work for justice, for example.

"In my cultural-history classes," Roth continues, "we talk about sexuality and identity, violence and revolution, art and obscenity, and the students are generally eager to weigh in. But when I bring up the topic of religious feeling or practice, an awkward silence always ensues." While he describes himself as an atheist Jew, Roth asserts: "I am not trying to convert any student to any religion. Yet how to discuss religious faith in class poses a major challenge for nonreligious colleges and universities. How can such an institution claim to educate students about ideas, culture, and ways of life if students, professors, or both are uncomfortable when talking about something that's been central to humanity throughout recorded history?"[6]

While much of our loss of fluency in Christian faith and language, as noted above, can be attributed to the politicization of faith, disillusionment with the church, disdain for faith-informed perspectives in nonreligious colleges and universities, the ubiquity of self-made spiritualities on the Internet, and the instability of family life, I will focus my observations in the upcoming six chapters through somewhat different frames. As I see it, the following problematic features have strangled our desire to speak about faith:

1. Our disillusionment or disappointment with the faith we inherited
2. The superficiality and artificiality of much Christian faith language
3. Our compulsive need for dogmatic belief certainties
4. Our discomfort with how faith relates to the *bodies* we live in
5. The nationalistic tribalization of white-dominated faith
6. Our lack of resolve to sustain the quality of family and community life necessary for forming faith and a rich vocabulary for speaking about faith

In each chapter in part 1, I offer several guiding motifs to help us examine the contours of our reluctance to speak about faith—with some variation in order.

Full of ourselves

When it comes right down to it, we hear only what we want to hear. We are preoccupied with ourselves, customize faith to our personal preferences, and use faith language to serve our own purposes, our assumptions about who God is, and our self-centered desires.

Out of tune

There are many ways in which our ears and hearts are not tuned to the frequency of the Spirit of God. We are inundated with voices from every conceivable direction—many of which hijack our imagination, reinforce our prejudices, stoke mistrust, and enflame our fears.

Disappointed in love

We talk a lot about love, yet more often than not, what we expected from love disappoints us. Love turns out to be more complicated and harder to obtain than we imagined. We don't know whether we can trust that love will come through. Much of what passes as love is superficial, truncated, or false. And the love we express often lacks integrity and is reserved for those we like.

Pulling the world apart

We are prone to cluster in exclusive tribal associations and affinity groups, throwing up walls of separation that push away and discredit those unlike us. We highlight the faults of those different from us, and our own rightness and godliness. We tend to make God look a lot like us and those we consider to be our people.

Silencing stories

We silence stories, questions, and insights from people who speak out of their own experience if they threaten us or call into question what we believe to be true. We privilege stories and language that confirm what we believe and turn a deaf ear to those that offer alternative perspectives.

In reflecting on the work of sociologist Wade Clark Roof, who helped us better understand the spiritual lives of the baby boomer generation, ethicist Laura Nash observes that although the religious language, symbols, and frameworks of meaning many of us grew up with may not capture our imagination or draw us toward faith now, it's *not* as if we're left without a desire for spiritual richness. In fact, she says, "the higher the education level, the greater the search for alternative blossomings of the spirit."[7]

It is my ardent hope that we can learn to give voice to these "alternative blossomings of the spirit." This hope is what compels me to *first* identify what I believe is rendering us deeply ambivalent about faith, and tongue-tied, and then to expand on how we can and must learn fluency in the beautifully rich, compassionate, and persuasive ardor and language of faith.

Chapter 1

Disillusioned with Inherited Faith

Perhaps we should examine more closely who it is that has the most difficulty talking about our faith, and why that is. From my observation and research, those of us who are white and college educated and consider ourselves politically progressive are the most tongue-tied. When a friend pointed this out to me, it was one of those proverbial elephant-in-the-room moments.

I am among those who sometimes struggle to talk about my faith. When I do, here are some of the reasons that give me pause—and I'm guessing a lot of my peers and their children struggle for the same reasons:

- Those of us who are educated or have learned enough to know that religious justification was used by government forces to violently displace Native peoples from the fertile lands that were sold to our forebears *feel uneasy and in some way responsible*.

- Those of us who succeed presumably because of our hard work, yet know that we benefit economically from underpaid or even enslaved workers in a global economy based on discrimination and colonization that was historically justified by so-called Christian nations, *feel uneasy and in some way responsible*.
- Those of us whose faith is parasitical on generations of privileged folk who rarely experienced discrimination or suffered for their ethnicity or race *feel uneasy and in some way responsible* for the horrors perpetrated by white Christian rulers and church leaders.
- Those of us whose lifestyle depends on law enforcement and armies to protect us from violent criminals and aggressive nations *feel uneasy about and in some way responsible for* the atrocities police and military forces have visited upon persons of color and other nations.
- Those of us who thought being Christian had something to do with caring for the stranger and loving the enemy *feel uneasy about and sometimes nauseated by* all the Christian talking heads who seem to be blind to immigrant children in cages, deaf to pervasive lies and hypocrisy, and enthralled by political and military power to dominate.

We feel generally paralyzed to talk about faith in any way that isn't laden with guilt and dismay for all that has been done over the centuries and to this present day, in the name of religion. While we may appreciate the religious moral vision of a Martin Luther King Jr. or a Mother Teresa and feel strongly about issues from a justice or human rights perspective, we really don't expect that God will intervene in our affairs. Few of us have a sense of "what it would even look like for God to act," writes theologian Andrew Root. "After all, in our secular age, divine action often seems unbelievable."[1]

FULL OF OURSELVES

The world simply doesn't feel like a place where the supernatural intervenes, writes culture critic Alan Noble. Our conversations are mostly about ourselves, how we define ourselves, how we promote personal fulfillment and success. The focus of our conversations isn't normally about a divine being who loves us and wants us to live full and abundant lives, or about someone named Jesus Christ.[2]

Many of my midlife and older educated peers are uninterested in talking about the Bible or traditional church teaching or personal faith. In university and college, we learned powerful new languages of profession, theory, and culture that opened our minds to infinite possibilities. I, and many of my peers from separatist, narrowly defined faith communities, became enamored with the big world of ideas and opportunities. We came alive to tools, skills, social constructs, and worldviews—both ancient and recent—that expanded the universe of meaning and possibility in exhilarating ways.

Higher education taught us to reflect critically on how the enclosed congregations of our childhoods were lacking—which was necessary and liberating. Higher education helped us grapple with the vast abuses of religion gone awry. Higher education helped us reflect on unjust systems, economic disparities, racialized violence, environmental exploitation, and the ways religion has both helped and hindered liberation for oppressed peoples. Higher education equipped us as skilled, responsible, even ethically attuned professionals. These emphases of higher education were hugely important—and must be enacted with even greater acuity and urgency going forward.

What higher education in large part neglected to do well was to model faith attuned to the Spirit of God—an active, alert faith equipped to critically discern what is of God, and what is not. What higher education in large part failed to do well was equip us to become outspoken people of faith—able to articulate a moral vision for God's just and peaceful shalom in the public spaces, work arenas, and neighborhoods we inhabit. And in our families. Naively, we bought into a notion that talking about personal faith, reading the Bible, and cultivating practices of attentiveness to the Spirit were antiquated, even embarrassing; that it wasn't sophisticated to draw strength from prayer or to daily learn to rely on God's provision. In large part, we neglected to learn that along with our desire to be good professionals, we needed to cultivate practices of deep listening and prayer in order to recognize and name that-of-God in the world. The prophet Micah holds together so well what many of us in our heady pursuit of professional fulfillment failed to do: "What does the Lord require of you but to do justice, and to love kindness, and to *walk humbly with your God*" (Micah 6:8, emphasis added).

Being full of ourselves has insidious dimensions that extend well beyond primarily seeking our own success—or neglecting to "walk humbly with God." In a disquieting article entitled "How America Lost Its Mind," writer and public radio host Kurt Andersen describes the ways "each of us is freer than ever to custom-make reality, to believe whatever and pretend to be whoever we wish." He describes at length how Americans increasingly blur the lines between actual facts and fictional fabrications. What we consider to be truth has become more and more open to negotiation, and is thought to be flexible, personal, and subjective. Not only those prone to paranoia about conspiracy theories but those in the intellectual mainstream itself have come to accept the notion that there are many valid realities and truths, Andersen says. This "new ultra-freedom" is heady stuff. We like it. And we've come to insist on it, even as "we fear and loathe the ways so many of our wrongheaded fellow Americans use it."[3]

What this "new ultra-freedom" has unleashed in our society is terrifying, particularly when we see how many people buy into all manner of conspiracy theories, including those fabricated by leading politicians. Yet there are a lot of us who consider ourselves fairly educated who are also enamored with the freedom to untether from Christian sources of wisdom and Scripture in order to customize our own spiritualities.

A dear friend spoke to me about the nature-based soul work some of her friends are pursuing and drew my attention to the website of a well-known retreat center where a mutual acquaintance works that reads: "You'll find the space and time to search within yourself and unearth your course. No matter which course you choose, you'll become more in tune with yourself—your aspirations, your priorities, your innermost desires, your health and well-being. You'll leave our . . . resort an enhanced version of yourself. Once you begin a new journey with us, you'll be equipped to continue on the path of living the way that's right for you, with meaning as you define it . . ." There is no mention on this website of a Loving Power that might contribute to becoming more in tune with oneself. Unlike the 12-step programs, which acknowledge as a core tenet that one is powerless over one's addiction and so must embrace a "higher power" as part of the recovery process, there is a self-absorption in what otherwise feels like a genuine search for greater authenticity and connection with nature.

Being full of ourselves and our own pursuit of an individualized, customized faith has contributed to being out of tune with a faith oriented to following Jesus, "the image of the invisible God," in whom "all things in heaven and on earth were created, things visible and invisible" (Colossians 1:15-16).

OUT OF TUNE

A former colleague, David Brubaker, dean of Eastern Mennonite University's School of Social Sciences and Professions, began a thread in one of his frequent Facebook posts meant to encourage dialogue about faith this way: "I believe that every human being is born with an innate desire to be part of something larger than themselves . . . to be part of a larger story. For millennia this need was filled by religion, but as religion declines in the western world we are seeing the rise of other more toxic identities to fill the void, such as white nationalism and toxic partisanship. This is an unanticipated consequence of growing secularization, and one that we need to be countering now. Any ideas how we might do so?"

If, as is widely attested to be true, each of us is born with an *innate desire* to be part of something larger than ourselves, then the all-important question that quickly arises is, What is that "something larger than ourselves" worthy of our life's devotion; our wholehearted labor and love? How will I find a "something larger than myself" that will provide the greatest, deep-down, lifelong satisfaction, and at the end of life, peace?

Renowned English theologian and philosopher of religion Sarah Coakley calls her new venture in theological writing *On Desiring God*. She pointedly acknowledges that she writes for "those who hover agonizingly at the edges of institutional religion" wondering how Christian faith can remain defensible as a worldview in light of "its massive historic collusion in gender blindness and abuse of power, its tragic (and continuing) mismanagement of the economy of desire." She devotes her imagination and reframing of theology, she says, to those "who continue to seek a vision of God for today, one attractive enough to magnetize their deepest human longings so as to *order* their desires in relation to God."[4]

I am captivated by Coakley's theological vision, and find it extraordinarily helpful as a framework for ongoing reflection about how we can learn to talk about faith in ways that both are personal (an ordering of our desires in relation to God) and move us beyond mere personal absorption toward a vision of who God is and how we can know God. But in order to talk about desire, we must talk frankly about the ways our desires can become disordered and our longing for love disappointed.

DISAPPOINTED IN LOVE

A friend wrote to me recently saying that it's been her experience that at least part of the problem of faith and faith language is that so few of us actually *experience* "God" as opposed to talking about God. Church dogma has diverted our attention, she said, and been substituted as a ruse for the real thing. She has been told and believed too many fabrications, she said. She used to believe the biblical stories, but no more. She has haltingly talked about mystical experiences with some folks over the years, but now is questioning whether all of that was her powerful (easy-to-fool) mind creating and shaping those "experiences." For her, the issue isn't speaking about God, but losing trust. Frankly, she said, while she always believed in a "separate guiding force," after years of desperately "wandering in the desert" with a troubled child, she no longer experiences that and questions the "belief system" that suggested that to be true.

Another friend wrote about a former colleague whose life-time of faith has been riddled by disappointments and very deep emotional and ethical struggles. He is not a mystic, she said, but a realist through and through. He is also not tongue-tied about his faith, but his life has included experiences that have been deeply wounding, have created fear and wariness. Real struggles have immensely complicated how he expresses his faith.

Another friend calls from time to time to talk about the trauma she experienced as a child because of the complete unreliability of her mother's love. Her mother, because of mental illness, essentially abandoned her as a child. She describes the depth of her loss as a black hole around which she's circled her entire life. Because of subsequent extremely painful losses, she's concluded that she's not worthy of love, that God doesn't love her. Despite seminary education, three beautiful children, and a gifted, loving husband, it's hard for her to hold on to hope that she'll ever find relief for the primal wound of her mother's abandonment.

It is the discrepancy we feel between the magnetic pull of our deepest longings toward a God of Love and a contrived, false God that renders us voiceless. We simply don't know how to negotiate the tension between the powerful attraction we feel for a God of Love and the unbearable pain and distress that wears us down. When what we had been taught or believed to be true doesn't bear up under the weight of disappointment, more often than not, we go silent. We bear our sorrow, disillusionment, and anger alone. Or we're perceived by "good Christians" as having lost the faith, given up on God, given in to cynicism and despair. Inviting each other to give voice to our disappointment with the inadequacy of inherited faith or a hand-me-down God may make it more possible to join in with the cries of the father who brought his desperately ill child to Jesus: "I believe; help my unbelief!" (Mark 9:24).

PULLING THE WORLD APART

Biblical theologian and former colleague Ben Ollenburger, upon learning of this book project, mentioned to me how theologian Karl Barth, writing in 1933 in Germany, said after something catastrophic had happened that it was important to do theology "as if nothing has happened." He meant that precisely in that moment, it was crucial that theology (that is, talk about God) pay even more careful attention to its subject matter for the benefit of the church and, thus, in resistance to the catastrophic forces of Hitler and National Socialism. "You are not writing (not expressly) about theology," my colleague said, "but something catastrophic has happened—is happening—in our day. Just as this country has proven to be unprepared for this accursed virus, we Christians have lost the language of faith, or unembarrassed skill in using it."

In these catastrophic times, it's urgent that, rather than going silent out of embarrassment for all the ways faith and faith language has been misused, we "pay even more attention" to the subject matter of our faith—to the character and vision of God, personified in Jesus Christ. While much public perception is that white evangelicals speak for Christianity, preachers like Rev. William H. Lamar IV, pastor of Metropolitan African Methodist Episcopal Church in Washington, D.C., won't let that stand. He writes, "I believe it is time for those who claim to follow Jesus to declare, without equivocation, that white evangelicalism is a morally bankrupt, bone-crushing theological system devoid of any semblance of the deity incarnate in Christ."

Lamar continues, "I am a preacher. So as I dust the COVID-19 crime scene, I am ultimately in search of theological fingerprints. What kind of God-talk makes possible a refusal to provide the universal health care that may have mitigated this crisis? What kind of God-talk makes possible a refusal to invest the money necessary to end homelessness? What kind of God-talk makes possible the racializing of criminality and poverty? What kind of God-talk gives political power to science-denying policymakers? The answer? White evangelical God-talk. The injustices that many communities are experiencing as a result of the novel coronavirus are inextricably linked to this theology. The evidence is irrefutable."

And he concludes, "This bad theology of who belongs and who does not, of who is worthy and who is not, has the blood of my parishioners on its hands. . . . How would the novel coronavirus be affecting my community if the God-talk of white evangelicals, whose theology controls our political landscape, sounded more like Jesus?"[5]

Rev. Lamar's prophetic truth-telling prompts me to ask how we might break through the tongue-tied sound barrier to tell our own stories and describe our struggles toward faith in ways that sounded more like Jesus.

SILENCING STORIES

We all have favorite stories to narrate the meaning of our lives—fragmentary incidents or full-blown epics, transformative personal and community moments, family and ethnic histories, birth and death events, Bible and faith encounters, stories of enchantment and mystery. When we describe events or tell stories, we tend to tell certain ones and not others. Which ones do we avoid, shrink back from, and why? Which ones do we make sure are not told? I wonder how we've missed hearing each other's experiences of God because we've inadequately created the conditions for people to talk vulnerably about life-changing events, mystical visions, heartbreaking disappointments, and God sightings.

Pope Benedict XVI said in a funeral eulogy for an Italian educator that "Christianity is not an intellectual system, a collection of dogmas, a set of cognitive, heady beliefs, or a moralism. Christianity is instead an encounter, a love story; it is an event."[6] Encounters, love stories, and events all become starting points for conversation about what we've longed for and lost in ways that disappoint us. Or found, in ways that astonish us. "It is nearly impossible to retell and remember the events with which we identify," writes Andrew Root, "and not use words of encounter, mystery, possibility, hope, fullness, and despair, saying, 'Only God knows why I said that,' or 'I'm not sure why I was there,' or 'I felt overwhelmed, almost outside myself.'"[7]

Pastor Lillian Daniel intentionally cultivated the practice of "testimony" in her United Church of Christ congregation for talking about events where we sense God's presence. She writes, "In our mainline Protestant church we defined testimony very simply: it was to be offered as a spoken word in the context of worship, and it could not omit God. That may sound like a ludicrous caveat for the church, for a community of believers, but it is my experience as a pastor that many church members have great difficulty expressing their faith. We had lost the art and practice of testimony."[8]

Daniel talks about how she missed the freedom of other church traditions, "especially born-again traditions," where they freely discuss their encounters with God. She says that while she has her own evangelical yearnings, she dislikes "the politics of exclusivity" that often comes with those church experiences. But, she wonders, might it be possible to hold together a vision of inclusivity with "the excitement of saving testimonies about a personal relation with Jesus?"[9]

Educated Mennonites I know are not unlike the people Daniel describes in her mainline congregation. We seem to have a strong bias for action, preferring to be the "hands and feet of Jesus" rather than to talk about our personal faith. Richard Kauffman, a friend and a former editor for the *Christian Century*, acknowledged to me that while active service is a good instinct, it is insufficient. "Our faith is based on a narrative, and we have to be able to tell that story," he said.

In fact, it is the "history-forming events" of the Bible, writes Root, that shake us loose from the assumptions of a secularizing frame of reference and its flattened worldview. Biblical stories about God liberating Israel from Egypt and God who raises Jesus from the dead awaken us to "the possibility of divine action." Root suggests, "Maybe one of the reasons that miracles and God's speaking seems so improbable to people in the secular age is because we never talk about them when they happen in our lives."[10]

For a contrast frame, we'll next listen to those of us from more conservative or evangelical Christian circles who seem to talk effortlessly about faith. We'll examine faith talk that flows freely yet often seems disconnected from real life and why that contributes to giving sacred words a bad name. I wonder, with Pastor Daniel, whether it might be possible to hold together a vision of God's expansive, hospitable love with more freedom to talk vulnerably and bravely about personal faith—both our disappointments and our encounters with God.

Chapter 2

Superficial and Contrived Christianese

I'm filled with reticence—even fear—when I try to speak about God. It's hard to speak about an invisible, immortal One whom most of us can't help but domesticate in some fashion simply because we're not God and have never seen God. It seems nigh unto impossible to speak anything about God without setting someone off. Every faith-laden word feels like a mini mine that could trigger an outcry or smirk of revulsion. If I am someone easily set off by religious words that others use—that don't ring true to me—who am I to think I can do any better? So why not keep quiet? Why talk about faith at all?

I have a vivid memory from an event when as a thirty-two-year-old I came home from a church meeting kicking myself for having spoken up—and feeling that I'd fumbled badly in trying to say what I intended to say. Why don't I just shut up, I fumed. I don't need to speak up at all. I know very well how to stay quiet. It would be a lot less costly than this self-loathing. I was serious—doubting my motives for speaking up and suspecting that what I had to say wasn't all that important anyway. The next morning, I happened onto Jesus' parable of the man who gave five talents to one of his servants, two talents to another, and one talent to yet another ("each according to his ability," Matthew 25:15 NIV). I identified with the servant who was given one talent—and especially his going off to hide his one talent in a hole. And then I was completely convicted as I read the man's reply on learning of the servant's impulse to hide his one talent: "And throw that worthless servant outside, into the darkness, where there will be weeping and gnashing of teeth" (v. 30 NIV). Oh my! Oh my! Oh my! So much for getting a pass on speaking up.

The truth is that countless times I've come away from speaking events filled with self-recrimination, mostly because I was sure I hadn't said what needed to be said in a way that was worthy of its beauty or truth. It is costly—this speaking up. Yet I feel with the prophet Jeremiah, who said: "If I say, 'I will not mention him, or speak any more in his name,' then within me there is something like a burning fire shut up in my bones; I am weary with holding it in, and I cannot" (Jeremiah 20:9).

And so I come somewhat trembling to this chapter—and the whole book project—because what I offer may sound like an unfair critique. I believe, even so, that I, and every one of us, should reflect on the language we reflexively use in order to become more aware of words and phrases that sound out of touch with reality, may be misunderstood, or worse, may be dishonest and even harmful.

There are several angles I speak to that overlap, but are also worth differentiating. One is a recognition that the faith language we use may work just fine for insiders to our community, our church, and our people. Any affinity group, profession, or workforce must have familiar language in common to communicate well with each other. In Christian circles, however, it is problematic when the language we use becomes code for who speaks correctly about God and who doesn't, who quotes Bible chapter-and-verse faithfully and who's suspect, who sounds spiritual enough and who doesn't, who's in and who's out.

Another angle, which is more difficult to get ahold of, is what I refer to as superficial or contrived Christianese. When the language we use as Christians doesn't describe our real experience as human beings, it's problematic for reasons other than its inability to be understood by outsiders. Hyper-spiritualized language sounds like we've taken leave of the real world, and our senses, in order to create a virtual world where we can make whatever claims we want about God, what God said to me, or how God did so and so on my behalf—or on behalf of my church or nation.

It's also the case that any person or group can use Christian jargon that is meant to sound Christian but serves as a cover for very un-Christlike ways of living. Since it can be hard to separate out who's sincerely using Christianese (because it's the only way they know how "to talk Christian") and who's using language to manipulate others or to curry favor, it's important to become discerning listeners.

Simple phrases that one hears all the time in some Christian circles can be baffling if you're not an insider to a group that provides context and interpretation. What does "Jesus died for my sins" mean, for example? Or "I got saved"? Or "I heard the voice of the Lord"? Or "God told me to do so and so"? Or "I'm born again"? Or "Until I met Jesus"? Or "Are you saved and going to heaven?" It's immensely helpful when people tell stories that shed light on what these phrases mean for them. Unfortunately, these phrases are often used as code with assumed meanings that don't translate well into ordinary life. And the language tends to start and stop with *me*—my heart, my salvation, my needs—without reference to how sin, salvation, being born again, or meeting Jesus may contribute to community-wide change that will free everyone to fairly and equitably experience the life-saving gifts of God's good Spirit and earth.

A couple of months ago, the memorial service of an elderly acquaintance of mine included the song "Jesus Paid It All." What does that mean, I wonder? The song states that "sin had left a crimson stain, He washed it white as snow." It continues, "For nothing good have I whereby Thy grace to claim. I'll wash my garments white in the blood of Calv'ry's Lamb. . . . Jesus died my soul to save."

Some of us grew up singing this song and others like it. Within particular communities of faith, these heart songs carry strong emotional resonance and communicate deeply sincere sentiments. The language does not translate well outside of these insular groups, however. As code language, it says one thing while meaning something else. To the uninitiated and to those with inquiring minds, these pieties sound absurd. Many of us go silent or murmur in disbelief because what we hear sounds out of touch with life as we know it.

In many Christian worship services, and in circles where Christianese or Christian jargon is prevalent, it's as if we construct a fantasy world that exists in another sphere. Some of us who grew up in the church, particularly those of my generation, know Bible geography better than we do our local watershed. We become starry-eyed romantics when a bottle of Jordan River water is on hand for a congregant's baptism, while ignoring the health and water quality of our local creeks and rivers. The make-believe world some of us live in allows us to travel from an "all is calm, no crying he makes" baby Jesus straight toward our heavenly home, carrying an entry ticket stamped "I asked Jesus into my heart." Our religiosity is so otherworldly that we rarely touch down on the ground— and our language reflects that artificiality. Talk about faith becomes a rehearsing of truisms that, when held up to the light of thoughtful reflection, seem out of touch with real life.

FULL OF OURSELVES

Americans have long indulged in "wishful thinking," writes Joshua Grace in a review of a book on the topic, titled *Fantasyland*, by Kurt Andersen. In reflecting on the national obsession with a then-current president, Grace summarizes Andersen, saying, "Never before has it been so easy to find fiction masquerading as fact. And our desire to believe what suits us isn't restricted to either the politically right or left. Both sides embrace their own self-serving realities." It may be too late for the American "fantasy industrial complex" to be uprooted, given how it is reinforced by the Internet, movies, advertising, theme parks—and "especially—Christianity," Andersen writes.[1] What Andersen observes seems particularly true for those of us in the dominant white culture of North America, who experience preferential treatment because of the color of our skin.

White Christians suffer from a "bad case of Disney Princess theology," writes pastor and blogger Erna Kim Hackett. Given that many of us tend to read the Bible for what it says to us as individuals, rather than focusing on God's vision for the good of all people, each of us sees ourselves as "the princess in every story." We are Esther, never Xerxes or Haman. We are Peter, but never Judas. We are the woman anointing Jesus, never the Pharisees. We are the Jews escaping slavery, never Egypt. For citizens of what is deemed the most powerful country in the world, a country that enslaved both Native and Black people, to see ourselves as Israel and not Egypt pointedly illustrates "Disney princess theology." Because we live unaware that we are privileged people whose power historically has hugely disadvantaged people of color, we're unable to correctly locate ourselves in Scripture or society, Hackett writes. We are blind and utterly out of step with the issues of power and justice the Bible really speaks to.[2]

The mash-up of fear, avoidance, delusion, fantastical thinking, and vaguely Christian notions creates a bizarre cacophony of superstition and manipulation.

Sitting on an airplane before takeoff, I once heard a panicky mother in the seat behind me telling her son not to use the restroom because it might suck him in, "or at least your weenie," and turn him into a girl. And then to both of her kids, a boy and a girl, she said that they'd better say they're sorry to God for everything they'd done wrong in case the plane went down so they could go to the place *up there* where God was rather than the place *down below* where bad people go, and she wasn't sure where she would end up. How is God related to Santa Claus? the children wondered. She said they were a lot alike.

Many cultural and religion observers point out how we commercialize Christian faith by making it simply another consumer preference in a vast sea of preferences we use to bolster our identity and define us as individuals. The Internet has dished up a virtual smorgasbord of possible belief systems, all of which compete with each other to attract followers. The cacophony of clamor for our attention makes the idea of a God who is transcendent, immortal, invisible, present-everywhere-with-the-power-to-stop-us-in-our-tracks harder to anticipate or perceive.

Rather than properly countering the runaway consumerism everywhere, the church ends up imitating it, writes theologian James Smith in his frequently cited book *Desiring the Kingdom: Worship, Worldview, and Cultural Formation.* Church folk merely substitute Christian kitsch, or "Jesus-fied" versions of products, reducing God to just another commodity.[3]

At the height of the Cold War, Tatiana Goricheva, a Russian intellectual and dissident, was forced to leave the Soviet Union because of her transformative conversion to Christian faith and the ways it affected her activism. On coming to the West, she was sobered by the superficiality and commercialization of faith talk. In her 1987 book *Talking about God Is Dangerous,* Goricheva observes: "I saw my first religious broadcast ever on the television. I thank God that we have atheism [in Russia] and no religious education," she writes. "What this man said on the screen was likely to drive more people out of the church than the clumsy chatter of our paid atheists. . . . He was a boring bad actor with mechanical and studied gestures. He was faceless. *For the first time I understood how dangerous it is to talk about God. Each word must be a sacrifice—filled to the brim with authenticity. Otherwise it is better to keep silent.*"[4]

OUT OF TUNE

Too often, congregational worship, especially among people who are white and quite comfortable, feels (if I may be frank) superficial and disconnected from real life. Maybe not for the regulars who are reassured by predictability. But for those looking for genuine connection to divine power and honest engagement with our daily struggles, it may not feel worth our time to show up. Scripture is read like lifeless words on a page. Over time, familiarity with what we hear breeds disinterest, if not contempt. Phrases, stories, and obscure biblical words—originally born in times of suffering, disorientation, oppression, astonishment, and liberation—are repeated with little appreciation for their power.

In some congregations, people sit passively in pews, with little bodily involvement in worship. In others, we sing lively worship songs projected onto a wall, songs whose primary focus seems to be about how *good* God makes us feel. We tell Bible stories so ancient that we have no idea what was really going on. Sometimes we tell the stories with grit and empathy, but too often, full-blooded, passionate biblical heroes are reduced to caricatures, like paper cutouts. Pastors preach, some of them with great authenticity, and some in stylized ways with no "skin in the game." It isn't surprising that many of us don't care to speak about faith when we've experienced religious language as privatized kitsch in congregations of reasonably comfortable, well-fed, don't-ruffle-my-feathers people.

Oscar Siwali is a peace activist and the founding director of SADRA Conflict Transformation in South Africa. He has dedicated his life to equipping communities with skills that embrace nonviolence and peaceful methods for resolving conflict. In June 2019, I heard him preach at Prairie Street Mennonite Church, in Elkhart, Indiana. He lamented how so many Christians in the United States seem to be immune to what's happening with the wholesale collusion of so-called evangelical Christians with political power. Do we see or even notice when politicians use the name of Jesus for their own benefit?

Why are we not concerned when Jesus is "being swapped for political power?" he wondered. "I'm here as a conscience," he said, "but when one side doesn't recognize the pain of the other, we're in serious trouble. Christians in the U.S. are assimilated to comfort. I'd love to hear a strong noise from Christians crying out '*Not in my name*.' But you have numbed yourselves. You are afraid to feel love, and to be involved in the world."

DISAPPOINTED IN LOVE

There are three excessively tall, blazing white, metallic crosses with powerful spotlights beamed on them along an interstate I frequent. Interspersed between the crosses are two gigantic American flags. I usually avert my eyes because this marriage of cross and flag is a desecration of the cross of Jesus—a Jewish brown-skinned man who was killed by the empire of his day on an instrument of torture, a wooden cross. While no words are spoken in this overwhelming display, it sounds to me, and I'm sure to many others, like a proclamation of white Christian nationalism.

In a *New York Times* opinion article titled "Why People Hate Religion," an agitated Timothy Egan observes that it's the "phonies, the charlatans who wave Bibles" whom we hear about "while those of real faith do Christ's work among refugees." A prominent government official, for example, "wears his faith like a fluorescent orange vest. But when he visited the border this summer and saw human beings crammed like cordwood in the Texas heat, that faith was invisible."

Egan cites multiple examples to show that in his view, Christian phonies "are legion," and he asserts that "young people are leaving the pews in droves because too often the person facing them in those pews is a fraud. They hate religion because, at a moment to stand up and be counted on the right side of history, religion is used as moral cover for despicable behavior."[5] The Pew Research Center reports that the decline in Christianity in the United States "continues at a rapid pace," with the number of American adults describing themselves as Christian dropping 12 points over the past decade to 65 percent, and the religiously unaffiliated increasing from 17 percent to 26 percent overall.[6]

PULLING THE WORLD APART

We sing, and demonstrate in countless ways, that "this world is not my home, I'm just a-passing through. My treasures are laid up, somewhere beyond the blue. The angels beckon me from heaven's open door and I can't feel at home in this world anymore." While we've been assured by none other than Jesus himself that he has gone to prepare a place for us, it was Jesus who came from "realms of glory" to break bread with human beings, wash dirty feet, delight in the birds and lilies of the field, bless children, open blind eyes, weep over the city of Jerusalem, heal the lepers, and show us what love for neighbors looks like—in the flesh. To be one-with-us in our down-to-earth humanity. So why do so many Christians talk in sentimentalized Christianese about that earthy, human Jesus?

The make-believe world some Christians have created neglects to take the real world seriously.

Two persons in a congregation I visited recently spoke about flooding of city streets near the Atlantic coast where they own some property. When my husband remarked on the impact of climate change and how that might affect property values, the woman replied adamantly to me, "I don't believe in climate change." When I responded that many around the world are experiencing the devastating consequences of climate change with crop failure and forced migration, she repeated, "I don't believe in it," and moved off to another conversation.

Climate scientist and evangelical Christian Katharine Hayhoe observed that there are many ways Christians offer religious-sounding objections to the catastrophe of climate change: "If God is in control, then nothing bad can happen," or "God gave us dominion over the earth, so we can do whatever we want," or "The earth is going to end anyway, so why does it matter?"[7]

The otherworldly superficiality of Christianese is the language of persons of privilege—persons whose babies aren't going hungry because their parents can't find work, whose children aren't at risk of police brutality because of the color of their skin, who in air-conditioned comfort can't imagine what it's like to be forced off their land because the rains haven't come for three years, or who've never been violently displaced from their homes because of their ethnicity or religion.

SILENCING STORIES

I worshiped recently in a church building completely devoid of windows. Instead, the congregation is met by virtual images projected onto a screen at the front of the sanctuary. Why, I wondered, when God gifts us with magnificent blue skies, swirling majestic clouds, grand and grace-filled trees, do we wall our places of worship off from the very gifts the good Creator provided to open our spirits for worship? Why do we surround ourselves with virtual images that reduce the grandeur of God's spectacular world to artificial, bite-sized projections? Why do we silence the "stories" of God's creation crying out to us in order to stare at a screen?

"I don't think most of us sense how much we trivialize our faith in our evangelical churches," writes Alan Noble. "We can't recite awe on cue: it bursts out of us when we're confronted by something worthy of awe. It strikes us *viscerally*. . . . We spend hundreds of dollars to *mediate* that creation and suck every bit of wonder and mystery and beauty out of it."[8]

Tatiana Goricheva recounts a trip with a church group in her first years after moving to Western Europe. "The young and energetic minister, a sporty type, talked the whole weekend," she observes—about airplanes, football, the elections and the food. He laughed a lot trying to keep everyone cheerful, like popular entertainers. "And all the time out through the windows was a world unexpectedly beautiful, with steep cliffs, lit with deep blue, violet, almost other-worldly colours, so I was quite naturally reminded of one of the psalms: 'How wonderful are your works, O God; with great wisdom you have created all things.'"[9]

So where does this leave those of us who want to be honest and firmly rooted in the real world? How do we put words to faith amid the mash-up and commercialization of religious language? How do we not simply reduce God-talk to pretty niceties? How do we not think of God as a favorite pet for our private comfort and security—tame enough to use for one's own pleasure? Those of us who've developed critical distance from religious code language or superficial truisms have had little opportunity to develop more honest, humble, and earthy ways to talk about how we experience God. Usually, we simply jettison the sentimental God-talk as childish and false.

"One of the common threads in the [Old Testament]," writes pastor Melissa Florer-Bixler, "is that humans frequently find ourselves trying to domesticate God. People want God to show up, but almost always on our own terms. . . . God isn't another object to be harnessed or controlled. There's an edge of danger to the story, this God who will not be contained in the appointed space."[10]

And if God is, as many stories suggest, a God of fearsome power whose name shall not be taken in vain, why would a mere human even *try* to speak about God? It's really not surprising that we turn to virtual worlds and Christianized code—because we're all fumbling in a thick fog about who God is and how God shows up.

Yet (and this is what gives me a modicum of courage) there are countless stories of persons caught off guard by a powerful love, surprised by release from debilitating guilt, comforted by beauty in the midst of brokenness; stories that describe what looks a lot like an encounter with the Holy One. The One we call by many names.

Rather than going silent out of fear or loathing for all the ways God-talk seems privatized, spiritualized, or false, we can fumble toward speech; speech that is grounded in gutsy, vulnerable life; speech that is at home in our flesh-and-blood bodies, wrapped in skin like swaddling clothes. We can forage for words to describe moments when we gape speechless in wonder, weep uncontrollably with relief, or are utterly undone by joy.

Chapter 3

Manufacturing Fake Castles of Certainty

I'm afraid of the unknown. I don't like uncertainty. I can't imagine that any of us isn't in some fashion afraid of things spiraling out of control or falling apart. New Year's morning 2020, I sat on my front porch, worrying about why it was so unseasonably warm even as I gladly soaked in the sunshine. I worried about my beautiful grandchildren and how to prepare them for an unknown future threatened by climate change, invasive diseases, and economic hardships. I found solace in the opening cadences for January 1 in *Take Our Moments and Our Days: An Anabaptist Prayer Book*: "He is the image of the invisible God, the firstborn of all creation. In him all things in heaven and on earth were created, things visible and invisible . . . O God, may your way be known upon earth, your saving power among all nations. Let the peoples praise you, O

God; let all the peoples praise you." And then I was promptly
unsettled by the psalm reading that followed:

> Long ago you founded the earth
> and the heavens are the work of your hands.
> They will perish but you will remain.
> They will all wear out like a garment.
> You will change them like clothes that are changed.
> But you neither change, nor have an end. (Psalm 102:25-27)[1]

The incomprehensibility of God, particularly when the
ground is shifting under our feet in times of uncertainty, grief,
and suffering, is one of the hardest realities we face, writes
Heidi Russell in her book *Quantum Shift: Theological and
Pastoral Implications of Contemporary Developments in Science*. That we can ask questions of God to which there simply
are no answers is profoundly disquieting. Yet the loss of certainty in the answers provided is a common phenomenon, in
both scientific and religious worldviews. In the modern era,
science thought everything could be explained and predicted.
With the twenty-first century, however, the age of uncertainty
dawned, not only for religion, but also for science. In both
theology and science, there are questions to which we do not
have answers.[2]

A common reaction to increasing uncertainty is a rise of
fundamentalist and extremist groups. The desperate need many
feel for certainty and absolutes has become a near pathological
obsession—putting at risk our ability to talk in thoughtful ways
about faith. Faith is about learning to trust God even when we
can't see or know for certain. Faith is making peace with the
mystery of unknowing—a peace that passes understanding.
Faith is about drawing from the wells of wisdom that countless
generations learned about how God can be known. Faith is
about believing we are held secure in God's love, no matter

what. Yet it is hard to hold together honest, thoughtful inquiry with belief in a God *everyone* wants on *their* side.

"My scientist friends have come up with things like 'principles of uncertainty' and dark holes," Franciscan mystic and globally acclaimed teacher Richard Rohr said in an NPR interview. "They're willing to live inside imagined hypotheses and theories. But many religious folks insist on *answers* that are *always* true. We love closure, resolution and clarity, while thinking that we are people of 'faith'! How strange that the very word 'faith' has come to mean its exact opposite."[3]

FULL OF OURSELVES

In a recent online women's meeting, a friend from our local, rural church mentioned that she has a bumper sticker on her car that reads "Science fact: The center of the universe is not you." I audibly laughed because, unbeknownst to her, I was working on this chapter. I love how bumper stickers, hashtags, and limericks say in a few words what most of us take many words to say.

In some Christian communities there's a resurgence of science denial and anti-intellectualism that claims biblical justification. This resurgence is accompanied by attacks on persons and schools that welcome young and old to ask tough questions about faith and hone the skills necessary to interpret the Bible honestly, with humility and integrity. Some of these attacks arise from ignorance dressed up in bogus theology and self-righteousness that smacks of a new inquisition. This anti-education, anti-science bigotry is depriving scores of gifted young people of conversation with the best of biblical wisdom and science.

On the other hand, those of us who benefit from higher education often exhibit a kind of intellectual arrogance that lacks genuine faith. We find little time to pray or meditate on the Scriptures ourselves, much less to model ways to do so for others. We teach critical thinking about any number of serious topics but struggle to mentor young people in authentic worship and life-giving prayer. We dismiss the power, relevance, and beauty of the Bible with a scorn that looks a lot like that of so-called biblical literalists who dismiss the relevance of science.

Many of us are reluctant to talk about faith because the Bible, albeit a silent partner in any conversation about faith, is so potent that everyone who uses a phrase here or a verse there wields a kind of shock-and-awe wand—with power to destroy, shame, divide, and conquer, or to heal, encourage, restore, and save. It all depends.

OUT OF TUNE

The Bible has been a battleground where the culture wars are fought. Those in power, often white men, use its potency to enhance their own dogmatic certainties about what it says, how God has spoken, and why we need to fall in line. Since many of us prefer to avoid conflict or are living with religious shell shock or wounded by abusive use of the Bible, we'd rather steer clear of conversations laden with Bible-talk.

Some Christians think the Bible came directly from God's quill and is without error or internal contradiction, and that what *they* think the Bible says *is* precisely what it says. This certainty is accompanied by a conviction that anyone who disagrees with what they believe the Bible says doesn't take the "authority of the Bible" seriously—and is not to be trusted.

While serving as president of Anabaptist Mennonite *Biblical* Seminary (AMBS), I was occasionally confronted by people who took exception to what they assumed our professors and graduates taught about the Bible. Rather than buying into the premise of their accusations, I normally chose to reframe what was at issue. On occasion, I used an analogy of an orchestra to describe what was in play. I wrote: "As I reflected on your inquiry, I thought of an analogy. I don't know if you appreciate Beethoven or Mozart or Handel. An orchestra has many instruments playing together that make for a full and beautiful sound. Yet if a listener declares that it's only violins that are playing—and entirely misses the trumpets, drums, woodwinds, and cellos—he's missing out on so much of what's in play. What we try to do at AMBS is to listen to all the instruments playing together, and to examine how each individual instrument contributes to the integrity of the whole, glorious music of the Word of God."

Christian Smith, director of the Center for the Study of Religion and Society at the University of Notre Dame, wrote a withering critique of the way many Christians use the Bible in a book called *The Bible Made Impossible: Why Biblicism Is Not a Truly Evangelical Reading of Scripture*. He laments the ways Christians who profess to have a high regard for the Bible show selective seriousness about some Scriptures, ignore others, and make arbitrary claims about others in ad hoc ways. In other words, he says, one might describe their approach as "uneven and capriciously selective literalism," often using what they select to support assumptions they already hold—whether on parenting, marriage, or whatever. Such an approach demeans Scripture, he claims.[4]

And not only does literalism demean Scripture, but it also demonstrates a "shamefully untrusting and ungrateful" reluctance to receive the magnificent, complex, raw, and sometimes contradictory texts as they are. It's as if these Christians "*want a Bible that is different*" from what it is, writes Smith. "They essentially demand—in God's name . . . a sacred text that will make them certain and secure, even though that is not actually the kind of text that God gave."[5]

PULLING THE WORLD APART

All claims of certainty about what the Bible says are exercises in power—for good or ill, depending on who's controlling the interpretation, who benefits, who is silenced, marginalized, empowered, or forgiven. Countless persons, both leaders and next-door neighbors, have weaponized the Bible against others, including women, Indigenous people, enslaved people, and LGBTQ individuals. But just as the potency of the Bible has been used to enflame discrimination and violence, it has proven over and over to be a revolutionary force for love, liberation, and restored life. While some of us clam up because everything about the Bible feels fraught, there are many Christians who see the loving-kindness, justice, mystery, and beauty of God shining through every page and find in it a mother lode of wisdom from our foremothers and fathers about how to live a good and profound life.

Most of our lives we strive to achieve mastery—which is the power to feed ourselves, manage our bodily functions, drive safely, be successful at a job, learn a skill, raise a family. It's not hard to see why each of us also desires mastery of knowledge about who God is, what God expects of us, what constitutes real faith, or how we're called to live. Yet when we presume mastery of what God thinks and try to dominate others with our certainty about what the Bible says, we abuse power. We undermine others' ability to speak about how they each experience God's presence or lack thereof. We disable each person's ability to listen for the promptings of the Spirit and to give voice to what they hear. We neglect to see how, by insisting that our cultural and gendered perspective about what the Scriptures say is the right one, we risk missing the ways God is speaking through those different from us.

DISAPPOINTED IN LOVE

If we accept the conviction, held by many wise people, that all truth claims—about the Bible, about God, about faith—are exercises in power, what will assist us to use that power wisely so that we don't disappoint those who genuinely desire to know God? What will enable us to enter into honest conversation that builds up community rather than tearing us apart?

I'll paraphrase Sarah Coakley's quite esoteric language to say: it is a contemplative or prayerful approach that will make all the difference in the world in how we talk about faith. Such an approach, "by virtue of its very practices of *un-mastery*," addresses the issues we're concerned about related to abuse of power, abuse of superior knowledge, and abuse of love by those bent on demonstrating *mastery* to show dominance.[6]

Coakley says that "unredeemed *desire*" is at the root of each of these challenges and that it is prayer, or what she calls the contemplative task, that refines our human desire. It is our desire and longing for God above all that will modulate and refine *all* human desires, freeing us from abusive uses of power because we are first and foremost seeking after God.[7]

In other words, it is our neglect to trust the power of God made known to us in prayer that results in our desperate need to build defensive castles of certainty. It is our neglect to deeply root ourselves in God's love made known to us in prayer that makes our need for the Bible to give us crystal-clear answers more acute. It is our neglect to trust that God's Spirit will speak through the Bible's apparent incongruities to show us its underlying orchestral harmonies that contributes to a need to be dogmatic in damaging ways. Unless we humble ourselves, acknowledge that there is much we don't know about God, and devote ourselves to being present to God in prayer and contemplation, we will continue to be disappointed in love. And we will continue to disappoint others who are made to believe they're not good enough to belong to groups that profess certainties about who is right and who is wrong about what God thinks.

SILENCING STORIES

Sadly, many Christians find it threatening to live with uncertainty when science and faith appear to be in conflict or when sincere people think the Bible says very different things about matters that to some are nonnegotiable.

A friend, whom I will call Scott Zehr, shared with me a letter he wrote to leaders of his church after a young man from the congregation, whom I will call Kent Miller, died by suicide. Scott wrote at a time when his congregation had lost many members because of disagreement about whether to welcome diverse views on sexuality and diverse individuals. I paraphrase to clarify and abbreviate Scott's letter below:

> I write this letter to you with a very heavy heart as this is not something I want to do, but . . . the 'small voice' (which I sense to be the Holy Spirit) keeps nudging.

> The Sunday morning sermon was about the authority of Scripture for the Christian life. The pastor began by reading from 2 Timothy 3. He talked about the authority of Scripture and mixed in comments about those "enlightened by the medical and science community." All Scripture is God breathed, he said, and on the issue of homosexuality, the medical and science community are on the wrong side of God, and of Scripture.

At that very moment, a "small voice" inside of me said, "Scott, be careful. You heard this before from the pulpit." A very clear image from childhood came to me—an event I hadn't remembered before. I said to that "small voice," if that childhood event turns out to have really happened, I will stand up for the voiceless among us.

The event is etched in my mind. I was very young, somewhere in the two- to four-year-old range. My father took my arm as we went out of church after worship one Sunday. There he confronted the preacher of the day and challenged him about his preaching that the Scripture teaches that the earth is flat. The Bible says it is flat, the preacher responded.

Several weeks after the 2 Timothy 3 sermon, I asked my uncle about the teachings of the preacher whom my father confronted. To my shock, I learned that what I had suddenly remembered was true. And for the record, I believe that science and the medical community are not on the wrong side of God, or Scripture.

The day I read the obituary of Kent Miller, a gut-wrenching question came to me: Did Kent struggle with his sexual identity? Did we fail this young man? Did he feel any safety in our congregation? Was there anyone he could safely confide in? I was troubled but . . . I let it go for the time being.

Last week, this "small voice" reminded me of my commitment to stand up for the voiceless among us. The question that I fought with was: "Did the leadership of the congregation do a review to see if we might have created an unsafe place which may have contributed to this situation?" I told myself, Scott, you can't let this young man die in vain. A heavy feeling came over me as I realized the responsibility I had to honor my commitment to stand up for the voiceless. To the church leadership, I ask the following questions:

- Is our church a safe place for those that are struggling with sexual identity?
- Are we praying for and open to walking with folks with divergent views?
- What safeguards or checks and balances are needed to ensure that preachers and teachers express their theology in humble, respectful, and nonjudgmental ways?
- Do we want preaching that focuses on moralistic purity codes or preaching that holds a high view of Scripture together with love, invites openness to our questions and struggles—and respects discoveries from the scientific and medical community?

Sincerely,

Scott Zehr

The young man who took his life is one of countless others who have found Christian communities to be unsympathetic to their struggles, lacking in empathy, and blind to their pain; communities that neglect to hold scientific evidence and biblical wisdom together for discerning how to care for those rendered voiceless under the weight of fear. Scott's gentle but direct advocacy arose out of his careful listening to Spirit and Scripture, new scientific data, and a suffering young man, along with a desire to rethink dogmatic certainties in order to more faithfully follow Jesus. Scott's questions to his congregational leaders suggest that with compassionate, patient listening, we may discover that it is the right questions, not the certainty of answers, that guide us forward in an adventure of faith. It is by learning to trust God and each other's diverse, discerning voices rather than throwing up immovable walls that we discover the Love from which nothing can separate us.

Chapter 4

Uncomfortable in Our Own Skin

Every single human being, no matter if rich or poor, healthy or ill, Black, Brown, or white, lives and moves in and as a body—and relates in some fashion to the bodies of others. Why is it, then, that most of us find it difficult or frightening to talk about our bodies—our desires, shame, regrets, and delights? We rarely feel as vulnerable as when our body—its shape, abilities, urges, failings, or pleasures—becomes a point of conversation.

We've all heard lots of harmful ways to talk about bodies, and not enough good and honoring ways. Our lack of practice and uneasiness with how to talk about bodies—*appropriately*—has a direct impact on our ability to talk authentically about faith. The desires of one's body are often experienced as a leading cause of alienation from God—much more often, in my experience, than as a way to connect with God or with others about our experience of God. There is nothing so close and personal to us as our bodies, so how we relate to them directly affects how we relate to God, the creator of these bodies that thrill and infuriate us.

One of the most universal claims of the Christian faith is that *every*one—translated, every human being or every human mind-spirit-body—is made in the image of God (Genesis 1:27). So what does "being made in the image of God" mean for how we cover up or expose our bodies, feed our bodies or fast from food, push our bodies to the limit or take it easy, abstain from drinking alcohol or enjoy fine wines, celebrate the goodness of bodies or support laws that demean or execute some bodies, offer marriage as a gift for those who seek it or deny marriage to persons of same-sex orientation, stay safe by avoiding risky encounters or put our body at risk to save someone in danger?

OUT OF TUNE

It is rare to hear a sermon that doesn't avoid direct mention of the fearful and wonderful reality that everyone listening *has* a body and that we all *are* bodies. The irony is that it was God becoming a body, a human being, one-with-us in life, death, and new life, that is the most revolutionizing good news of the Christian gospel. Yet truth be told, a lot of us struggle to be comfortable in our own skin. I like the way poet Jane Kenyon described our embodied experience as a "long struggle to be at home / in the body, this difficult friendship."[1]

Over the years, it has become increasingly hard for me to go to church, in large part because nearly every congregation I go to expects people to sit still, stand in place, sing songs without any bodily movement that would draw attention to oneself—even though the music is sometimes exhilarating and has a powerful beat. As young adults, my husband and I, with two small children, attended a church where dancing with the music was a beautiful and expected part of the worship service. We all loved it, especially the children. Since then, I've been in countless churches and found that it is a rare congregation of white North Americans that invites full-bodied worship. It's an entirely different story for churches of other ethnicities and continents.

"Protestants centered their lives around 'a lecture,'" writes Krista Tippett, host of NPR's *On Being*, "and squeezed the faithful into pews where they had to sit up straight." With appreciation for Pentecostals she had seen in worship, she recounts how "the transformative power of their whole-body spirituality was palpable," noting how for herself, "becoming wiser about spiritual things has meant learning to live in my body, not just my head."[2]

Sustained attention to the vulnerabilities, sufferings, pleasures, and confusions of the body, writes theologian Stephanie Paulsell, "has helped faithful people throughout history to deepen their relationship with God and others." And she continues, "Christian conviction about the goodness of the body, coupled with a recognition of the body's vulnerabilities, has nurtured a profound sense of responsibility for the protection and nourishment of bodies throughout the history of the church. . . . Bodily vulnerability is something we all share—rich and poor, male and female, enslaved and free. . . . [Early] Christians knew that . . . everybody is a fragile temple of God's Spirit and worthy of care."[3] Yet faith language has been deployed throughout Christian history and in a heightened way again today to suggest that some bodies, some races, faith groups, genders, or sexual orientations are of greater value than others.

PULLING THE WORLD APART

Conflicts between people of faith are perhaps nowhere more fraught than in the way we talk about managing individual and communal sexual well-being and the way we talk about sexual abuse, sexual orientation, and who gets to say under what circumstances sexual intimacy between partners can legitimately be expressed. It's no wonder that many of us avoid talking about faith altogether. We've seen *so much harm* done in the name of religion to real people whose bodies have been not only dishonored, but despised—and treated as less than human.

In my work in theological education, I have worked with survivors of sexual abuse and, sadly, with professors who have been perpetrators of abuse. Many victims of sexual abuse have come to trust me with their stories. It has fallen to me, on multiple occasions, to partner with them in the truth-telling required to bring these violations of body, mind, and spirit into the light. *Silence*, and an inability to talk honestly about our bodies—desires, fears, regrets, power dynamics, and shame— has exacerbated the harms we do to each other, often in secret.

My experience is magnified many times over in the larger church as more and more stories have come to light from Catholic, Southern Baptist, Amish, and all manner of faith groups. Perpetrators have abused others by using religious language to manipulate victims and cover up their sexual exploits. Faith language has been deployed by church leaders to silence or discredit victims and keep communities in ignorance rather than to cry out for justice, offer a public accounting of what went wrong, and witness to personal and community-wide sexual health.

FULL OF OURSELVES

Faith language has been used to reinforce prejudice against the bodies of persons of other races, ethnicities, and faiths.

I speak more to this in the next chapter, but include a story here that illustrates why many of us shrink back from using a language that some deploy out of their presumed white superiority, thus poisoning the most fundamental relationships between neighbors.

Willie James Jennings, in his book *The Christian Imagination: Theology and the Origins of Race*, describes at length a chilling incident that bewildered him as a child. He recounts that both his mother and father were "magnificent storytellers" and that foremost in their stories was Jesus. "They knew the Bible, but, far more important, they knew the world through the Bible." Jennings describes how one day, two men from the First Christian Reformed Church down the street abruptly walked into his backyard while he and his mother, Mary, were working in the garden. In stilted, rehearsed fashion, they talked about their church, the activities they had for kids, and what they were hoping to do in the neighborhood.

"The strangeness of this event," Jennings says, "lay not only in their appearance in our backyard but also in the obliviousness of these men as to whom they were addressing—Mary Jennings, one of the pillars of New Hope Missionary Baptist Church. I thought it incredibly odd that they never once asked her if she went to church, if she was a Christian, or even if she believed in God. . . . The depth and complexities of Mary's faith were unfathomable, as unfathomable as the blindness of these men to our Christian lives. . . . Our house . . . was about two hundred yards from where [their] beautifully majestic church stood."[4]

Jennings uses the incident described above to ask the dumbfounded question: "Why did these men not know me, not know [my parents], and not know the multitude of other black Christians who filled the neighborhood that surrounded that church?"[5]

Indeed! Why? I ask myself the same question over and over. As someone who grew up in a white church—albeit a small, quiet one—I was brainwashed, along with so many others, to imagine that our white faith was superior; that it was our responsibility as those who knew best to be the instructors, the saviors, the purveyors of faith. While there was much in my faith community that moderated this brainwashing, it was so pervasive in the water and air of the dominant culture I moved in that I, along with so many others, assumed that the color of my body meant I knew better than others who God is and how we should talk about God. I am deeply grieved for the years I tended to think this way, and profoundly grateful for the persons like Jennings who have helped me see.

DISAPPOINTED IN LOVE

If becoming wise about spiritual things and deepening our relationship with God requires paying attention to our bodies and the bodies of others that are different from ours, what has *inhibited* us from learning to talk vulnerably about what is closest to us—our aching, amazing, and different bodies? Rather than celebrating how our bodies are wonderfully *and* fearfully made, Christian leaders and congregants have often behaved in ways that shame those with bodies who don't measure up to communal expectations. Those with positional power have often used faith language to make us fear our own bodies and disrespect those who are deemed to have bodies less worthy.

I offer a couple of family stories:

My mother long carried the deep shame of a family secret about having been conceived out of wedlock that profoundly affected her self-image, and that of her mother. Thankfully, as an eighty-year-old, she finally felt free to share her story not only with her children but also in the memoir she and my father narrated.[6] She described the incident in an interview with her granddaughter Deborah Good for that memoir.

Mother recounted how when she was nine years old, she found a record of births and deaths in a "big, fat family Bible" and noted that her birthdate was seven months after her parents' wedding date. She remembered sitting at the kitchen table, cleaning brussels sprouts with her mother, and asking, "Mother, how is this that I was born seven months after you were married?" And her mother said, "Oh, Jane. I wanted to tell you before you would hear it from anyone else. I'm sorry you had to ask."

Her mother told the story of how, as a little country girl, she came to town to get a job as a secretary in a jewelry store, of all places. She wouldn't wear jewelry, as she was a plain Mennonite girl. She was the next to youngest one in a big family of girls, and she was the only one in her family who had a high school education. She had to trade farm work with one of her sisters in order to get permission to go to high school because they were required to work for their parents for a certain number of years. After the city boy, who was to become her husband, began dating her, he wanted to "go to bed" with her. She didn't think this was the right thing to do, but she went to somebody for counsel, who said, "Well, you'd better give him what he wants, or you might lose him." As a result, "she was pregnant with me," my mother said. "And so that's a story that my family did not tell. I kept this in my heart. And my mother and I never talked about it again."

My mother continued, "My mother was a very spiritual person, and I am sure this was excruciatingly difficult for her. And I am sure she prayed much. I know she did. I am sure she prayed that God would somehow not have me suffer because of her indiscretion. I don't think your generation can under-stand the scorn and shame and suffering this was. She had to stand up in front of the church and make a confession."

When asked whether she felt if it somehow made her less good, even though she had nothing to do with it happening, my mother responded, choking up with tears, "Somehow, I think that was deep inside of me, but I don't think I acknowl-edged it. If I could have talked about it through the years, I think it would have been much, much healthier. It was the silence that made it seem so shameful." And then she wept for her mother, who she was sure was doing penance for her "indiscretion" her whole life.

The challenge to talk appropriately about how bodies are shamed, violated, neglected, marginalized, or abused is so fraught with difficulty that often the choice has been to *avoid* conversation all together—and choose silence.

SILENCING STORIES

Perhaps it was knowing some of the cost of shameful secrets on his beloved wife that led my father to work with me on writing "An Open Letter to My Beloved Church"—which after being published in *The Mennonite*, a publication of Mennonite Church USA, in November 2014, went viral. By September 1, 2020, it had been viewed some 418,524 times on that website with more than 700 shares and has appeared countless other places, including being referenced in *People* magazine and in an interview with bestselling author Malcolm Gladwell for an episode of his popular *Revisionist History* podcast entitled "Generous Orthodoxy."

The letter begins: "I am profoundly reluctant to write this letter because I know there are those it will wound deeply. But I have also come to the conviction that I can no longer hide the light the Lord has lit within me, under a bushel. I want to share with you what the Lord has been telling me and my dear life companion."

In the long letter, my father describes the many ways he has lovingly and loyally served the church. He mentions the grief he and my mother felt when their third son, my brother, who came out as gay, was excommunicated from the Mennonite Church as a young adult and how, many years later, when that son and his committed partner of twenty-seven years asked my father to marry them, he happily agreed.

The letter includes personal dimensions of my father and mother's story, but it also functions as a biblically informed case for the church to authorize same-sex marriage—coming from someone wholeheartedly devoted to the authority of the Bible: "When my wife and I read the Bible with today's fractured, anxious church in mind, we ask, what is Jesus calling us to do with those sons and daughters who are among the most despised people in the world—in all races and communities? What would Jesus do with our sons and daughters who are bullied, homeless, sexually abused, and driven to suicide at far higher rates than our heterosexual children?"

The letter invites a new boldness on the part of the church, stating:

> We invite the church to courageously stake out new territory, much as the early church did. We invite the church to embrace the missional opportunity to extend the church's blessing of marriage to our homosexual children who desire to live in accountable, covenanted ways.

> We know that while many of us hear different things from the Scriptures, God's deepest desire, as made known in Jesus Christ, is "to seek and to save that which was lost." We believe this is an opportune moment for the church to

boldly proclaim a pastoral, grace-filled readiness to include both homosexuals and heterosexuals within the blessing of a marriage covenant designed to be wholesome and God-honoring.

And toward the end, the letter states, "This is the light that has been burning more and more brightly under my bushel, and I am now prepared finally, as a 96-year old, still zealous missionary, to let it shine."

The letter set off shock waves in our family—and in the broader church. A brother of mine astutely observed that it was "breaking the silence" that was a bigger problem for many people than the deed of officiating a same-sex marriage itself. If my father had stayed quiet about what he'd done, his action would not have caused a significant stir. As it was, "breaking the silence" opened countless, animated conversations about faith and bodies. My father's public testimony was widely received with tears of relief, overwhelming affirmation, and heartfelt gratitude. But there were those who took strong exception to what he did. Rather than seeing his public witness as an integral and logical extension of his widely respected missionary work, it was perceived as harming the witness of the church.

Author Nora Gallagher describes herself as an Episcopalian dropout in the 1970s, along with droves of others who dropped out over the next thirty years or so. Many of those who left are returning, she said. "But if the church hadn't changed, I wouldn't be here." Years later, after returning, Gallagher participated in a workshop where the facilitator remarked: "There's divorce, living together, sexual revolution. We haven't talked about any of this in church." His comment provoked Gallagher to wonder: "Where was the church when I slept with my boyfriend in college? When I found the one doctor in town who would prescribe birth control pills to students? When during an early and painful marriage, I wrestled with divorce? . . . I see, then, partly why I left the Church. It simply wasn't there for any of these events in my life, either to help me sort them out or to give them dignity. I could bring none of them with me when I prayed." She further observes, "This was partly how the Church became irrelevant. By standing on the sidelines or insisting on rigid standards while a whole generation dealt with sudden sexual liberation and confusion. And thus the Church lost a moral ground—a real moral ground, rather than what passed for one."[7]

So given that Christian communities have generally avoided talking straightforwardly about our bodies—and that much of the talk that has happened has caused harm to those who don't measure up or whom we value less—what can and should we do? I believe we can wrestle with the messiness and complexity of these questions without fear by focusing on a couple of guiding principles that are both simple and profound. For the simplicity and profundity, I turn to two wise sages.

"God is clearly more comfortable with diversity than we are," writes Father Richard Rohr. "God and the entire cosmos are about two things: differentiation (people and things becoming themselves) and communion (living in supportive coexistence)."[8] We readily see this in the natural world—diversity and mutual interdependence—but we've neglected to fully appreciate the beauty of diversity and mutual interdependence in our human communities.

Rohr expands his point by talking about how Jesus honored the differences of people he met, diverse in their economic status, lifestyle, religion, ethnicity, righteousness, success, gender. Despite that diversity, he kept the law very simple in order to bring them to God. When a legal expert asked him, "Teacher, which commandment in the law is the greatest?" Jesus replied, "'You shall love the Lord your God with all your heart, and all your soul, and all your mind.' This is the greatest and first commandment. And a second is like it: 'You shall love your neighbor as yourself.' On these two commandments hang all the law and the prophets" (Matthew 22:35-40). The way Jesus held together the diversity of human beings with the powerful simplicity of the law's guiding principles is beautiful to see.

Sarah Coakley shines a light from another angle on a guiding principle that can help us discern how to talk appropriately about bodies and faith. Coakley talks about how more basic than desire for sex, or consideration about one's gender, for example, is a "naked longing for God." When every bodily desire is considered for its nearness to or distance from God's love, our desire for God helps regulate and refine our human desires.[9]

Because faith language has often been used to reinforce prejudice against those with bodies we value less or consider to be wrongly designed, many of us regard it with suspicion. Instead, faith language should be used to help us discover and name a *shared* desire to honor God *with* our bodies. With the wisdom of these two contemporary sages in mind, we can become fluent in both body-honoring and God-honoring language. We can become more transparent as human beings who are different from one another and yet dependent on each other to make life work. We can become more accountable to each other as human beings who are all made (with our differences) in the image of God and called together to love God first and foremost and love our neighbors as ourselves.

Chapter 5

Us-versus-Them Default Thinking

While reflecting on the increasing number of fractures in North American Christian denominations and congregations in our day, a mythical image reared up out of the deep recesses of my memory—a Hydra—a nine-headed, terrifying sea monster of ancient Greek lore. Every time a head was cut off, two more appeared in its place. It's a disquieting image to ponder on both national and church landscapes as multiplying numbers of angry heads compete for airtime, marketing space, and diminishing loyalties.

Many of these "talking heads" call themselves Christian. Some of them weaponize faith language against people they don't consider part of their "tribe" and speak as if God were exclusively their own tribal god. "You can safely assume you've created God in your own image when it turns out that

God hates all the same people you do," writes Anne Lamott, totally hitting the nail on the "talking heads."[1]

It's also true that those who make God in their image "can't make sense of the Christian faith of Harriet Tubman, or her children," Christian ethicist Reggie Williams observed in a public Facebook post in November 2019. "Like Christians who took up arms to kill for the right to own and sell black people, they call mother Harriet Tubman a heretic and a thief. But it helps to remember that Jesus wasn't condemned by atheists." He was condemned by religious leaders who whipped their followers into a frenzy, goading them to believe their tribe's faith was under siege.

FULL OF OURSELVES

There was a lot of talk in my growing-up years as a Mennonite girl about being "separate from the world." Some of the markers of that separateness were the centuries-old stories of martyrdom we told, our avoidance of popular culture, and that our young men chose to be conscientious objectors to war. Vigilance of the boundaries between us and the world was a constant preoccupation—with sermons on nonconformity expressed in how we dressed, simple living, minimal use of televised media, love of enemy, and truthfulness—"Let your communication be, Yea, yea; Nay, nay" (Matthew 5:37 KJV). I acquired the strong impression that if we did everything right, obeyed the bishops, the Bible, and Jesus, we could keep the nastiness of the world out; that within our carefully guarded subculture, the purity of the church would be preserved.

I value much of the faith language I learned as a young Mennonite girl, the kindness of the thickly woven community that surrounded me, and the courageous, countercultural identity I was given. But one of the unfortunate lessons I also learned along the way was a default *us-versus-them* way of thinking. Faith language was used to reinforce "our tribe's" rightness and sense of moral superiority. We tended to be dismissive of the faith language of other "tribes." There was "the church" (our version of Christianity) and the rest was "the world." The white Swiss Germans among us had almost no awareness of how our majority status privileged most of us, keeping those who didn't fit the "ideal type" at a disadvantage, and everyone else at a distance.

The ancestors of my family migrated to North America from Switzerland and Germany in the early eighteenth century because of religious persecution. They found freedom of religion and land to farm primarily in the eastern United States. Not until recently did we stop to reflect on the Indigenous peoples who were displaced so our ancestors could begin a new life. Beginning in the late 1800s, Mennonites sent missionaries to Africa, Asia, and Central and Latin America to teach others about our faith, often using religious language that reflected our tribal preferences. Faith language has sometimes been used in patronizing ways with peoples of other continents. Rarely have we reflected on the power and privilege that has come with being white Swiss-German North Americans.

OUT OF TUNE

"Although 'tribe' is often a negative word in contemporary usage," writes historian of Christianity Diana Butler Bass, "it is helpful to remember that 'tribe' is a rich source of history, identity, and solidarity among native peoples. The problem is not the idea of tribe per se, but what happens when tribes become exclusive (when belonging is based on some form of superiority) and interested primarily in their own survival (when other tribes are viewed as a threat.)" Building communities on the basis of "likeness," Bass writes, isn't really the problem, as human beings have always built neighborhoods around some shared sense of "likeness." The problem is when those strong, shared ties "mutate into exclusion and conformity," become increasingly isolated from each other, suspicious of those who are different, and are surrounded by an "invisible fencing of fear."[2]

"Identity-formation-through-difference-and-tension mechanism helps to explain the vitality of many religious groups in the Unites States, especially American evangelicals," writes Christian Smith. Faith communities "need" others with whom they disagree "in order to help sustain their internal identity commitments." Membership numbers that swell "may have nothing at all to do with spiritual vitality or faithfulness or truth" . . . but may be because "Christian groups 'benefit' from conflict, disunity, and fragmentation and use such disagreement and distinction from others to build and sustain their in-group strength."[3]

I've watched this dynamic play out over and over again in the relatively short span of my lifetime. Issues that often show up as the reason for "retribalization" or a church split, whether at the local congregation, church conference, or denominational level, frequently revolve around women in leadership, authority and interpretation of Scripture, membership guidelines, policies regarding persons of same-sex attraction, and how to relate to governing authorities.

When talk revolves around who is more right, who gets to wield the power for defining the boundaries, and where boundaries need to be set, most of us seem prone to falling out of tune with each other, and with God's vision for shalom. The practice of hospitality, Bass and others say, is what saves tribes from "tribalism."[4] Tribes can learn to coexist with mutual respect and appreciation for what we each bring to the banquet table.

Jesus tells the parable of a great banquet, recorded in Luke 14. He begins with this striking command: "When you give a luncheon or a dinner, do not invite your friends or your brothers or your relatives or rich neighbors, in case they may invite you in return, and you would be repaid. But when you give a banquet, invite the poor, the crippled, the lame, and the blind. And you will be blessed, because they cannot repay you, for you will be repaid at the resurrection of the righteous" (vv. 12-14). Jesus continues with a parable about a master of a household who gave a great dinner and invited many people—who one after another sent back some excuse for not being able to come. The master became angry and told his servant to "go out at once into the streets and lanes of the town and bring in the poor, the crippled, the blind, and the lame" (v. 21). And when there was still room after that had been done, the master said, "Go out into the roads and lanes, and compel people to come in, so that my house may be filled. For I tell you, none of those who were invited will taste my dinner" (vv. 23-24).

This is a parable about the kingdom of God. Jesus' implication is that those on the margins value the opportunity to feast and fellowship at the banquet table. The rest of us are preoccupied—distracted and out of tune. We don't notice that a table is set every day for us to commune with God, to revel in God's bounty, to feast even on a busy day in the company of others welcomed by the master. We prefer to throw our own parties and draw up our own list of invitees. We feel pretty cocky about who is welcome and who is not.

PULLING THE WORLD APART

The Bible, because of all the stories in the Old Testament about God's chosen people and God's relationship with a *particular* tribe, lends itself easily to a "reading of tribal chosenness," acknowledged Walter Brueggemann in an address to a Sojourners Summit for Change.[5] He pointedly pivoted, however, to emphasize that there are all kinds of signals in the Old Testament and in the New Testament to the contrary—stating that "chosenness has to remain open" and "that God is in the business of choosing many *other* peoples."

But that doesn't change the pervasive historical reality that biblical notions of chosenness have often been interpreted as exclusivist and have been horribly abused. Countless politicians and white church leaders in Europe and North America over the centuries have exploited assumptions about a special "chosen" status to promote ideologies of white supremacy and to justify racial hierarchies, brutal slavery, the genocidal removal of Native peoples from the land, and violence toward people of other faiths.

Exclusivity and extreme views on one's own tribal superiority are evident not only in church or denominational groups, but in ideologically driven groups as well. As some "tribal affinities" and denominational loyalties weaken or break down for Mennonites, United Methodists, Catholics, Episcopalians, Presbyterians, Lutherans, Baptists, and other North American Christians, it seems we're prone to retribalize along new fault lines. Rather like the Hydra's multiplying heads, many of us cluster into ideologically driven groups variously called traditionalists, progressives, conservatives, evangelicals, pro-lifers, pro-choicers, anarchists, environmentalists, feminists, rural churches, welcoming churches—on and on. While many of these groups do wonderful faith-oriented work, they can also manifest an arrogant sense of exclusive rightness. Extremists and fundamentalists show up in every group, both on the left and on the right. And many of us in the middle catch the disease as well, out of some idealist expectation of perfection or deluded notion that we know best about the right way forward.

In politicized ways, Christians have been pushed to choose sides on abortion, same-sex marriage, political party affinity, religious liberties, attitudes toward people of other faiths, and immigrants. Faith language has been used to draw battle lines and to pull human communities apart into competing camps of loyalists. Rather than testimonials of winsome faith drawing people toward Christian communities because of how we love each other and have "the goodwill of all the people" (Acts 2:47), religious-sounding partisan platforms are used to conquer and divide. No wonder persons who thought being Christian was about unifying love are put off by weaponized religious words!

In an interview, religious historian Martin Marty spoke to Krista Tippett about extremists, often called fundamentalists. Religious fundamentalism, he said, "is always reactive, born when there is an assault on values that people have *and are uncertain about*. And around the world in our time . . . people are having trouble with identity—what do I believe, whom do I trust, who trusts me? . . . There is presently a 'massive, convulsive ingathering of peoples into their separatenesses and overagainstnesses to protect their pride and power and place from others who are doing the same thing.'" Marty didn't divide the world into conservative and liberal, writes Tippett. He divided it into "mean and non-mean."[6]

"This whole business of demonization, I've been deeply concerned about it," civil rights legend and public theologian

Ruby Sales said in an *On Being* interview.[7] She's concerned, she said, "because it does not locate the good in people. It gives up on people. And you see that most especially in the right and the left. I have been very concerned about the demonization that comes out of right-wing communities and also the demonization that I've heard on the left. And it comes from the same source of displaced whiteness."

DISAPPOINTED IN LOVE

After acknowledging, in his Summit for Change address, that the biblical theme of chosenness has been exploited throughout history and by white supremacists in our day, Brueggemann highlighted the Old Testament's best "anticipatory text" at the end of Isaiah 19. The prophet says: "On that day Israel will be the third with Egypt and Assyria, a blessing in the midst of the earth, whom the LORD of hosts has blessed, saying, 'Blessed be Egypt my people, and Assyria the work of my hands, and Israel my heritage'" (Isaiah 19:24-25). This text, Brueggemann said, "is a recognition that there are many blessed chosen peoples." And in the New Testament, the lead text is surely "Peter's incredible vision in Acts 10, where God tells him to eat impure food to violate the old purity codes of Leviticus, and out of that comes this incredible dawning on Peter and Paul and all the apostles that the good news of God's transformative love in the world is not a monopoly of any race or tribe or nation or tongue."[8]

As human beings, made in the image of God, we are designed to be in relationship with others. We will not flourish without the all-important wisdom we learn from others, often from those whose experience, perspectives, bodies, and beliefs are very different from our own. "The church of Christ ecumenically embraces the whole inhabited earth. She is not a tribal religion, nor a Western religion, nor a white religion, but the church of all humanity," declared Jürgen Moltmann, renowned German theologian. "The church of Christ is present in all the people on earth and cannot become 'a national religion.'"[9]

Lest we be constantly disappointed in love, we must find our voices in order to condemn the diabolical collusion of Christian faith with racist, nationalist talk. We must find our voices to cry out, "Not in my name! And not in the name of Christianity!" We must use our voices to name what a blasphemy it is to wrap Christ in an American flag, or any national flag. We must rediscover the Bible, not to maliciously manipulate it to justify hatred and violence, but as the clarion call it is to join Jesus' mission to bring good news to the poor, proclaim release to the captives, and recovery of sight to the blind, to let the oppressed go free, and to proclaim the year of the Lord's favor—the shalom vision of God on earth as it is in heaven (Luke 4:18-19).

SILENCING STORIES

Drew Hart is the author of *Trouble I've Seen: Changing the Way the Church Views Racism* and *Who Will Be a Witness? Igniting Activism for God's Justice, Love, and Deliverance.* I was fortunate to host Hart during my tenure at AMBS, and have learned much from him. Soon after George Floyd's brutal murder on May 25, 2020, and the protests and public outcry that exploded around the United States and the entire world, I listened in on a Facebook Live panel among Black church leaders in Harrisburg, Pennsylvania, on June 9, 2020, called "How the Church Views Racism." Hart talked about how many of us who are white condemn slavery and Jim Crow laws, but we've never wrestled with the theology that justified those brutalities—and so it continues to undermine the credibility of the church. The ugly truth is that the church in the West sanctioned slavery and conquest, beginning in the fifteenth century. We can't be silent about the church's role, he said. We have to name it—that it was the church who permitted the brutality and exploitation of people of color. What might have happened, Hart wondered, if when Columbus landed in the Bahamas he had shown love to the Native peoples, and said, let us learn from you how to live in this place. Instead, he and his so-called Christian compatriots enslaved and slaughtered the Native peoples.

Furthermore, Hart said, we need to be truthful about who Jesus was. He wasn't white or Western European. Gentile Europeans were grafted into someone else's story, and yet they co-opted Jesus and used him to dominate others in ways that are *anti*-Jesus. Hart compared racism in the church to the demons Jesus cast out of the troubled man who lived among the tombs on the "other side" of the Sea of Galilee. The demons that possessed him were called Legion, because there were many of them. Jesus cast them out, restoring sanity and peace to the man (Mark 5:1-20). We need to exorcise, or cast out, the white Jesus from the church, Hart said. Anything we do with discipleship, teaching, or talking about what it means to follow Jesus must be explicitly anti-racist.

It is often people of color—including African Americans, Latino Americans, Native Americans, Asian Americans—who model ways to talk about faith that those of us who feel tongue-tied need to learn from. "Ours is an alternative narrative, not one of genocide of Native peoples and exploitation of people of color to create a 'white land,'" declared Sales at a conference I participated in at Hampton, Virginia. "We are a countercultural people who remember the meaning of the spiritual journey conveyed in our Scriptures: a journey of faith that frees all people to be fully human, that deeply disciples communities even in the midst of oppression to revel in song and to know the sweet, sweet Spirit that inhabits all of us, giving us agency and hope."

As I write this on Martin Luther King Jr. Day, I'm reminded of his words: "We have inherited a large house, a great 'world house' in which we have to live together—Black and white, Easterner and Westerner, Gentile and Jew, Catholic and Protestant, Muslim and Hindu—a family unduly separated in ideas, culture and interest, who, because we can never again live apart, must learn somehow to live with each other in peace." King continues, "Together we must learn to live as brothers [and sisters] or together we will be forced to perish as fools."[10]

Learning to live together in this "great world house" requires learning to talk with each other about faith, the faith that inspired King, Hart, Sales, and countless other moral giants and ordinary people throughout history and to this day, a faith that we must learn to speak about more honestly, humbly, and courageously.

Chapter 6

Community-Based Language Learning Is Vanishing

For children to learn a language, they need to hear that language consistently spoken over months and years. Children can learn multiple languages at the same time, but they need sustained practice over a long time. One of the most devastating reasons we're losing our ability to talk about faith is that we have little opportunity to experience the heartfelt expression of parental or congregational faith or to hear and practice faith language that convincingly names our experience. The loss of intact, faith-infused communities and families, where faith stories are told with love over time so we see how our personal story fits into the cosmic story of God's shalom vision, is rendering us and our children tone-deaf and illiterate.

Christian faith can't exist without words, writes Jonathan Merritt, "because someone spoke to someone who spoke to someone who spoke to someone about God." The language of faith, like any other language, and perhaps more so, "provides the glue that binds a community together." Sacred words like mercy, trust, peace, justice, wisdom, sin, evil, confession, forgiveness, truthfulness, and prayer are vessels carrying precious information that reveals "deep and often invisible realities." Sacred words, developed and honed by our ancestors, help us perceive, categorize, and make meaning, and when words die, so does the knowledge carried by those words.[1]

Formation in the language of faith is about the quality and consistency with which we talk to each other and do small, everyday things. My family life growing up revolved around faith—both when my parents were American Mennonite missionaries in Ethiopia, and later in my high school years, when they cultivated ministries, businesses, fruits, flowers, and vegetables in southeastern Pennsylvania. Faith was central to everything we did in my parental home. Most days began with prayer and a Scripture reading at the breakfast table. While we lived in Ethiopia, every Wednesday evening there was a prayer meeting with others from the missionary team with whom my parents served. My brothers, sisters, and I participated in these prayer meetings. We learned to kneel down with the adults and bury our faces in the couch cushions or hard wooden benches. Every Sunday we gathered with those we called our brothers and sisters in Christ to worship the God we believed created us, called us each by name, and sent us into the world to share the news of a Savior who loves the world in ways that are good news for everyone.

My parents loved telling us Bible stories, which they mixed with stories from "when I was a little boy in Chesapeake,

Virginia," or "when I was a little girl in Lancaster, Pennsylvania." They told the stories with suspense, wonderment, and love so we could feel the emotion of the characters. Their stories laid a narrative seedbed for my imagination to take root in rich humus; stories of real people who showed qualities of daring, heroism, resilience, grace, and transformation; stories that included miracles and mystery. Stories helped me see how people from centuries ago experienced God and how my own parents took risks, recovered from loss, stared down fear, and lived amazing lives. Life was unpredictable and frightening in many ways. There were always uncertainties and much to worry about. I found profound security, however, from observing my parents' steady trust in God, the ways they stayed attuned to God, and their thoughtful conversations with Christian friends about how to discern God's will; how to make decisions in light of what God may desire for how we live and the work we engage.

After becoming a parent myself, I grew more and more intent to pass on my faith to my children. I pondered and often wrote about how families can create a culture that nurtures faith, family identity, and personal character.[2] I exercised my theological muscles in writing about how children transformed my own faith in phenomenal ways. Being a mother taught me new dimensions of humility, responsibility, empathy, solidarity, tolerance, interdependence, what it means to be converted, and hope.[3] As I have watched my children grow into adulthood and now become parents themselves, I frequently give thanks for the wisdom my life with them has nurtured in me. I give thanks for the courageous, faith-filled adults they've become.

OUT OF TUNE

Many of us assume that because talk about faith is weighted with consequence, we're not knowledgeable enough to speak about God's presence in the world with each other, or with our children. We're only too happy to leave that religious stuff to the professional theologians and preachers. Over and over I've heard people give a disclaimer when they start to say something about faith that "I'm not a theologian, but . . ." They then proceed to make what are essentially theological statements about their faith or thoughts about God's ways in the world. Why the felt need for a disclaimer? I wonder. It's great to have theologians who've made the study of God's ways in the world their primary focus—and those who've studied the deep histories of theological traditions and who construct theological frameworks for guiding our communal discourse about who God is. But the unintended downside of having specialists is that some of us then think that speaking about God belongs only to the professionals. We think of theology as an elitist undertaking and so take a pass—concluding that since we're not specialists, we're not *able* to talk meaningfully about our desire to know God or about events where we sensed God's presence. Which is simply untrue.

I believe every human being is born with an innate desire to be part of a larger story. Every one of us can reflect on what the larger story is of which we want to be a part. We can ponder what it is we love most, what it is that makes life good—and why. Reflecting together on these questions is essentially a theological conversation, particularly if we touch in any way on God. Yet many of us don't choose to talk about these questions with friends—or with our children. Why is that?

DISAPPOINTED IN LOVE

My observation is that, taking their cues from persons in my generation, many of those in midlife professions or who are parents of growing children have decided what's most important is to succeed professionally and economically— which means getting into the best schools and bending every effort to get good jobs and keep them. The Great Recession, soaring unemployment numbers, and renewed fears of economic collapse accentuate their determination to succeed financially. I applaud and give thanks for responsible, skilled professionals and public servants every day. But I grieve when professional or economic success becomes so all-consuming that it squeezes out practices that help us stay aligned with God's shalom vision.

Earlier I noted Andrew Root's observation that many of us aren't even curious about what it might look like if God were to act, since divine action seems unbelievable in our secular age.[4] With our pell-mell rush to manage the craziness of our lives, whether intentionally or not, we've concluded that paying attention to God or God-talk is unnecessary or optional. For one, it's way too complicated, loaded with strong emotions, slippery, and intangible. We resist being guilted into going to church or giving money. We're disappointed with what we've seen and heard of the hypocrisy, nastiness, and impotence of religious talking heads, and prefer to work on what's right in front of us—the need to stay focused on making ends meet.

What we're left with is a flattened universe. Skills and acuity for detecting God's Spirit go inert. Many of us can no longer imagine what an encounter with God might be like. Within a flattened world, we give ourselves to activism or business or family life or fantasy without any expectation of divine intervention. We rarely take time to imagine with our children or grandchildren how we might listen for God, respond to God's call to action, anticipate God's intervention, or give ourselves in service to the shalom vision of God for the world.

The secular age tempts us to believe that any action from God seems implausible. By not cultivating daily life practices—like morning prayer, calling on God to bless, thanking God for gifts, or crying out for help—we narrow our frame of reference and become deaf and blind to the supernatural.

And yet, though we pay little attention to God in our hustle to make life work, and though God may seem absent and inaccessible, it is often the case, writes Root, that when life is upended and stress overwhelms, "God arrives . . . right when things seem so hard." Why is that?

Root talks about how the life of faith is not to assume that every circumstance will bring God's arrival, but rather is to open our eyes in anticipation that God, who is a shepherd, a minister, a loving parent, "may just move over these waters of impossibility." To stay alert, we must learn to call out to this God, he says, and listen for how God may speak to us. And when God does come, Root says, "we must tell others of the arrival, for right in our places of death, God has ministered life."[5]

The tragedy is that so many of us aren't even watching for God, or teaching our children to watch. We don't take time to open the space, create the conditions, lay the groundwork for detecting divine action, because we're full of our own worries, priorities, agendas.

FULL OF OURSELVES

A good friend lamented to me that she fears families have by and large lost something that she feels can never be reclaimed. Many households have two working parents and children in the care of non-family members, which limits the amount of time together in any twenty-four-hour period. Most parents she knows aren't making choices that prioritize prayer or Scripture readings at mealtimes, prayers at intervals throughout the day, or conversation about how God may be present in the normal activities of a day. With time needed for household chores, shopping, sporting events, music lessons, (you-name-it), on weekends there's no time for church or gathering with other Christians to be immersed in worship, public prayers, or testimonies about experiences of the holy. The pace of life is beyond exhausting, with little time for conversation about how we learn to love God and neighbor unless it's in the car on the way to soccer practice.

Alan Noble writes at length about how living in "this distracted age" affects our ability to respond with passion and conviction to matters of faith. The incessant distraction of social and entertainment media, if not well managed, can rob us of the focus needed to talk with each other about basic things—like what we believe about human worth, why we exist, what we think is true, and what mystical or spiritual hopes we have. Social media has two primary goals, writes Noble: to capture our attention and to gather our data. Gathering our data "has troubling implications for our privacy," but the goal to *capture our attention* "has a direct effect on our ability to encounter and contemplate the holy."[6] Unlike books or long essays that invite us to grapple with an idea or wrestle with stories that have many layered meanings, social media is a "sound bite" arena offering only short tidbits that grab our attention here and there and there and there.

Nearly everyone now holds within their hands a source for millions of diverse conversational threads, countless news stories, and a blizzard of images. How does anyone begin to process such an overload of information or contradicting construals of what matters? We become "addicted to novelty," writes Noble, and like other addictions, this takes a toll on our bodies. We become *mentally fatigued*. A fatigued mind considers a conversation about God as just another "superficial distraction."

Since many of us are not well equipped to distinguish between what is trivial and what is crucial, it feels like everything is important all the time, and we must keep up or lose out. With all that shows up on our screen or smartphone, we must make "millions of tiny decisions"—about what song to play, how to reply to a text, or what to share on social media—which can lead to "decision overload." *Decision overload* is a problem for faith and spirituality. We wonder why we should try to discover what is true because the "expanding horizon of possible beliefs" is just overwhelming.[7]

The editors of the *Christian Century* noted their concern in August 2019 about a *JAMA Pediatrics* report that "the number of children and teens hospitalized for suicide attempts or suicidal thoughts doubled between 2007 and 2015." What's making life unbearable for more and more people, young and old? they ask. For teens and young adults, "researchers trace the increase in mental health issues to the rise of social media." Among the recommendations the CDC makes to prevent suicide is this: "Offer activities that bring people together so they feel connected and not alone." The editors conclude: "That's the holy work of any community, including congregations."[8]

Social media, when used well, can help us stay connected with family and friends, enhance discourse about faith, and provide resources that enrich faith. When not managed well, social media and the distractions of popular culture figure large in pulling us away from the kind of shared family and community life that cultivates faith and the language of faith. So does the dishonest and uncivil manner in which we talk to each other.

PULLING THE WORLD APART

In Proverbs, we learn that "speech and community go hand in hand" and that "speech is important because it has the power to build or destroy community," writes Glenn Pemberton. For the sages of Proverbs, speech functions rather like a thermometer, indicating how well a person's heart is. Truthful, kind, and gentle words signal a wise heart. On the other hand, lies, gossip, flattery, and slander are symptoms of a confused, self-centered heart. The character of the heart is ultimately responsible for our speech, which in turn affects the health of our communities, families, and our own character development. The sages talk about this heart-and-speech relationship throughout Proverbs.[9]

The sages recognize four types of speakers that destroy community life: the false witness, the mocker or scoffer, the gossip, and the wicked. People who do not tell the truth when called to witness endanger communities. A mocker or scoffer who is proud and acts with arrogance in ridiculing others endangers communities. Those who listen to and repeat rumors and separate close friends by relaying gossip endanger communities. People who hide violence behind their words and set deadly ambushes that are meant to destroy their neighbors endanger communities.[10]

Violent speech and actions are ubiquitous as a way of life in the United States. Many of us have become immune to pervasive violence in the ways we talk to each other and the entertainment we consume, and rarely reflect on how violence contributes to breakdown in family and community life.

Peace theologian Malinda Berry describes herself as passionate about nonviolent communication. She observes that Swiss theologian Karl Barth "is known for describing the starting point of all theology and theological reflection as a *communication*—God's self-revelation to us in and through Jesus Christ isn't just 'incarnation'; it's also 'communication.'" "Incarnation" describes a deity or spirit who becomes a person—in the flesh. "Communication" is a message with information or news that is successfully shared.

We make a faith claim, Berry says, when we affirm that Jesus is an *incarnation* of God. But when we also see him as a *communication* (the Word of God who became human), "a whole new horizon opens up for considering the manner and style of incarnation. When incarnation meets communication, breaking old, harmful communication habits and creating new, connective communication patterns is *gospel work*." Berry urges her readers who might normally fight or flee or passively go silent when in conflict to consider another option. How might we be nonviolent in the ways we communicate with each other? How might we cultivate qualities like curiosity and compassion rather than violent talk—and look a lot more like Jesus?[11]

Centuries after the sages of Proverbs spoke, Jesus, a sage par excellence, polishes the point, saying: "The good person out of the good treasure of the heart produces good, and the evil person out of evil treasure produces evil; for it is out of the abundance of the heart that the mouth speaks" (Luke 6:45).

Where better to form hearts filled with "good treasure" than in families and communities that invite conversation about good and evil and the complex situations where there is no pure good or pure evil? Where better than in family and community to talk about how we are more complicit in evil than we're normally able to see unless others help keep us accountable for the choices we make? But given what we're up against when deaf to God's Spirit, distracted by social media, false witnesses, scornful mockery, and violent denigration of entire groups of people, we need more than mere words to deliver us from evil.

SILENCING STORIES

It often seems that what many of us are experiencing in the West and particularly in the United States, a nation that thinks of itself as the most powerful on earth, is an acceleration of confusion, violence, polarization, and community breakdown that some describe as spiritual bondage or a "demonic grip on our common life." The writer to the Ephesians describes our reality this way: "For our struggle is not against enemies of blood and flesh, but against the rulers, against the authorities, against the cosmic powers of this present darkness, against the spiritual forces of evil in the heavenly places" (Ephesians 6:12).

The writer of Ephesians encourages his readers to "be strong in the Lord and in the strength of *his power*" (Ephesians 6:10, emphasis added). Persons of privilege (often white North Americans) manage to control most contingencies in their lives. We associate power with money, position, race, military might, education, and home address rather than "for yours is the kingdom, the *power*, and the glory." Many of us simply don't associate power with prayer.

Which brings me to perhaps the most disabling of all silenced stories—our failure to pray together, as families, in praying circles in our homes or congregations. Neglecting to pray together has contributed to the breakdown of our ability to talk meaningfully about faith. We rarely stop to talk about what prayer is or how we pray or to tell stories about what prayer means for us. In fact, many of us are quite embarrassed about participating in prayer, pausing to pray, or leading a prayer. Only if life stirs up crises might we call out to God, try to figure out how prayer works, and go searching for the alternative power source that the Spirit of God might be. We rarely think of prayer as a genuinely powerful force for good—a practice that aligns us with the Spirit-power required to withstand the "cosmic powers of this present darkness."

The fascinating thing in our flattened secular age is that often those who hear God speak are those who pray, writes Root. Prayer is important, powerful, and central "only because God speaks, sees, and hears." That it is those who pray who hear God speak may simply be proof that people of faith are deluded, Root says. Or "it could be that reality is larger than our perceptions, and so taking on practices that broaden our attention can disclose new dimensions to reality itself. Prayer is the broadening of our attention on the world around us, looking again for the arriving of God."[12]

When we don't take time to learn to pray or to participate in praying families or communities, we lack the opportunity to actively "look for the arriving of God" in the unfolding of our days or to learn language that names whatever fledgling faith we may have.

Root recounts a story about much loved pastor and author Eugene Peterson. Peterson was visiting a desperately ill parishioner. He asked her, "Is there any way I can minister to you?"

To Peterson's surprise, the woman responded shyly, "Yes. I've been thinking a lot about it. Would you teach me to pray?" Peterson understood this to mean, "Would you teach me . . . to see divine action? Would you be my pastor and help me to see that indeed God sees me?" This was a breakthrough.

Peterson said, "I had been a pastor . . . for three years. It was the first time anyone had asked me to teach them to pray." He further recounted how the woman's shy request gave him "a focus that I had come to believe was at the very center of my pastoral vocation."[13]

We can begin with a prayer as simple as saying thank you—and watch how kindness and alertness blossom from that most elemental prayer. "Imagine raising children in a culture in which gratitude is the first priority," writes Robin Wall Kimmerer, a botanist and member of the Citizen Potawatomi Nation. While lamenting the violence we've perpetrated against each other and against the plants, animals, and earth on whom our lives depend, Kimmerer implores everyone to imagine: "What would it be like to be raised on gratitude? . . . No declarations of political loyalty are required, just a response to a repeated question: 'Can we agree to be grateful for all that is given?'"[14]

For children to learn a language, they need to hear that language consistently spoken by their parents and community leaders over a long time. The seedbed for germinating faith is genuine prayer: deep listening, silence, thankfulness, readiness to come clean and to be embraced by love.

A young mother I know described how patterns of praying together have changed. She recalled how, in her own formative years, she heard and participated in spontaneous, spoken prayers at church. The church where she and her small children attend now rarely practices spoken, spontaneous prayers, focusing instead on forms of written prayers.

We can all learn to cultivate practices of prayer, both written and spontaneous. When we are able simply to say thank you, our spirits open to the divine. When we say thank you, over and over and over, we learn to focus on what is in front of us, rather than being endlessly distracted. We recognize how dependent we are on others and the good gifts of the earth. We stay attuned to what is good around us—and find the power to stand up for what is right and just. Saying thank you prompts us to search for more words to describe how God is present and to learn from others about their experience of God's good gifts. With a simple thank you, we begin to gain fluency in a new language—learning to give voice to our faith—an art that will restore joy and vitality to our families and communities.

PART 2

LEARNING FLUENCY— STEP BY STEP

How Can We Discover Freedom, Honesty, and Resolve When Talking about Faith?

Recovering a lost language or learning to speak a language doesn't happen overnight. But a *desire* to learn will unbolt the door—swinging it wide open—and fill our lungs with sparkling morning air.

We can learn to talk about faith in ways that are honest. We can recover winsome beauty that was lost. We can salt our talk with tears and astonishment. We can capture the grief, joy, and power of what we long for, believe in, and love—with strange and wondrous sacred words that reach out to each other and to God. When we vulnerably speak what we know to be true in our own bodies, minds, and spirits, we will be on our way toward fluency. We will provide children with anchoring language to resist manipulation by the superstitious scaremongers of the world. We will give ourselves language with the gravitas needed to repent of family-, community-, and earth-destroying patterns of living. We will regain moral resolve to help save the world for our children and grandchildren.

Unfortunately, we don't have many models for how to speak in trustworthy ways about faith that don't sound like insider Christianese or religious code speak. Many of the voices we hear in public sound affected, pushy, or offensive. Yet people of faith throughout history have demonstrated countless times how sacred language used well can bring out the best of our humanity, inspiring culture and conscience, sacred music and science—mobilizing vast movements of ordinary people to pursue a vision for God's peaceful, just, and beautiful shalom.

Rather than faith being something we go mum about, and hold in secret—or as sociologist Peter Berger is reported to have said, something that is only "done in private between consenting adults"[1]—we can find the resolve to name what we love and lament; to express something true from the depths of our longing; to acknowledge how hard it is to trust that all will be well, and to describe our desire to know and be known by God.

"As I've tried to talk about God," writes Melissa Florer-Bixler, "which I do almost every Sunday from the pulpit, I'm grateful to discover the grace in speaking the unspeakable, a grace in learning to fail, a grace in finding new ways to talk about a God who is always appearing in and out of view."[2] In my fumbling attempts to speak vulnerably about what I do and don't know of who God is, how we come to know God, and what the Bible, nature, and other cultures teach us about God, more often than not, I fail. With Florer-Bixler, I'm grateful for grace. Grace to fumble out loud. Grace to fumble forward by daring to break open fresh ways to talk about God.

What, I wonder, might guide our flawed and yet fervent desire to become fluent and speak honestly about our faith? Woman Wisdom steps up as a trustworthy guide:

> Hear, for I will speak noble things,
>   and from my lips will come what is right;
> for my mouth will utter truth;
>   wickedness is an abomination to my lips.
> All the words of my mouth are righteous;
>   there is nothing twisted or crooked in them.
> They are all straight to one who understands
>   and right to those who find knowledge.
> Take my instruction instead of silver,
>   and knowledge rather than choice gold;
> for wisdom is better than jewels,
>   and all that you may desire cannot compare with her.
> (Proverbs 8:6-11)

In the company of Woman Wisdom, I offer several principles that have guided me and that, I believe, can guide our shared desire to learn the art of talking about faith—giving voice to what we know and don't know about God. These principles will provide the framework for our further reflection on gaining fluency, in each of the following chapters.

The principles are as follows: (1) First listen! (2) Submit to mystery. (3) Talk about what we love. (4) Hold the world together. (5) Speak from storied, holy ground. These are ground rules for learning to talk about faith with authenticity, humility, love, and conviction. They will give us the best chance for flourishing in these stressful times. They will provide sturdy ground from which to speak with moral integrity to our children—and to the listening world.

FIRST LISTEN!

To speak about faith with authenticity, we must always first *listen.* A favorite Scripture that has guided my stumbling ventures to speak is from the prophet Isaiah: "The Lord God has given me the tongue of a teacher, that I may know how to sustain the weary with a word. Morning by morning he wakens— *wakens my ear to listen* as those who are taught" (Isaiah 50:4, emphasis added). Speaking with genuine understanding first and always requires listening. Many spiritual traditions name listening as indispensable to spiritual understanding, calling it by different names: contemplation, meditation, mindfulness, reflection, prayer, silence.

The question of how to become better listeners is the taproot of all that infuses the language of faith with truthfulness. Listening to each other, to our own bodies, to the trees, sky, and bees, to the wisdom tradition, the daily news, the Scriptures, and the "still, small voice" that speaks despite the earthquake, wind, and fire that threaten to overwhelm; listening for the Spirit.

Listening is learning to give careful attention to ordinary moments. It is, as Stephanie Paulsell writes, staying with the ordinary moment long enough for it "to begin to shine its light on us, on the history to which we belong, and on the world all around." She quotes literary standout Virginia Woolf, who said that "every moment is the center and meeting place of an extraordinary number of perceptions which have not yet been expressed."[3]

This undertaking to listen well will involve risk. For those of us who have reasonably reliable primary relationships, security, and a faith-based moral framework, the risk may not seem all that great. We've not lived with constant fear, and so have the emotional space to wonder and be inquisitive. We can afford to risk expressing what our bodies know, respond to the presence of beauty, and follow nudges of curiosity. But not all of us. Awakening to a desire to see and hear how God is active in our world will be harder for some of us than others. Learning to listen well will require considerable time and patience—among people we learn to trust. We do this learning step by step, with (at least in my case) many course corrections over the long haul.

SUBMIT TO MYSTERY

Leaning in to listen—whether to the pain of persons I know or to the complexity of the natural world—has deepened my love for God, and also shown me how little I really know about God. The more I know, the more aware I am of what I don't know. The odd thing is that the less I presume to know for certain, the more a quiet assurance that I am known and loved grows within—along with a readiness to speak what I believe about God. It may seem ironic, but my experience is in keeping with what the spiritual masters say about how submission to the *mystery* of God will reveal God to us or open up our awareness of God "hidden in plain sight."

Another way to describe "submission" is to reflect on humility—and what it means to be humble in the face of the mystery. A definition of humility that has served me well came from feminist theologian Rosemary Radford Ruether in a seminary class I took with her many years ago. She said that humility is about accurate or realistic self-knowledge. In other words, it's not about being down on oneself, or passively acquiescing to other strong-willed persons. Being humble is about being *honest* with oneself—naming one's strengths and limitations, what one is good at and may not be good at, what one knows and doesn't know. I like this definition because it frees me to be honest about what I can say with a measure of confidence and what I don't really know enough to speak about. It frees all of us, Sarah Coakley suggests, to acknowledge "mystery and unknowing."

"Once there is a full and ready acknowledgement that to make claims about God involves a fundamental submission to mystery and unknowing," Coakley writes, "the issues lose their edge. God is not an extra item in the universe to be known and so controlled, by intellect, will or imagination. God is, rather, that without which there would be nothing at all; God is the source and sustainer of all being, and, as such, the dizzying mystery encountered in the act of contemplation. . . . To know God is unlike any other knowledge; indeed, it is more truly to *be* known, and so transformed."[4]

The challenge then is to find words to speak the unspeakable. Theologian Rowan Williams reminds us that language is an imperfect means of expressing what we know, which we will always struggle with until "something greater than language is here." We each, in our own way, along with countless poets, scholars, theologians, sages, mothers, and fathers, struggle to find words, metaphors, word images, and stories to talk about "the simplest yet most inexhaustible of all subjects, the life upon which all life depends and the embodiment among us of that life in a human life and human words, in the person of Jesus of Nazareth."[5] It is a struggle—but also a marvel—to find words that begin to name the wonder of it all.

IT'S ALL ABOUT BEING IN LOVE

In the introduction, I spoke of faith as a love story with a vision of God that is attractive enough to "magnetize" our deepest human desires toward God. We become a distinctive people of faith, writes James Smith, when our loves and desires are rightly ordered—aligned with the desires of the Creator for our good. We thrive as human beings when our vision of "the good life" or ideal picture of human flourishing runs with the grain of the universe envisioned by the Creator.[6]

Learning to talk about faith will mean figuring out how talking about God is like telling our own love story. Many people wonder why the Song of Songs made it into the Bible. No one knows for sure, writes Paulsell. Scores of both Jewish and Christian interpreters "have found in it the song of the human yearning for God and God's desire to be in relationship with humanity. It is a song about desire, which is also a song about the pain of separation and absence. It is a song about how God loved the people of Israel and desired their good. As a song, it testifies to the beauty of the human body, mutuality in love, the goodness of sexual desire, and the power of love.[7]

We can speak about faith honestly when we remember that, ultimately, faith is all about being in love—learning to trust that one is loved and to vulnerably offer love in return. As with any love story, however, honest talk will need to grapple with when love is twisted toward selfish ends. Or when love is embedded in a grand delusion about myself, my family, my church, or my nation. Any talk of love will need to discern what is true and false, up-building or self-destructive, just or unjust.

A friend, Chris Rice, who is the Mennonite Central Committee United Nations liaison, posted a Facebook comment soon after the murder of George Floyd in Minneapolis: "An unarmed black man in handcuffs, pleading to breathe, killed by a white police officer as other officers remain silent and do nothing to intervene. Another terrible injustice in too long a series. Another sign of unhealed sicknesses in the soul of America (myself included). Love is patient, yes. Yet loving those who do wrong doesn't mean ignoring injustice. Love does not minimize sin or evil. Love is not blind to cancers which have gone deep into the body politic. Love does not mean pretending that everything is okay. Because love without truth lies . . ."

When talking about faith, we must tell the truth about love, our disappointment in love, failure to love, fear of love, and longing for love unfulfilled—along with the joy of knowing one is beloved and expressing love even toward those it is hard to love.

HOLD THE WORLD TOGETHER

I spoke at length in part 1 about the regrettable ways that faith language has been used to push people apart. Speaking about faith with integrity will require learning how to "hold the world together" amid no shortage of polarizing tensions. We can both be real with our own convictions and learn from another's convictions. A little humility (or maybe a lot) is required to admit that one doesn't know it all—and has much to learn from how others encounter God.

None of us can have meaningful conversations about faith if we're not willing to gently hold together the tension of opposing perspectives, to ponder the truth on both sides of a divisive issue, and to let the tension of the division pull our hearts open to a larger and larger love—an image I learned from education philosopher Parker Palmer.

One of the marvels I experienced while serving as president at Anabaptist Mennonite Biblical Seminary was observing how students and faculty from across the theological spectrum related to polarizing issues. We invited everyone, whether so-called conservative or liberal, to submit pre-formed convictions to be tested by persons with different convictions, by the deep wisdom from our faith traditions, by the best scientific and experiential data available—and above all, by the Scriptures. Together, as a learning community, using the best interpretive tools available, we called on the Holy Spirit to bring us from the different places we stood, closer to each other and to Jesus Christ, in whom "all things hold together," and through whom "God was pleased to reconcile to himself all things . . . by making peace through the blood of his cross" (Colossians 1:15-20, excerpted).

SPEAK FROM STORIED, HOLY GROUND

Rather than assuming that faith talk is about obscure doctrines, we gain fluency step by step with stories—real stories about the messy, beautiful stuff of ordinary days. The sturdy ground needed to speak both to our children and grandchildren and to the broader listening public is best acquired by coming to know God in conversation with the stories of others different from us, the stories of the saints, and the stories of the Scriptures.

Rebecca Slough described storytelling to me in this way: "We tend to think that a story has a beginning, a middle, and an end. God's story is a big story with an arc that we can anticipate. But, most of our stories are fragmentary, episodic, sometime long on description and short on action (or vice versa). Our fits and starts in telling stories are important, even though they will be revised, and occasionally scrapped in the future. Most often, we are creating many short folksongs that tell about one event in our lives and not a grand epic opera."

We share stories because, while God may seem absent to many of us, some of us have God moments that remain unspoken unless we're invited to describe what we've seen and heard—even if not fully formed, coherent, or verifiable. As I shared in chapter 1 about pastor Lillian Daniel's cultivation of testimony in her United Church of Christ congregation, we can learn (on the road to rediscovering the lost art of talking about faith) how to speak a personal word about a life event . . . and not "omit God."[8]

And it isn't just our own stories that ground faith, friend and theologian Richard Kauffman said to me, but the stories of those who have gone before us—the heroes of faith often referred to as saints, and the testimonies that fill the pages of the Bible. In our desire to discover stories that shed light on what it means to have faith, we are a lot like the disciples on the road to Emmaus in Luke 24. The two disciples poured out their confusion and despair to the stranger who joined them on the road, lamenting about recent events which involved the crucifixion of the one they had hoped would "redeem Israel" (v. 21), often referred to as the Messiah or the Christ. The stranger, "beginning with Moses and all the prophets," pointed out to them all kinds of things about Christ found throughout the scriptures (v. 27). Later, when they discovered that it was Jesus, the crucified Christ, who had been walking and talking with them, they exclaimed: "Were not our hearts burning within us while he was talking to us on the road, while he was opening the scriptures to us?" (v. 32).

In the chapters that follow, we will look first at how the power of sacred words is ultimately derived from the Word of God, who lived among us full of grace and truth. We will reflect on how learning to talk about bodies awakens us to our shared humanity and how faith gains life force in hard times. We will reflect on how Woman Wisdom, the Bible, and Christian tradition are fonts of sacred language and stories. We will celebrate how curiosity and Mother Nature refresh our language. We will exult in how language is ennobled by beauty and how scientific discoveries open windows on God's face. We will see how language is renewed at its core by worship and prayer, confirming that the art of talking about faith is now and forever a love story.

Listening well, leaning into mystery, talking about what we love, and holding our convictions in gentle tension with others' convictions, while standing on storied, holy ground, will restore a greater sense of our shared humanity and desire to know and be known by God. Our children and grandchildren will be blessed—as will the watching world.

Chapter 7

The Power of Sacred Words Rediscovered

LEARNING TO "SPEAK GOD"

I've heard the story of the wilderness temptation of Jesus many times. When reading it again recently, I was newly intrigued by Jesus' response when the devil taunted, "If you are the Son of God, command these stones to become loaves of bread." Jesus answered, "One does not live by bread alone, *but by every word that comes from the mouth of God*" (Matthew 4:3-4, emphasis added).

Jesus didn't deny that bread (food) is necessary to sustain life. Matthew (a tax collector and disciple of Jesus) described how in contrast to John the Baptist, who "came neither eating nor drinking," Jesus "came eating and drinking, and they say, 'Look, a glutton and a drunkard, a friend of tax collectors and sinners!' Yet wisdom is vindicated by her deeds" (Matthew 11:18-19).

What Jesus declared to the devil is that bread alone is not enough to sustain life. What we need in an ultimate way are words from God. Words that reveal, encourage, rebuke, fortify, bless, and empower. Words that sustain life in its full-orbed pathos and magnificence.

With all the ways words about faith have been twisted beyond recognition, and because many of us have been hesitant to talk freely about what we believe, the language of faith is in peril, with devastating consequences.

"Once a community of speakers realizes that their language is in peril," Jonathan Merritt writes, "they must decide if they want to save it. And some are successful." Hebrew, for example, is the most famous "comeback language." Irish was nearly extinct at the end of the nineteenth century and now has some two million speakers. Hawaiian almost disappeared as a spoken language in the 1800s and now is surging.[1]

Reviving sacred language, writes Merritt, doesn't mean treating words as if they are fossilized—with meanings already locked in. Nor does it mean merely substituting problematic words for ones that seem less offensive—which is really only a way of avoiding the problem. Rather, Merritt proposes that we must muster the courage and imagination to play with sacred words, since words are malleable, open for fresh interpretations, already carrying within themselves many possible meanings.[2] It's as we imaginatively reengage sacred words that they take us on a journey into sacred space and dimensions of love that awaken body, mind, and spirit.

Merritt offers the beautiful image of a Native American tradition for carrying fire from one settlement to another—carefully sheltering live embers in an animal horn. The horn becomes a metaphor for sacred language, he suggests, and words are like the embers we carry to light a torch or start a fire in a new location. The embers don't originate with us, but we need them to light our own torches and community bonfires. Sacred words, like embers, have been carried to us by messengers from generations past. While millions of fire carriers have carelessly dropped or lost live embers, we can discover where they still glow and can reignite a torch to pass on to another generation.[3]

The prophet Ezekiel was a fire carrier of powerful sacred visions and words. The Old Testament book of Ezekiel is filled with spectacular images used extensively throughout history in synagogue and church worship. One of Ezekiel's visions is of a sapphire-looking throne, with a human form above it gleaming like amber enclosed in fire, with splendor all around like "the bow in a cloud on a rainy day" (Ezekiel 1:28). This, says Ezekiel,

> was the appearance of the likeness of the glory of the LORD. When I saw it, I fell on my face, and I heard the voice of someone speaking. He said to me: O mortal, stand up on your feet, and I will speak with you. And when he spoke to me, a spirit entered into me and set me on my feet. . . . He said to me, Mortal, I am sending you to the people of Israel, to a nation of rebels who have rebelled against me; they and their ancestors have transgressed against me to this very day. The descendants are impudent and stubborn. I am sending you to them, and you shall say to them, "Thus says the Lord GOD." (Ezekiel 1:28–2:4)

Ezekiel and his people had been violently uprooted and forced to migrate to a foreign land called Babylon, at about 590 BCE. They were disoriented and traumatized, desperate for a glimmer of hope. Ezekiel reminds his people that they've survived throughout their history, and will survive this exile, not because of their own ingenuity, but because of who God is, the Holy One of Israel. He recounts for them how it was God's spiritual and moral power that led them through the exodus from Egypt generations before. He reminds them that even now, it is the spiritual and moral power that flows from God's temple, not from the king's palace, that will liberate them—a power that is centered in worship.

Unlike the previous prophets Isaiah and Jeremiah, whose proclamations were written down after oral delivery, Ezekiel experiences the word of God as a written scroll.[4] "I looked, and a hand was stretched out to me, and a written scroll was in it. He spread it before me; it had writing on the front and on the back, and written on it were words of lamentation and mourning and woe. . . . He said to me, Mortal, eat this scroll that I give you and fill your stomach with it. Then I ate it; and in my mouth it was as sweet as honey" (Ezekiel 2:9–3:3).

Ezekiel is not merely to speak the word but to ingest it, take it in bodily. The scroll, though written with words of lamentation and mourning and woe, becomes as sweet as honey when eaten. Astonishing!

Where does this all end up for a despairing people? The trajectory of the book of Ezekiel brings us to a vision of the new temple: "[I] will set my sanctuary among them forevermore. My dwelling place shall be with them; and I will be their God, and they shall be my people" (Ezekiel 37:26-7). A stream of water flowing from the sanctuary begins as a trickle and then grows into a vast river that restores fertility to barren, dry lands. Stagnant waters become fresh, and everything lives where the river goes—every living creature, swarms of fish, and all kinds of trees for food, whose leaves are for healing (Ezekiel 47).

The rejuvenating river flows not from the king's palace but from a worshiping community who knows God's Word and glorifies God as the source of peace and freedom. The end of the story, writes biblical scholar Millard Lind, isn't enslavement by an empire but freedom and restoration that flow out of worship; a people emboldened by the Word of the Lord, spoken, in this case, by a defenseless prophet.[5]

So how might we be invited to "eat the scroll"? I'm drawn to studies on resilience—a widely studied phenomenon. Some communities have the capacity to absorb a disturbance—like a forest fire (in an ecological system) or a pandemic (in a social system)—and reorganize while remaining true to who they are. And some don't. Disruptive events can destroy communities, or they can release new potential, said social innovations analyst Frances Westley in a November 19, 2012, public address on "Social Innovation and Resilience." What, I wonder, will empower us to be resilient in these disruptive, chaotic times? What will free us to reorganize, innovate, and release new potential while remaining true to who we are? I believe it is all about the Word of God—and the many ways we learn to listen, ingest, and embody "every word that comes from the mouth of God."

Merritt reports that younger generations are having more spiritual conversations than older generations, and in fact, he claims, "millennials are having more conversations about religion or spirituality than any other generation."[6] I've observed in the seminary communities I related to over my decades as a teacher and administrator that international students from around the world talk freely about their faith, and students of color, most of whom know far more about resilience than their white peers, show how faith and faith language is alive and well in their communities.

I have been privileged to participate in many communities who bring intense interest to understanding the meaning and power of sacred words, mining their rich depths of meaning and discovering their power to liberate and heal. I engage in this work because I know that "speaking God" with each other will make us more resilient, fortify us for facing the harsh reality of climate change, equip us to counter racialized violence with strong love, and provide solace in the midst of economic hardship. As we learn to carry embers from bonfires that warmed communities since ancient times into our own backyards, and from there to start new fires wherever we go, we rediscover the power of sacred words.

FIRST LISTEN!

Reengaging with sacred words that help us speak about God will require honesty, imagination, and (dare I say) a measure of playfulness. When we listen to how words are being used, we quickly discover that we mean quite different things when we say "God" or "salvation" or "world" or "peace" or "gospel" or "kingdom of God" or "sin" or "justice." Word meanings have histories, stories, multidimensional depths of wisdom that can be teased out when we're ready to listen to what's in play for others from different cultures and communities. There are experts to whom we can turn for meanings of words in original languages, ancient cultures, particular contexts, but what we most need to do first and always is listen to each other around the kitchen table, over lunch breaks at work, or while out walking together. What does "God" mean to you? How do you understand the meaning of "salvation"? What is the "gospel" really? Listening well, without becoming reactive or dogmatic, can be hard, hard work. Most of us assume these words are fossilized, to use Merritt's word, with precise, tamper-free meanings. We can quickly become defensive when a word precious to us is being poorly used. Yet reacting in haste before hearing someone out will be counterproductive in the long run.

I prefer to think of sacred words as if they are like skin. Skin is our body's largest organ—the one we wear on the outside. Adults carry around some eight pounds and twenty-two square feet of skin. It's elastic, responds to touch, is sensitive to changing temperatures, and replaces dead cells with living ones while constantly maintaining bodily integrity—staying intact and covering and protecting our bodies.

It can be hard work to get inside the skin of sacred words, but gaining fluency will require that we do. For us to examine word meanings from the inside out, we need to create spaces where we feel safe enough to speak our own perspective and honor what we hear from one another. I remember working as a teacher to create a space that felt both safe and challenging—safe enough that people could openly bring their full selves into the conversation and challenging enough to dare to think in new ways about important matters. I like the way others have described the listening, learning space needed for personal growth as "brave space."

Krista Tippet writes that Parker Palmer likens the "nature of the soul to a wild animal deep in the woods of our psyche that if approached brusquely or cross-examined will simply run away. We have to create quiet, inviting, and trustworthy spaces, Parker says, to keep the insights and presence of soul at the table." And another educator noted that "we put words around what the soul knows . . . not through what we *think*, but through what we *are*, through the story of our lives."[7] In committing ourselves to listen first, we must create brave spaces where we can dare to listen well, speak honestly, and examine word meanings from multiple perspectives, without undue fear.

SUBMIT TO MYSTERY

A frequently cited quote from Michel de Montaigne (1533–92), an influential philosopher of the French Renaissance, brings a smile of recognition to my face: "I speak the truth not so much as I would, but as much as I dare, and I dare a little more as I grow older." He describes it well for me. With the years, I become more daring for examining the meaning of words, and more humble about my own limited perspective, more open to the mystery of God at work through many cultures, and thus more eager to learn from others at home and around the world.

Among the people with whom I share a common Mennonite Swiss-German ancestry, there's a strong tendency to avoid hard conversations about faith-related matters. We learn to be nice in passive-aggressive ways and save what we really think for select insiders who agree with us. Or we simply withdraw in silence. Learning to speak respectfully in the midst of disagreements and carefully listening to discover what can be known from another's story are skills some of us are slowly gaining. We learn these skills if we're willing to submit to Christ's plea: "Just as I have loved you, you also should love one another" (John 13:34). Loving each other will mean staying in the circle to listen even when it's hard instead of hurrying to form privatized associations that reflect our tribe's purity brand. The more often we model honest, respectful conversations to get inside the "skin" of sacred words, of core beliefs, of deep longings for God, the more we'll regain moral credibility as Christians.

The mystery of sacred words is their power to transcend cultures, leap over national boundaries, speak truths that link us in our shared humanity to God no matter where in the world we live. As a child, I first heard faith talked about in what was for me a foreign land. I spent much of my childhood in Ethiopia, and watched how the language of faith transcended cultural, ethnic, and national borders. Ever since, I've been fascinated with how the heartbeat of faith has strong resonance in vastly different cultural contexts and yet dresses up in widely varied "clothes." There is really nothing so liberating for sacred words as to hear them spoken by persons of other cultures experiencing their power for the first time. Persons from other cultural and racial communities provide white Westerners with a window into the Spirit-power of sacred words. We have much to learn from Christ followers around the world about how faith infuses all of life, and how to get inside sacred words.

In the end, sacred words flow out of worship and a people who are freed, as Ezekiel declared, by the Word of the Lord—and the fullest expression of that Word: the earthshaking life and love of Jesus Christ.

IT'S ALL ABOUT BEING IN LOVE

I read Toni Morrison's book *Home* last summer. In an essay about Morrison's religious vision, Amy Frykholm talks about how the eventual salvation for the book's two main characters, Frank and Cee, is the women of the town who offer what Morrison calls a "demanding love," a love that can heal what was broken while helping them tell the truth about their lives. Frykholm observes that while the women of the town "harshly criticize the choices Cee has made in her life," they also show her "a delicate mercy and work to rebuild Cee in body and spirit." They say, "You good enough for Jesus. That's all you need to know." The reviewer further observes that almost every novel Morrison wrote contains women who are "straight-talking, hardworking, and nurturing to a degree that is holy, perhaps divine."[8]

Morrison's story reminds me of a story my father told Malcolm Gladwell while they sat in my parents' living room. Gladwell included the interview in the first season of his *Revisionist History* podcast in a popular episode called "Generous Orthodoxy." The story tells about how as a young adult, my gay brother unloaded his deep distress to our parents after a high school class reunion where former friends "hit me over the head with the Bible." He declared angrily that he wanted nothing more to do with the church. On his way out the door, my mother called after him, "Don't give up on Jesus." My brother turned and looked at her with a warm smile.

How do we love one another in situations of breakdown and intractable disagreement? I have seen it happen when we're invited to tell our personal stories in spaces where leaders and participants hold together straight talk with mercy. When we stay at the table, honoring each other enough to listen with open minds and hearts, we can be direct about our own convictions even as we listen for the source of others' convictions. When we honor each other's stories about God encounters or disappointments, we find ourselves in a sacred space.

Disagreements are a normal part of human communities—and acutely so in the church. Yet many of our congregations remain "shallow and immature" because we do all we can to avoid any appearance of disagreement, observes community organizer Christopher Smith. Leadership that is authoritarian "imposes a sharp order on a world that is not nearly so neat," including the right meaning of words. Authoritarian leaders are quick to punish and exclude those who question their interpretation of word meanings. In contrast, non-anxious, healthy leaders transparently acknowledge where there is disagreement, find ways to facilitate honest conversation, and bring people together to talk about the Jesus way, holding together the wisdom of Scripture, the traditions we've inherited, and what we know from daily experiences and scientific data.[9]

When we commit first-first-first to love each other and sort out our differences with negotiated protocols for conversation that help us feel safe and brave, we will experience what Jesus longed for: "By this everyone will know that you are my disciples, if you have love for one another" (John 13:35). Finding ways to speak honestly about what wholesome sexuality and spirituality entail, for example, is essential for the well-being of our children, families, and faith communities. We've failed miserably and can patiently learn how to hold together straight talk and delicate mercy.

HOLD THE WORLD TOGETHER

"Be truthful, not neutral," Christiane Amanpour, CNN's chief international correspondent, said in an interview. I like that. Truth-telling was a noted feature of my nine years as president at AMBS. I, along with other colleagues, offered straight talk about the sexual violations of a famous former professor several decades before and about the seminary's inadequate response then, which significantly exacerbated harm to victims. We offered long overdue apologies, seeking with everything in our moral fiber to hold straight talk (rooted in evidence and facts) together with mercy.[10]

My public communication during the years I served as president was received with appreciation by many and offended others. I am grateful for those who spoke directly with me about where they perceived I might have misspoken and also listened carefully to me when I disagreed with their assessment of what I was doing. As I wrote at the time, "Giving-and-receiving-counsel, when wedded with giving-and-receiving-mercy, provides the comfort and courage we all need for communities of faith to flourish."

While the raw pain of prejudice and fractured relationships throbs, there is comfort within communities who do the hard work needed to learn to trust each other enough to be directly truthful with each other. There is comfort in communities who offer forthright apology for the pain we cause each other. There is comfort in communities that embody radical hospitality strong enough to embrace those different from ourselves. There is comfort in communities that are spiritually mature enough to tenderly hold each other within the wideness of God's mercy. "Comfort, O comfort my people, says your God. Speak tenderly to Jerusalem" (Isaiah 40:1-2).

SPEAK FROM STORIED, HOLY GROUND

"A meaningful life is woven with stories," novelist Amy Gottlieb has written, and "generous compassionate listening may be the most sacred act of all."[11]

My story is one that includes truth-telling after listening to the stories of victims of sexual abuse. Along with truth-telling comes the question of moral authority—or whose truth, whose stories, we deem authoritative, worth heeding and believing. I often ponder what it was about Jesus' authority that astonished the people of his day. Jesus was an exemplar of moral indignation. He minced no words about those who harmed children, for example. In fact, Jesus says it would be better for such persons "if a great millstone were fastened around your neck and you were drowned in the depth of the sea" (Matthew 18:6).

When I hear a church leader describe how fellow bishops used a "machete" to cut off those who mingle with the wrong people, I begin to understand what prompted Jesus to turn over the tables of the money changers. Jesus got most riled up at righteous purists who used their power to keep those deemed unworthy or the wrong race or of little value or diseased or impure out of the temple, outside of the community of God's beloved.

Many of us, including myself, know what it's like to be silenced by those in authority, to be put in our place, to be told they don't want to listen to what we think or engage with why we think it's important.

I want to be among those who hold together conviction with kindness, and truth-telling with mercy. I want to be among those who speak with moral authority on behalf of victims and disenfranchised persons. I want to be among those who don't shy away from the power of sacred words grounded in the wise, compassionate, justice-seeking, and righteous authority of Jesus.

For too long, many of us have been silent about our faith. We are long overdue to break the silence and learn to be personal and public truth-tellers—unafraid to speak and act with authenticity and authority. Yet if followers of Jesus are to have any transformative impact in these troubled times, we can't be like other self-righteous bullies out there.

I want to be someone who uses sacred words wisely, in ways that dignify every person and every created plant, animal, rock, and river I encounter. I want to show such reverence toward that-of-God in another created being that I am willing to listen rather than shut them down, cherish rather than harm, revere rather than destroy. I want what moral authority I speak with to be filled with grace and truth.

Jesus proclaimed in life and word the dawning of the kingdom of God—or as some like to playfully call it, the kin-dom of God. Jesus, the Word of God in human form, taught us to pray, "Thy kingdom come, Thy will be done on earth, as it is in heaven." In the most extraordinary story of human history, Jesus inaugurated God's kingdom of shalom. Some two thousand years later, in the company of the Holy Spirit, each of us is invited into this everlasting kingdom whose kin are known by their fearlessness, compassion, peaceableness, daring, creativity, patience, kindness, just living, and joy.

As with Ezekiel of old, when we "eat the scroll," we will be surprised by how sacred words become as sweet as honey in our mouth. Those sweet words, even when filled with lamentation, mourning, and woe, are the words that make it possible to tell our part of the greatest love story of all time. A poet of both original and borrowed text described that love story this way:

> O love of God, how rich and pure!
> How measureless and strong!
> It shall forevermore endure
> the saints' and angels' song.
>
> Could we with ink the ocean fill,
> and were the skies of parchment made;
> were every stalk on earth a quill,
> and everyone a scribe by trade;
> to write the love of God above
> would drain the ocean dry;
> nor could the scroll contain the whole,
> though stretched from sky to sky.[12]

Chapter 8

Coming Home to Body and Voice

IT'S ABOUT BEING HUMAN

Language that isn't filled with the pathos and wonder of living and dying as human beings on Planet Earth becomes an empty shell. When we try to describe the pathos and wonder of being human, we also find ourselves reaching for ways to talk about God. Language about God and about the meaning of life rings true only when rooted in the bond of humanity we share with every single person the world round.

A wonderful example of this comes from the biblical letter to Christians in Asia Minor—a letter likely written by the early church leader Paul in the later part of the first century. In the letter, Paul talks about "the plan of the mystery hidden for ages in God who created all things; so that through the church the wisdom of God in its rich variety might now be made known" (Ephesians 3:9-10).

The phrases from this ancient letter sound at first blush like shells of wordy esoterica. New Testament scholar Tom Yoder Neufeld, however, shows the pathos and wonder that fill these words in a way that astonishes me. The mystery revealed in Jesus Christ is that, along with the insider Jews, "the Gentiles have become fellow heirs, members of the same body, and sharers in the promise in Christ Jesus through the gospel" (Ephesians 3:6). The body, or the church that emerges from the joining of two formerly antagonistic people groups, is the manifestation of the *wisdom of God in its rich varieties*.[1]

In other words, the *wisdom of God in its rich varieties* is that insiders and outsiders (or Jews and Gentiles) discovered that the humanity they shared was just that: *a shared humanness; a shared longing to be loved and live in peace, without abuse, fear, or condemnation.* That people long alienated from one another, oppressed because of their race or gender, formerly victims of violence or prone to use violence *could be a new people together* was a source of great wonderment in the early church. When persons from all walks of life comprehended the new freedom and personal dignity made possible by Jesus Christ, the language of faith exploded in a tumult of amazement. Christian faith spread like wildfire.

Richard Rohr observes in a public post called "Universal Dignity in a Debauched Empire" that the revolutionary character of the Christian movement was the profound sense of the inherent dignity of every human person—"which was unheard of before [Paul's] time"—dignity for every human being regardless of race, religion, gender, nationality, class, education, or social position. Paul's teaching had tremendous influence. Why? Because human dignity was at such a low ebb—with widespread slavery, women regarded as property, temple prostitution, and wholesale injustice toward the poor and outsider. When Paul declares, "You, all of you, are sons and daughters of God, now clothed in Christ, where there is no distinction between male or female, Greek or Jew, slave or free, but all of you are one in Christ Jesus" (Galatians 3:26-28, Rohr's translation), this would have seemed both impossible and "utterly attractive and hopeful to the 95% who had no dignity in that society."[2]

Much has changed since Paul was writing nearly two thousand years ago, but when it comes to the desire for human dignity no matter who we are—*nothing has changed!* Yet now, as then, evil disrespect is promoted from the highest rulers in the land on down. One way to describe what we're experiencing in the United States, at least, is a "crisis of contempt" with wholesale contempt for people we disagree with or deem to be different, other, alien.

There is perhaps no more urgent reason we must learn to speak persuasively about faith than to resist the diabolical forces driven by contempt and to reclaim the distinct beauty of every single human life. "We need to tackle the evil together— equal in the presence of God," South African peace activist Oscar Siwali declared in a sermon at Prairie Street Mennonite Church. "Is the color of our skin most important, or our identity in Jesus Christ *and* as human beings more important? We might have different colors, but we are blood brothers and sisters. We might be different, but we are one; and together we can do so much more."

FIRST LISTEN!

It's unlikely that we'll have any enthusiasm about being blood brothers and sisters in faith, whether with the neighbor next door or across the world, unless we're more candid about our own humanness—including our vulnerable, sometimes bewildering bodies. Faith language will evaporate in clouds of empty vapor, disconnected from anything real, unless we listen first to our bodies and learn to be comfortable in our own skin.

Much of my life has been marked by a quite high level of anxiety. This may be attributed to having grown up as a "third culture kid"—born in Ethiopia to American parents, then suddenly thrust as an adolescent back into American culture when my family returned to the United States. To protect myself from what was unfamiliar and frightening, I withdrew internally. I learned to project an external shell of self-confidence quite out of sync with how I felt inside.

Learning to be present in the moment—to be vulnerable and real—has been hard, hard work for me. One revelatory, life-changing encounter as a young adult was reading Thomas Merton's *New Seeds of Contemplation* for a college creative writing class in 1973. I had never read Merton before. The entire book, now yellowed, has underlining on nearly every page. There are two paragraphs, however, that indelibly etched themselves into my consciousness. They named my reality so spot on that it was as if the lock on an internal prison cell suddenly sprang open.

Merton described a "false self" around which I wind experiences, covering myself with pleasures and glory like bandages in order to be perceptible to myself and to the world, "as if I were an invisible body that could only become visible when something visible covered its surface. But"—this I starred in the margin and underlined—"there is no substance under the things with which I am clothed. I am hollow, and my structure of pleasures and ambitions has no foundation. I am objectified in them. . . . And when they are gone there will be nothing left of me but my own nakedness and emptiness and hollowness, to tell me that I am my own mistake."

Thankfully, Merton didn't leave me there—naked and empty. He continued, "The secret of my identity is hidden in the love and mercy of God."[3]

A lot of persistence, encouragement, failure, intense struggle, and digging myself out of holes to try again and again have brought more harmony between my inner and outer selves; between my scared, uptight body and a body that knows how to wholeheartedly laugh. Over time, I've discovered that the more comfortable I am in my own skin, the better I'm able to be present to others—listening calmly in high-anxiety moments; less intimidated by persons different from me and circumstances beyond my control. It was with no small measure of surprise in the last decade that I received commendations for being a non-anxious leader.

I've seen a similar transformation happen for many others who, in finding a trustworthy context to open up, felt free to vulnerably talk about shame, regret, and failure that had locked them in. With an invitation to risk being candid about the inner stuff that was hidden away in fear, persons come home to themselves and alive to the presence of God. Lillian Daniel, who cultivated the practice of testimony in her United Church of Christ congregation, writes, "I began to notice recently that testimonies are usually stories about some sort of transformation. They often tell a story that could be summed up: 'I used to feel, or be, or behave this way, but now something has changed.'" Furthermore, she says, "Over and over again, people told me that testimony was opening up our church, not only creating excitement in worship, but in the coffee hour discussions as well. We were making new friends, hearing new stories of faith, being woken up by the Word."[4]

SUBMIT TO MYSTERY

Learning to talk about faith is all about learning to be vulnerable and present to other people and to God. The irony is that the more comfortable we are in our own skin, and submit to our humanness, the more we will flourish not only as human beings, but also as spiritual beings. This is bound up in the mystery of what it means to be created beings for whom being oriented toward the Creator is a necessary condition to being "fully or properly human," observes James Smith. He notes that Irenaeus, a Greek bishop from the second century, put it this way: "The glory of God is a human being fully alive."[5]

Growing up, I was taught that dancing is provocative and bad, so to discover as an adult the joy it releases—especially in worship, or with persons I dearly love—was amazing. It's hard to sit still when great music fills the room. My body wants to respond. The exuberance that accompanies a full-bodied response, swaying with the beat, is exhilarating. But unless I'm with people who also love to move to music, I must stifle the impulse. It makes me far too vulnerable. Given that the staid worship of most white North American churches I frequent precludes dancing, I do it in the privacy of my own home, with my husband or grandchildren.

A recent Facebook post by friend and missiologist James Krabill highlighted an amazing comment that East African theologian John Mbiti reportedly said: "We do theology with our feet. If you can't dance your theology, it becomes superficial, disembodied, and eventually disconnected from life's realities." I could not agree more. Our talk about God has become so disembodied, so disconnected from life's realities, that it's like "a noisy gong or a clanging cymbal." Dancing, singing our hearts out, washing feet, kneeling, sharing a meal, wailing in grief are bodily practices. Ironically, it is precisely because they're rooted in our bodies that, mysteriously, they open our spirits as well.

IT'S ALL ABOUT BEING IN LOVE

"With my body I thee worship" is one of my husband's favorite lines. It may seem too personal a line to share in public—and yet the line is taken directly from a public liturgy; a marriage liturgy of the Anglican Book of Common Prayer. The language is a tad archaic. Updated contemporary vows use alternative phrases about honoring and cherishing. But something beautifully solemn is lost in the alternatives. "With my body I thee worship" boldly declares for all to hear that marriage includes bodily devotion to one's partner. This public declaration, with its poetic beauty, is held within the deep wisdom of a traditional, communal recognition that keeping faith (*fidelity*) with one's partner is profoundly good. That this bodily honoring of one's partner is declared within public worship of our creator God makes all the difference in the world.

I long for more honest conversations in church communities about why thoughtful consideration about who will have sex with whom matters, and why finding public ways to honor bodies belongs in public worship. It is in our communal interest, our children's interest, and our personal individual interest to reclaim the wisdom of the traditional assertion that for all involved, a decision to have sex with a partner should involve a public declaration of devotion to the body of that partner in the context of worship. This declaration belongs in the church as the body of Christ for the safety, integrity, and shared goodness of all involved.

"In our day, when 'sexual freedom' seems to signify only multiple sexual partners," writes Stephanie Paulsell, "it is good to remember that postponing or refusing sexual relationships can also be a gesture toward freedom. It is good for young people, whose sexual selves are still unfolding, to know that delaying full sexual expression might preserve for them the freedom to live into a deeply satisfying sexual life as adults. It is good for couples practicing the discipline of sexual fidelity to remember the freedom that unfolds over time when two people remain committed to one another's pleasure in a context of trust and faithfulness."[6]

Paulsell suggests that "young people who have grown up learning that the body mirrors back to us something important about God and that the body's desires are a precious gift from God . . . have a compass to help them negotiate the road to sexual maturity." Communities that frequently talk about the "goodness of the body will be better able to resist viewing the body as a source of shame." And communities "that greet the image of God in gay bodies and straight bodies, in bodies of all sizes and shapes, all races, all colors, create a harbor for all who are growing into their sexual selves."[7]

Finding ways to honor each other's bodies will amplify our regard for the One who "knit" our bodies together, evoking praise with the psalmist, "For it was you who formed my inward parts; you knit me together in my mother's womb. I praise you, for I am fearfully and wonderfully made. Wonderful are your works; that I know very well" (Psalm 139:13-14).

HOLD THE WORLD TOGETHER

In so many ways, we're all alike—as human beings. We all want many of the same things: food in our stomachs, fresh air and clean water, safety from abuse, shelter from the elements, personal dignity, and love in our families. We all feel pain and pleasure in some of the same ways. Yet each of our individual and peoplehood stories is unique. That we are so alike as human beings with bodies and yet so very different as ethnic groups, nationalities, and religious bodies is a source of immense intrigue and enormous pain.

The biblical narratives provide a framework that holds open both a wide embrace of everyone (all peoples, tribes, and nations) centered in our shared humanity, and the freedom to be a distinctive, called out people. This is a *real strength* of a biblically grounded faith—and one that in our talk about faith, equips us to celebrate each person's or tribe's or ethnic group's distinctive gifts and to call out ways those particular gifts are a blessing for the good of all.

In an *On Being* public radio interview for reimagining the public good of theology, Ruby Sales spoke about the tension of holding commonality and difference together. "We live in a very diverse world, and to talk about what it means to be human is to talk with the simultaneous tongue of universality and particularities," she said. "As a Black person, to talk about what it means is to talk about my experience as an African American person, but also to talk about my experience that transcends being an African American, to the universal experience. So I think we've got to stop speaking about humanity as if it's monolithic. We've got to wrap our consciousness around a world where people bring to the world vastly different histories and experiences, but at the same time, a world where we experience grief and love in some of the same ways."[8]

In a livestream conversation between theologian Drew Hart and two other faith leaders from Harrisburg, Pennsylvania, soon after the murder of George Floyd, pastor and ministry founder Roma Benjamin illustrated what I heard Sales saying, which I paraphrase: "What is it that those policemen couldn't feel for this human being? God called us all humankind. Yet we must be mindful of the divider that's come between us.

America has two sets of forefathers. My forefathers came in chains. Another set of America's forefathers had slaves. We have to go back and reeducate people. We have to help our colleagues have these conversations."[9]

SPEAK FROM STORIED, HOLY GROUND

Telling stories seems to be a universal human activity that is common to all and yet highlights what is unique to each of our histories. Who we are as individuals is always a part of larger conversations and stories. The story of my birth in Nazareth, Ethiopia, is always situated within the story of the death of our next-door neighbor a day later, and the impact of that death on the name my parents chose for me. My childhood family's story is always situated within the Jesus story, and his great commission: "Go therefore and make disciples of all nations, baptizing them in the name of the Father and of the Son and of the Holy Spirit, and teaching them to obey everything that I have commanded you" (Matthew 28:19-20). My own children's stories are situated within the particular identity of our church as one of the historic peace churches and their parents' calling to be peacebuilders across the polarizing divide of East and West during the Cold War in what was then a communist country, former Yugoslavia. My grandchildren's stories are situated within stories of a global pandemic, climate change, and the Black Lives Matter movement, along with other movements to assure justice for all peoples in a world God created for human flourishing.

Tom Yoder Neufeld writes that the history of the Christian movement "is full of stories of diverse people bound together in congregations—women and men, rich and poor, highly educated and uneducated, native peoples and foreigners—worshiping and working together in the same church community."[10] In fact, the church is most powerful "when it is diverse ethnically, racially, culturally, and socioeconomically—when it is made up of those who should not be able to coexist."[11]

I was struck by Roma Benjamin's questions about the lack of church-based diversity, which I paraphrase: "Who gave us this language—white church? Black church? Hispanic church? Chinese church? Who segregated us this way? How many Gods do we serve? God of the white church? Of the Black church? Of the Chinese church? Jesus said 'Thy kingdom come. Thy will be done.' It's heartbreaking to see the lack of biblical response from white evangelical Christianity. We have turned our churches into Democratic and Republican—and try to make everyone see and think the same things. We are all evangelicals. We really need to address this with our white pastors. We need to sit down and have a serious conversation."

In the same conversation, Hart talked about how he constantly sees that young people are attracted to churches which are grappling with these things and fleeing from churches which aren't willing to deal with the issues that are affecting them. None of us should be satisfied to go back to church as it was before, he said. Too often we have simplistic, sentimental answers to complex problems. We have to name what's been happening, be honest about our past, and talk about what it means to be Christ's body on earth.

Paul writes eloquently about the church as the body of Christ. "For just as the body is one and has many members, and all the members of the body, though many, are one body, so it is with Christ. For in the one Spirit we were all baptized into one body—Jews or Greeks, slaves or free—and we were all made to drink of one Spirit. . . . If one member suffers, all suffer together with it; if one member is honored, all rejoice together with it. Now you are the body of Christ and individually members of it" (1 Corinthians 12:12-13, 26-27).

Bodies are amazing—strong and agile. They are also extremely vulnerable. They become ill and are broken and crushed. Bodies are resilient, with the capacity for regeneration and healing. It's hard work to keep a body in good shape or to restore a broken body. What a wonder it is to observe healthy bodies with the capacity to bless and heal others. And even more, to observe entire congregations who are healthy— honoring the human dignity of everyone.

In writing about his congregation's intentional commitment to promote healthy conversation, Christopher Smith describes the communication patterns of a body as an unceasing, round-the-clock conversation among a vast network of neurons that tells us how to move, respond, talk, and think. Data from our senses is passed at light speed from outside the body to the brain. The brain instantaneously and constantly processes data, discerning what it means and sending instructions to all parts of the body.[12] So it must be for communities of faith; for the church. We must cultivate conversation as blood brothers and sisters to fill the skin of words like justice, worship, evangelical, sexual fidelity, freedom, body of Christ, and Spirit with stories of lived faith. We will rediscover the power of sacred words when they are filled with the pathos and wonder of living and dying as people with bodies—bodies that share humanness in common even though we carry very different stories of what it's like to be human.

Chapter 9

Fortifying Words Needed in Hard Times

RESILIENT FAITH BLOSSOMS IN HARD TIMES

We all love to hear good news—big news like a grandbaby's safe arrival, a Supreme Court decision coming down fairly, a salary increase, a successful surgery, a church conflict that resolved amicably. Or less important fun news like the unexpected call we got a few years back from the travel agency: "You won. You won." Won what? "Oh, don't you remember? Our customer name drawing. We pulled your name. You won two free round-trip tickets to Las Vegas." (Las Vegas? Hmm. Could I divert the tickets to some other destination?)

Perhaps we love good news so much because it seems we're generally awash in bad news—sudden onset of serious illness, tragic death of a family member, elderly parent isolated in a nursing home lockdown, neighbors grabbed by ICE and deported, worsening economic woes, boiling over racial tensions, frightening climate events.

We deal with bad news and the hard times that ensue in lots of different ways: anger, bitterness, despair, anxiety, shaking our fists at God, blaming the government, organizing protests, throwing things, crawling under the covers, eating comfort food, rolling up our sleeves, praying.

When I was particularly distraught by a double tragedy affecting people in our community—my dear friend's husband and her daughter's husband, both killed within ten days of each other in separate horrific accidents—I sat at the piano, tears streaming down my face, wondering what in the world there was to sing that might assuage the confusion, anger, and grief. I happened onto the song "Halle, Halle, Hallelujah!" (a traditional Caribbean song arranged by John Bell). As I began singing, my rational brain kept vetoing the song. Wrong song! Wrong song! Who sings hallelujahs when experiencing such loss? Where's the mad, sad, angry song I should really be singing? Yet as I pounded the keys, the song began to possess me. I played and sang on and on and on, louder and louder, with no desire to stop. In the process I found that I was transported to another place. A place where *God is God*, no matter what. The change happened inexplicably. Without expectation. And it was real.

Bitterness, grief, and anger come easily for me. Much of it is a healthy response, arising out of deep comprehension that tragedy, injustice, abuse, and illness are not right or good or fair. The prophets of the Old Testament railed against injustice. The psalmist cried out in distress amid tragedy and lament amid the horror of violence. Jesus turned over the tables of the money changers, called Herod a fox, and wept over Jerusalem. We must not lose our edge or the ferocious passion to name brokenness for what it is. Without the sacred language of lament and anger animated by a fierce devotion to justice, love, moral righteousness, and peace, we can become trapped in fatalism and despair that the world is broken beyond repair.

The scriptural visions that are born from among a suffering people, whether in the wilderness, after forced migration, or under Roman persecution, have an unbelievable power. The Hebrew Scriptures, writes Walter Brueggemann, are the stories of a people's encounters with God, a new God whose name was not known before; a God who, unlike other gods, is responsive to the groans of the uncredentialed, the enslaved; a God who answers groans with mercy, compassion, justice, and liberation from oppression. The Hebrew Scriptures are stories of miracle and wonderment from a people who emerged out of nothing to become a named, free, and beloved community; a people with whom God forged a covenant of love.[1] I am convinced that it is only profound suffering that makes human beings wise enough to comprehend what is truly at stake—and open enough to perceive our utter dependency on God's provision and love from which nothing in all creation can separate us.

The import of this chapter is not at all to suggest that an experience of suffering is a virtue to be sought out, or that we should go looking for opportunities to suffer. Nor is it meant to flippantly imply that it's good for people to suffer because it will make them strong or wise. Nor am I saying that people victimized by abuse or discrimination or persecution should welcome or prolong their suffering because there is some elevated spiritual merit to be had. These are serious and evil distortions of what is one of the most profound and difficult truths at the heart of Christian faith—that suffering awakens us to our mortality and our need for each other and God. It is in the midst of suffering that many people search for faith with a backbone and for sacred words with enough real power to sustain hope.

Given that most faith-infused poetry, prayers, practices, and stories arise among people who cry out to God from a place of debilitating suffering, those of us who live in relative comfort have little genuine appreciation for their transformative power. Coming to Western Europe from a context where religion was repressed and believers were persecuted, Tatiana Goricheva observes that "in the churches here, one soon notices that everyone's attitude is somehow not an attitude of prayer. . . . That is something that I could never have imagined, that people can get used to church. It shows that the church can become the most boring institution in the world. It shows that one can dissolve into banality the miracle of faith that moves mountains and raises the dead."[2]

Many Christians view the decline of Christian faith in Western countries with alarm, but the history of God's people is a history of life cycles, writes theologian Elaine Heath. A new movement is born out of resistance to oppressive powers. First there is clarity about call and identity as a resistance movement. This is followed by a season of relative comfort, which leads eventually to complacency. A desire to maintain the status quo leads to collusion with the powers, and then catastrophic loss. The season of loss and marginalization has the impact of restoring the church, Heath writes. It is those on the margins of society who, during this "dark night of the soul" find voice again for their faith—and increasingly organize to resist the powers of oppression, which begins the cycle again.[3]

Faith is reborn, over the centuries, among people who experience the bald face of hatred and injustice and find that learning to trust God provides a strong spine of resilience in hard times. Faith is reborn in hard economic times, frightening times like a global pandemic, and worrisome times when we face a possible ecological collapse because of climate change. Faith is reborn when we name the crushing harms of racism, militarism, sexism, consumerism, and the despoilment of our world's flora and fauna. Faith is reborn when we examine ourselves and repent of personal sins of selfishness, dishonesty, jealousy, sexual exploitation, hatred, and fear. Faith is reborn when we repent for our participation in systems of injustice and devote ourselves to walking with fellow human beings who are suffering. Faith is reborn when we rediscover the deep wells of wisdom from our ancestors—and the power of sacred words they cherished.

FIRST LISTEN!

Over the years, when feeling fearful, vulnerable, overwhelmed, I've learned what a relief it is to simply say so. Somehow, letting go of any pretense otherwise frees me to lean into trust. I've often been buoyed by what I believe is the Holy Spirit, encouraging me to not be afraid. Over and over, I've turned in some fashion to this anchoring language: "Surely God is my salvation; I will trust, and will not be afraid, for the LORD GOD is my strength and my might; he has become my salvation" (Isaiah 12:2). It is in listening first to our *own* vulnerability before God that our hearts are opened to attend to the suffering of others and to speak up on their behalf—a solidarity at the heart of Christian faith. Jesus said, "Truly I tell you, just as you did it to one of the least of these who are members of my family, you did it to me" (Matthew 25:40).

Howard Thurman, professor of philosophy and religion at numerous colleges and universities, was revered by leaders of the civil rights movement for his mysticism and pastoral presence, writes theologian Myles Werntz in a feature on Thurman's life. Remarkably, as a key inspiration for Martin Luther King Jr. who was himself inspired by Gandhi, Thurman was a man committed above all to prayer and spiritual discipline. He believed that it is a transformative encounter with God that opens the soul to a nonviolent way of living. "In the mystical encounter of prayer," writes Werntz about Thurman's mysticism, "not only do people transcend the doctrinal particularities which divide Christians and divide one faith's claims about the nature of God from another; in prayer people are driven to confront the core issue of violence—the self-righteous and egoistic self. The ego is thereby displaced from its throne, replaced by the desire for union with the beauty of God. Our false selves are undone, and we realize the dignity of every person."[4]

Thurman believed, writes Werntz, that "those who would be contemplative must identify with those who are suffering, and those who would address suffering must be contemplative. To know the God who joins with the oppressed, whose 'backs are against the wall,' is to submit oneself to that God in prayer. In doing so, our transformation goes all the way down to our bones; we become people who can embody the way of Jesus, chastened in prayers and quieted in our anger, steeled with a moral courage that no violence can efface."[5]

SUBMIT TO MYSTERY

For five years, my husband and I gave leadership to a start-up experimental church we called The Table. As a gathered body, we shared communion every week, allowing it to become a vital heartbeat of congregational life, an altar call of recommitment, a flesh-and-blood encounter with the wounded, resurrected Jesus. As a group, we often talked about the biblical and theological meaning of the Lord's table practice. Regular participants spoke of how moving it was to enter the story of Jesus in a physically tangible way each Sunday. They testified to being met at the table and ministered to by the Spirit. I, along with others, often sensed the presence of the risen Christ, evoking tears and joy.

The suffering of Jesus is a central mystery of our faith—one that never ceases to generate intense conversation, theological disputations, countless books, no end of speculation, images, rituals, and prayers. Jesus crying out on the cross "My God, my God, why have you forsaken me?" is a striking contrast to images of God Almighty as invincible and all-powerful. Jesus' wounded, bleeding body stands in stark contrast to Jesus as King of kings and Lord of lords.

Jesus showed, with a beauty beyond belief, how power is made perfect in peaceableness; how what appears like weakness is instead the most potent power in the universe—"This is my commandment, that you love one another as I have loved you. No one has greater love than this, to lay down one's life for one's friends" (John 15:12-13).

Jesus chose to lay down his life rather than take another's life. He chose to love his enemies rather than hate those who resented him. He chose to forgive rather than berate those who harmed him. He chose to peacefully stand his ground rather than resort to vengeance. He chose to be vulnerable to insult and wounds rather than react with violence. He chose to face down death with a love stronger than death, shattering death's power with the power of resurrection; the victory of love over hatred.

All of us who carry wounds sense a profound solidarity of vulnerability with Jesus when we're invited to remember his death at the Lord's table: "This is my body broken for you." "This is my blood shed for you." At the table, a space opens up where we can bring whoever we are, with all our despair and hunger, to Jesus—and pray, "Wounded Savior, heal our wounds."

IT'S ALL ABOUT BEING IN LOVE

How we view the cross and suffering of Jesus affects how we think of the need for salvation, who the Savior is, what salvation entails, and how salvation is received, historian James Payton Jr. writes in a discussion about differences between how Eastern Orthodox Christians and Western Christians instinctively view the cross. What does Jesus' cry "It is finished" mean, for example, in Eastern Orthodoxy? Theologian and hierarch Kallistos Ware responds: "What has been fulfilled? We reply: The work of suffering love, the victory of love over hatred. Christ our God has loved his own to the uttermost."[6]

One of my faith heroes is Dorothy Day, who founded the *Catholic Worker* in 1933, a paper that for some fifty-three years was the voice of a movement that concentrated on the basics of the gospel. She helped found more than forty houses of hospitality and about a dozen farms that became places the poor could call home. One could use any number of stories from Day's life to illustrate how the work of suffering love gives rise to the victory of love over hatred. I found this reflection on failure and love written by her granddaughter especially poignant:

> When [Dorothy] was seventy-nine she said, "I feel like an utter failure," and she warned us that we always must

expect failure. "The older I get the more I feel that faith-fulness and perseverance are the greatest virtues—accept-ing the sense of failure we all must have in our work, in the work of others around us, since Christ was the world's greatest failure." Still, she said, we must keep moving. Take as many steps as you can. Bear witness, stand fast, hud-dle together in faith and community. And dream. We have, she said, a responsibility to hope and to dream of a better world. And being a practical mystic, she said one's spiritual life takes at least three hours a day. . . . Always, always, Dorothy spoke and wrote of love. As she said, there is no end to the folly of love, and there is nothing else to write about. . . . Christ understands us when we fail, and God understands us when we try to love.[7]

Speaking and writing about love, even when only failure is apparent, require fortifying practices for sustaining trust and hope in hard times. Those of us who grasp in small part, at least, what it looks like when suffering love triumphs over hatred, failure, and despair will no doubt find our talk about how we notice God's presence in hard times extraordinarily animated.

HOLD THE WORLD TOGETHER

Dorothy Day liked to quote St. Teresa of Ávila, who is reported to have grabbed her castanets and danced in the cold convent, saying, "One must do something to make life bearable!"[8]

In a public radio interview titled "An Invitation to Brave Space," minister Jennifer Bailey talked about when everything seems "dark and dim," what could be "more revolutionary than declaring that there are things that are worthy of our laughter, that there are things that are worthy of celebrating"? There's a reason, she continued, why elders of the civil rights movement were singing songs, cooking together, and just being together. "And so much of that relationship, that trust, is built over late-night bottles of wine on front porches," she said, "And man, if that Jesus guy didn't live that example. He was drinking, too, and sharing tables all the time."[9]

Krista Tippett, who has interviewed many guests for her public radio programs, ranging from poets to physicists, doctors to historians, artists to activists, writes, "My radio conversations teach me that people who bring light into the world wrench it out of darkness and contend openly with darkness all of their days. . . . They were flawed human beings, who wrestled with demons in themselves as in the world outside. For me, their goodness is more interesting, more genuinely inspiring, because of that reality."[10]

Resurrection and hope spring up from honest reckoning with sorrow and death. When we talk frankly about what it means to hold together what is wrong, broken, and harmful with laughter, castanets, and singing, the language of faith rises on powerful, joyful wings.

SPEAK FROM STORIED, HOLY GROUND

I was pleased to be able to listen in (via YouTube) on a conversation between Croatian theologian Miroslav Volf and African American theologian Willie James Jennings about a theology of joy after a Yale Center for Faith and Culture consultation on that theme in September 2014. Volf asked Jennings, "What is joy?" Jennings responded with these observations, which I distill and paraphrase:

> I look at joy as an act of resistance against despair and all its forces. Joy in that regard is work and can become a way of life. The work of joy resists despair and all the ways that despair wants to drive us toward death; all the ways life can be strangled and presented to us as not worth living. In contexts where we have plenty, the commercial spheres

of entertainment and advertisement offer us "joy" that doesn't fully take hold. In contexts where energies must be focused on survival, the work of joy become serious work. You learn how to have a good time when you have nothing. That's when we need people around us who know how to sing songs in a strange land and people who can make us laugh when all we want to do is cry. There is something absolutely beautiful about the joy created by oppressed peoples. There's something powerful about a womb of joy that helps constitute identity. I'm a child of the church. Not every church space is a space of joy. But multiple churches have been places of surprising joy for me. Extreme joy. Places where I've been stunned by joy.

I love the story that a former AMBS colleague, New Testament professor emerita Mary Schertz, shared with me a couple years ago in an email. She tells about the joy that arose in a circle of folks who had come together "to study the Bible as if your life depended on it." After several days of intense engagement, they concluded with deepened resolve to stand firm in hard times:

We are standing in a circle. We are not holding hands. We are together but also separate. We have been together for some significant time and some significant conversation. We pass the song "Stand firm. Stand very firm" around the circle, naming each person present, and encouraging them to stand firm, stand very firm. Something happens bodily. Our feet move apart, our hips and shoulders square, our chins lift. We are both still and ready to move. When the song comes to us, we dissolve in tears. We feel the earth under our feet, we feel that energy flowing into us, the earth where the bones of our beloved ancestors reside, the earth God created and enjoined us to care for and keep, the histories to which we belong, the earth to which we also will return. We feel the energy around the circle, our brothers and sisters in Christ, and from [our song leader]. We feel the energy of the Spirit hovering over us, strengthening, challenging, comforting. Above all, we are not alone. We are not perfect—little hard to be perfect with snot running out of your nose—but we are deeply loved, deeply valued. And here is the saving grace. We are more ready to go out, more ready to love more deeply, more ready to lead from our true selves, rooted, responsible, in community, filled with the Spirit.

It is in hard times when we have nowhere else to turn that we discover more of what it might mean to trust God with our lives. It is in hard times when we discover that joy is the work of the people who grab their castanets to sing and laugh when all you want to do is cry. It is in frightening, unsteady times when we lean especially hard on the sacred words in Scripture which tell us that when we stand firm in the love of God in Christ Jesus, *nothing* in all creation will be able to separate us from that love—no hardship, distress, persecution, famine, nakedness, peril, or sword (Romans 8:35-39).

Chapter 10

Wisdom Raising Her Voice

THE FEAR OF THE LORD IS THE BEGINNING OF WISDOM

For some reason, as a child, I was moved to pray for wisdom. I remember being struck by the clear instruction in James 1:5, "If any of you is lacking in wisdom, ask God, who gives to all generously and ungrudgingly, and it will be given you." I had no idea of the cost involved in acquiring a measure of wisdom. Nor did I know how truly precious wisdom would become.

I remember a comment a colleague made to me years ago about someone chosen for a prominent leadership position. I don't remember who it was. It may have been a U.S. president, a denominational executive, or a congregational leader. Her comment was that she had misgivings about his ability to lead well because he hadn't known much suffering. At the time, it was a new thought for me. I've often reflected back on her observation and noticed how leaders I most trust and admire for their humility and wisdom have been tempered by suffering—sometimes caused by their own acknowledged mistakes and failures.

Years ago, I began making a list of crucible events in my life because it seemed they'd begun to add up. Some of them included deaths and mental illness of close family members, excruciating stress at work, unrelenting self-doubt, marital conflict, distress from victims of sexual abuse and homophobia, threats of lawsuits for administrative decisions, risks of family rupture over contentious issues—on and on. In most respects, my life as a white, economically secure U.S. citizen is enormously privileged. The suffering I've known pales in comparison to those who live in poverty, at risk of physical abuse, with unrelenting physical pain or disabilities, or at risk of job discrimination, police brutality, starvation, war, and forced migration. Yet what suffering I have known has tempered my faith in ways that put real skin on sacred words and phrases like "trust and don't be afraid"; "peace that passes understanding"; "signs and wonders"; "salvation has come to this household"; "the steadfast love of the Lord"; "strength made perfect in weakness"; "the fear of the Lord is the beginning of wisdom."

I don't often hear talk about the "fear of the Lord" today. "Fear" implies a harsh, judgmental God, so my impression is that those of us who don't resonate with a "fire and brimstone" version of God have simply dropped the archaic reference from our lexicon. Talk I hear about God tends to imply that God is approachable and safe or that we know God well and rather expect God to do our bidding.

Somewhere I heard indirectly that the fear of the Lord is all about knowing where *real power* lies. I wish I knew the source because it resonated so deeply that it's become my preferred interpretation. Knowing the source of real power puts all other powers in perspective—which renders me speechless, rather like Isaiah, who on seeing the Lord "sitting on a throne, high and lofty" amid six winged seraphs covering their faces and feet, cried out "Woe is me!" (see Isaiah 6:1-5).

The sages of the Scriptures talk about how the beginning of wisdom is first of all overwhelming awe—which evokes fear. Why else does story after story in the Bible of an encounter with God or a messenger from God include the response "Fear not" or "Be not afraid"? There is that about such an encounter that puts us back on our heels—bowing, kneeling, utterly undone by our recognition of where the real power lies.

"People who have really met the holy are always humble," asserted Richard Rohr in an NPR interview entitled "Utterly Humbled by Mystery." "It's the people who don't know who usually pretend that they do. People who've had any genuine spiritual experience always know they *don't know*. They are utterly humbled before mystery."[1]

Job is one of the "wisdom" books of the Bible. Job, an upright rich man, loses everything he owned and suffers from terrible sickness. At the conclusion of all sorts of argumentation about why evil has befallen Job, God shows up. We call it a theophany; an appearance of the sacred.

After all the torturous days of accusing friends, nagging doubts, and lonely abandonment, God answers Job out of the whirlwind. But God answers with a whole lot of questions:

> Who is this that darkens counsel by words without knowledge?
> Gird up your loins like a man,
>   I will question you, and you shall declare to me.

Where were you when I laid the foundation of the earth?
    Tell me, if you have understanding.
Who determined its measurements—surely you know!
    Or who stretched the line upon it?
On what were its bases sunk,
    or who laid its cornerstone
when the morning stars sang together
    and all the heavenly beings shouted for joy? (Job 38:1-7)

When God shows up, we listen as we've never listened before; we notice how small we are in the whole scheme of things. We stare with mouths agape—stuttering as Job does:

See, I am of small account; what shall I answer you?
    I lay my hand on my mouth.
I have spoken once, and I will not answer;
    twice, but will proceed no further. . . .

I have uttered what I did not understand,
    things too wonderful for me, which I did not know. (Job 40:3-5; 42:3)

We become wise only as we listen in humility—allowing the suffering, wonder, complexity, and beauty of the world to astonish us and move us to bow down, in worship.

FIRST LISTEN!

The sages of Proverbs tell us that before creation, "the Lord God created, brought forth, or gave birth to Wisdom," writes Glenn Pemberton. Then she was at the Lord's side at creation, "frolicking, playing, or rejoicing." The Lord took pleasure in Wisdom, and Wisdom delighted in the human race. Now Woman Wisdom "shares what she knows about how the world works from what she saw at creation, with those who will listen."[2]

When, in humility, we're prepared to listen, we discover, as the sages of Proverbs tell us, that Woman Wisdom speaks everywhere: in the street, in the squares, at the busiest corners, and at the city gate. She raises her voice, cries out, and offers good counsel to all who will listen in the midst of our daily activities. Because her voice is everywhere, the only challenge is learning to recognize it in the hustle of everyday life.[3] This is what I love about Woman Wisdom—and more generally about the wisdom tradition. While the prophets of the Scriptures draw on visions to proclaim the word of the Lord, and the priests expound on the law of God, the wisdom writers of Scripture, often through the voice of Woman Wisdom, draw from the experiences of daily life to teach about God's ways in the world. Woman Wisdom, in other words, is all about helping us see how the stuff of direct experience—navigating friendship, poverty and wealth, hard work and laziness, slander and truth-telling, marriage and family—instructs us in shaping a life that is satisfying and good.[4]

A related dynamic in play with the wisdom writers of the Bible is that they seem to be, as Walter Brueggemann writes, "in touch with a mystery that cannot be too closely shepherded." What I hear in this is that somehow in comprehending that the beginning of wisdom is the fear of the Lord, and that as human beings we don't know a whole lot about how things really work, there must be latitude for review of old answers, testing of new solutions, exploration of unknown territory, and openness to what new discoveries reveal about life. The wisdom writers tried to take all experience into account, even new and perplexing experiences, because of their "sure confidence," writes Brueggemann, "that rightly understood, new experience will not subvert old Torah [the law of God], but will enhance it and give it vitality for fresh coping."[5] In other words, Women Wisdom models for us, in the wisdom writings of the Scriptures, how in our day we might bring new scientific data about our bodies, new challenges such as climate change and social media, into conversation with the ancient "law of God" and make new judgments that don't undermine the law of God but provide "vitality for fresh coping."

The law of God isn't a brittle thing, meant to be applied uniformly across time. Rather, the way of Wisdom is one that keeps faith with the deepest intent of the law even as we find new ways for that law to be realized here and now. Such an undertaking requires active listening and animated conversation to discern what will be most life-giving for us and our children. We can wholeheartedly engage in this deliberation when we stand on the bedrock conviction that "the fear of the Lord" *is the beginning* of wisdom. When the "fear of the Lord" brackets our days, writes Brueggemann, we are freed to live responsibly and even playfully in "the daily riddle, the daily freedom, and the daily burden" of life.[6]

SUBMIT TO MYSTERY

In recent years, if I awake early and am awash in anxiety, I occasionally turn on the Beatles song "Let It Be"—which moves me to tears and prayer. Mother Mary's words of wisdom become a calming invitation to release worry and open my spirit to watch for surprising provision. Paul McCartney wrote it about his mother, Mary. Many people think it's the Beatles' best song, and some claim it's one of the best songs ever. It became meaningful to me only as an adult in my late fifties but I was delighted when Samuel, my two-year-old grandson, said out of the blue during a visit: "Grandma, turn on 'Let it be' song, please." After it looped back—maybe ten times—I asked if we could move on to another song. "No.

More 'Let it be' song, please," he said. He's an exceedingly polite little boy, and a lover of Beatles' songs in general.

Mary the mother of Jesus is a boundary person—a woman who stands in the liminal space between earth and heaven; a woman who is one of us, yet who becomes in a mysterious way the entry point for the divine. She is not a passive wallflower but free, it would appear, to accept or reject the angel's overture. She listens carefully to what is being proposed, and thoughtfully chooses to say yes. When the angel says in Luke 1 "Do not be afraid, Mary, for you have found favor with God. And now, you will conceive in your womb and bear a son, and you will name him Jesus," Mary doesn't lose her wits. She boldly asks a very delicate question. "How can this be, since I am a virgin?" I love this about Mary.

When Zechariah asks, after being told by an angel that he would have a son, "How will I know that this is so? For I am an old man, and my wife is getting on in years" (Luke 1:18), he's given an answer but told that he would be mute for not believing. Mary, on the other hand, is simply given a respectful answer. And she responds, having done her own critical assessment: "Here am I, the servant of the Lord; *let it be* with me according to your word" (v. 38, emphasis added). Mary—speaking words of wisdom—humbly submits to the mystery.

When I pray, "Let it be," on anxious mornings, there is for me an intentional letting go of worry, along with the recognition that, while I will do everything in my power to engage the challenges of the day with skill and integrity, I am ultimately powerless to make things come round right. By consciously placing my life into the keeping of the One whose name is I AM Who I Am and inviting the illuminating wisdom of the Spirit, I find the courage to walk into the day with anticipation.

IT'S ALL ABOUT BEING IN LOVE

The wisdom writers tell us that Woman Wisdom "loves those who love her" and that what she gives is "better than gold or silver." She will come only to those who pursue her as a lover, holding her close and marrying her. Only then will Woman Wisdom's lover enjoy the blessings she so generously provides, writes Glenn Pemberton. What Woman Wisdom offers isn't "the good life" but a life that is good; a life that is full and genuine. She "walks on the paths of justice and righteousness and provides for those who walk with her." She is "no less than a tree of life," write the sages, providing "the life God has always intended for humanity,"[7] a life characterized by shalom.

To become wise, writes Pemberton, a person "must acquire a sense of harmony, a sensitivity to what is fitting and right, in all realms of attitude and behavior." In other words, to become wise, we must come to understand and practice justice—which is an "underlying principle of world order." Justice is the "ethical focal point around which the sages construct life," Pemberton writes, especially when the power of wealth and the vulnerability of poverty threaten to undermine what is just. The wisdom writers of the Scriptures share an ethical outlook that imagines "the world as it could and should be," the prophetic vision for justice to "roll down like an ever-flowing stream" (see Amos 5:15, 24).[8]

The sages' counsel to become a lover of Woman Wisdom isn't limited to ancient times. Holding her close is the only way to achieve harmony and discern what is fitting and right in our day. The answers we discern together about how to walk the paths of justice and righteousness may change how we think about family roles, same-sex attraction, parental discipline, and mental health, for example. Jesus seems to embody Woman Wisdom when he says, "Do not think that I have come to abolish the law or the prophets; I have come not to abolish but to fulfill. . . . You have heard that it was said to those of ancient times . . . but I say to you" (Matthew 5:17, 21-22). The wise ones among us know how to hold together new experiential and scientific data with the law of God in order to make new judgments that don't undermine the law of God but provide "vitality for fresh coping."

HOLD THE WORLD TOGETHER

One of my favorite Scriptures in the whole Bible, and one I've often preached on, is found in Paul's letter to the Christians in Colossae:

> [Jesus] is the image of the invisible God, the firstborn of all creation; for in him *all things* in heaven and on earth were created, things visible and invisible, whether thrones or dominions or rulers or powers—*all things* have been created through him and for him. He himself is before *all things*, and in him *all things* hold together. He is the head of the body, the church; he is the beginning, the firstborn from the dead, so that he might come to have first place in everything. For in him all the fullness of God was pleased to dwell, and through him God was pleased to reconcile to himself *all things*, whether on earth or in heaven, by making peace through the blood of his cross. (Colossians 1:15-20, emphasis added)

"All things" is repeated five times in these verses—for emphasis apparently. In Christ, all things hold together. All things. Surely, despite all the polarizing evidence to the contrary, we *can* learn to live within the creative tension of both/ and rather than either/or. We can learn the Wisdom personified in Jesus who was filled with grace *and* truth; Jesus who modeled, as I mentioned above, how to make new judgments that didn't undermine but fulfilled the law of God and provided "vitality for fresh coping."

Jesus, in whom all things hold together, came visually to life for me in the art gallery at James Madison University. A friend invited me along to see an art showing by an acquaintance of hers—an undergraduate student of art, Bethany Tobin. I wasn't prepared to be dumbstruck, but that is exactly what happened. I stopped by one small golden green print with geometric circles and lines superimposed on fragments of the Colossians 1 text entitled *In Him, All Things Consist*. As I stood in stunned silence, reading, tears began streaming down my face. I read:

> There are three themes in this cluster of works (of which this is one piece): elaborate patterns, use of text, and bright expressionistic use of color. The patterns symbolize order, harmony, coherence, and unity in the universe. I use circle frameworks from Islamic artists for whom geometric patterns and mathematical ratios refer to the absolute, infinite God. Numbers, with their ratios and harmonic proportions are seen as "keys to the structure of the cosmos and symbols of the archetypal world." As patterns found in the natural world, they reveal intelligence and purpose embedded in creation. The circle symbolizes wholeness and unity. For me, it all flows from the one who made it all and for whom it all exists—revealed in Jesus Christ. The text is a "philosophic constellation" circling the "concept it would like to unseal, hoping that it may fly open like the lock of a well-guarded safe-deposit box; in response, not to a single key of a single number, but to a combination of numbers." I'm drawn to concepts in physics. The verses are from Colossians 1—a picture of the mysterious, cosmic Christ. It's about everything—particles and people—getting "fixed and fit together in vibrant harmonies." The colors express the energy, electricity and discovery I felt while making this

work. I hope they carry the simple joy (and yes maybe fixation) I have about God, particles, patterns and ideas.[9]

My husband bought the small print for me after he saw how moved by it I was. It becomes a focal point for meditation from time to time, holding particles, patterns, and ideas within a frame that testify to how in Jesus Christ *all things* hold together. Jesus—the Wisdom of God—who walked among us (1 Corinthians 1:24).

SPEAK FROM STORIED, HOLY GROUND

"People who've been through hard things are the keepers of wisdom," said Dave Isay, StoryCorps founder, in a PBS interview in January 2020. He and his colleagues have recorded interviews with some sixty thousand persons (to date) in thousands of towns and cities in all fifty U.S. states. And indeed, I have found Isay's comment about "keepers of wisdom" to be true, over and over.

One of those keepers of wisdom is Diana Hayes, an African American womanist theologian. Hayes worked for years as a lawyer and had a passion for the great outdoors. But something more kept calling, which she discovered, over time, was a call not only to become a Catholic, but to serve the church as a theologian and professor at Georgetown University. She was the first African American woman to earn the pontifical degree doctor of sacred theology. Hayes for many years has also suffered from debilitating rheumatoid arthritis. She writes, "African-American women's wisdom emerges from an experience of triple (or more) oppression. Denied the dignity of womanhood, condemned for their skin color, whether too dark or too light, and often imprisoned by mis-education, demeaning and meaningless work, and a denial of their very humanity, African-American women have yet managed to forge a spirituality of hope and survival that has sustained them for centuries."[10]

In her most recent book, *No Crystal Stair*: *Womanist Spirituality*, Hayes writes:

> I know what it is like to be poor, to be discriminated against because of my poverty, my race, my gender, and my disabilities. These many years of struggle and pain, which continue to this day, have forged me in the fiery furnace of God's love. . . . My growth from anger and despair to acceptance and perseverance is one that I believe is repeated in the lives of many around me who struggle daily with pain, whether its form is physical, mental, or spiritual. . . . It is not over. The anger still bubbles to the surface at times; the despair creeps in unannounced and side-swipes me, leaving me befuddled and confused, but the knowledge that through it all God is steadfastly present in my life sustains and strengthens me.[11]

When I ask myself who are most like Israel's sages today, Hayes, Brueggemann, Tobin, and Pemberton come to mind as four examples from this chapter—along with countless others. Wise men and women are those who hold spaces open to make new judgments based on new data in a way that doesn't undermine the law of God, but rather interprets its meaning for a new time and context. Organizations and families where these sages hold forth become places filled with good oxygen, sparkling conversations, low anxiety, and an unusual attentiveness to the Spirit. Theologians, scientists, counselors, teachers, grandparents, pastors, bishops, builders, and nurses are among those who I've experienced as sages throughout my life. Whenever they raise their voice, the room becomes roomier, the conversation less anxious, the stories more in touch with the beauty, complexity, and suffering of our world; in a word, more honest and hopeful.

The sages among us help show how hard times like the turmoil over same-sex attraction or polarizing political charades—as hard as they are—are opportunities to reactivate lively discourse and intense discernment for making new judgments and finding new approaches. People of wisdom bring people together around our shared desire to live in peace because they remind us, as biblical scholar sage Willard Swartley sums up: "No fear of the Lord; no wisdom; thus no moral discernment between good and evil; and no *shalom*."[12]

Chapter 11

Curiosity Germinates Faith Talk

LISTENING FOR ANY HINT OF TRANSCENDENCE

We don't need to be expert Bible scholars or theologians to speak about our faith. What we are called to be is honest seekers, with a healthy curiosity about the nature of things. What we need are hospitable spaces for playing with God stuff—not in a careless, irreverent kind of way—but with inquiry that is animated by wonder, exploration that carries a good compass, experimentation that is guided by generational wisdom, and artistic design that takes its blueprint from the sages and Jesus.

"Dictatorial rigidity" is one of the hazards of religion that novelist Toni Morrison identified, which can show up in many guises, including in renderings like egalitarianism, environmentalism, and feminism. In a fascinating review of Morrison's religious vision called "Improvising Freedom," Amy Frykholm says that it's not that Morrison is opposed to these ideas, but that "she objects to any religious vocabulary that is inauthentic to her subjects or that fits easily into a consumer culture." Her desire is to "communicate through her characters a religious life that is at once mystical, practical, and communal—and that leads above all to spiritual freedom."[1]

As a child of several cultures, I have never felt at home anywhere—and yet I find aspects of home everywhere. Much crossing of cultures has made me endlessly curious, constantly alert to what people are doing and why. I hold everything at arm's length, curious about what informs or underlies particular beliefs and ways of doing things. I listen, for example, to the original music of a popular local band or to the compositions of an extended family member for what preoccupies the lyrics, whether activism, mental health, beauty, culture critique, faith, or a political agenda. In all kinds of venues—music, entertainment, conversation, art, or public lectures—I am eager to hear any hint of transcendence, murmurs of something mystical, or recognition that we are participants in a reality larger than ourselves. My spirit immediately quickens when I hear it, and sags a bit when I don't. I love what poet Jan Richardson asks in an Ash Wednesday Lenten prayer: "Did you not know what the Holy One can do with dust?"

My daughter brought me an aging 1967 hardcover book, written by an Episcopal priest and professor of theology, titled *The Supper of the Lamb: A Culinary Entertainment.* Despite her encouragement to sample its delights, the book sat on my coffee table for a long time. Then one day I picked it up and discovered its sumptuous feast. Father Robert Capon rhapsodizes about food. And about transcendence. Here's an appetizer:

O the humorless neatness of an intellectuality which buys mass-produced candlesticks and carefully puts one at each end of every philosophical mantelpiece! How far it lies from the playfulness of Him who composed such odd and needless variations on the themes of leaf and backbone, eye and nose! . . . A shout of rejoicing for the fish who wears his eyeballs at the ends of long stalks, and for the jubilant laughter of the God who holds him in life with a daily *bravo* at the *bravura* of his being! . . . Food is the daily sacrament of unnecessary goodness, ordained for a continual remembrance that the world will always be more delicious than it is useful.[2]

The grim determinism of religious and ideologically wired folks at both extremes of a conservative-liberal spectrum is deadening. I am more wired to curiosity and playfulness when it comes to God-talk, a playfulness that knows all about reverence and holy hilarity. Our conversations about faith will take off with surprising exuberance as soon as we allow curiosity about anything and everything to oxygenate the room.

FIRST LISTEN!

Poet Mary Oliver concludes her poem "Yes! No!" with this line: "To pay attention, this is our endless / and proper work."[3] In reflecting on her poetry, author Franklin Foer notes Oliver's conviction that what is "unnoticed can't possibly be loved" so we must "dilate . . . because a world worthy of attachment exists outside ourselves, and the alternative is numbness and narcissism."[4] It is in attending to what is right in front of us—the spiderweb's gossamer symmetry, the pulsing heartbeat under our rib cage, the skin's repair after a burn, the river of blue violets in the backyard—that our curiosity is awakened into an ever-expanding astonishment.

Foer cites a quote from Oliver that gives me chills: "Attention is the beginning of devotion."

This single claim speaks the truth at the heart of my spiritual journey. When I pay attention—no matter the subject, no matter the time—it's like riding a ray of sunlight toward its source. I can't help but notice what is right in front of me without my spirit leaping toward the Maker of all things bright and beautiful—even when dark clouds threaten to obscure everything.

Oliver's observation tracks with that of Capon—who exults about the wonders of the many layered onion in *ten pages of euphoric prose*, and concludes:

> I shall give the summation of my case for paying attention. [Humanity's]real work is to look at the things of the world and to love them for what they are. That is, after all, what God does, and [humanity] was not made in God's image for nothing. . . . If an hour can be spent on one onion, think how much regarding it took on the part of that old Russian who looked at onions and church spires long enough to come up with St. Basil's Cathedral. Or how much curious and loving attention was expended by the first [person] who looked hard enough at the insides of trees, the entrails of cats, the hind ends of horses and the juice of pine trees to realize he [or she] could turn them all into the first fiddle.[5]

SUBMIT TO MYSTERY

One of the songs my husband and I most enjoy singing together at the piano is a prayer to the Holy Spirit, drawn from common prayers of the Eastern Orthodox Church: "O heavenly King, the Comforter Spirit of truth. Who fillest all things, Who art in all places; O treas'ry of good things. And giver of life. Come and cleanse us from ev'ry stain. And take up Thine abode in us, O God. And save our souls, O Holy One!" It's a mystery to me why this song on a photocopied page in a music binder from Reba Place Church, where we worshiped decades ago, has so wedded itself to my spirit.

"Who fillest all things. Who art in all places." In standard theological terminology, this would be referred to as the omnipresence of God. Richard Rohr, in a public post called "Beholding," speaks of the omnipresence of God not as a theological doctrine, but "as the great silence that is present in every moment—but from which we are usually distracted by an overactive mind that refuses to wait in a humble unknowing for a pure wisdom from above (James 3:17)."[6]

In my line of work, we spend a lot of time with the Scriptures; the story of God. The immense wild and natural world is also a divine manuscript that tells of the breadth, length, height, and depth of the love of God—a love that surpasses knowledge. "The number of cells in the human body is almost exactly the same as the number of stars in the Milky Way," observes David James Duncan in his book *God Laughs and Plays*. "Is this meaningless coincidence or a purposeful symmetry devised by our Creator? I have no idea," he answers. "I only know that some facts make me happy, and that a flurry of such facts have begun to whirl through me now."[7]

Out the window on a blustery New Year's Eve, I suddenly see dense swirls of snowflakes offset by occasional brilliant sunlight. The cardinals, chickadees, tufted titmice, juncos, Carolina wrens, downy woodpeckers, and flickers snatch at seeds in our bird feeder, letting loose with an occasional song. I sit between the Blue Ridge and Allegheny Mountains pondering, with Duncan, "a celestial cloud whose 'snow' is stars and a terrestrial cloud whose 'stars' are snow," and smiling with the happy awareness that "we each have a Milky Way's worth of cells burning in our bodies; and our galaxy has a human being's worth of star-cells shining in its vast swirl."[8]

Christian faith talk is constantly in danger of becoming boring. Anyone with a healthy zest for life wants nothing to do with such tedium. Contrary to what most of us think, theology, or talk about faith, is rooted primarily in curiosity—a desire to know more about God and about everything that swirls around our daily universe of moments. As we listen to what we notice, we may ask, Where is God? When we follow the question, we'll discover that God is all over the place—up there, down here, inside my skin and out, within the bird's song and the neighbor's kind offer to help. When we submit to the mystery, we come alive to the wonder that God's love isn't doled out in small packages. God's love is more like a web of energy revealed in a vast network of interactions and relationships that animate all of life.

IT'S ALL ABOUT BEING IN LOVE

What if education wasn't first and foremost about what we know, but about what we love, asks James Smith.[9] When we love, we become genuinely intrigued. We ask good questions that arise from a fired-up curiosity.

As an illustration, my mind is drawn to the early monastics—those desert dwellers who, as mystic Thomas Merton observes, "sought a way to God that was uncharted and freely chosen, not inherited from others who had mapped it out beforehand." Our time is in need of their kind of simplicity—a practical and unassuming wisdom. They weren't fanatics, but "humble, quiet, sensible people, with a deep knowledge of human nature and enough understanding of the things of God to realize that they knew very little about God," Merton writes. They repeatedly insisted on "the primacy of love over everything else in the spiritual life."[10]

The desert hermits who left the world of their day to head to the desert "as though escaping from a wreck, did not merely intend to save themselves," Merton writes. "They knew that they were helpless to do any good for others as long as they floundered about in the wreckage. Once they got a foothold on solid ground, things were different. Then they had not only the power but even the obligation to pull the whole world to safety after them."[11]

HOLD THE WORLD TOGETHER

Faith talk rooted in curiosity takes us not only into natural wonders or into the desert in search of a foothold on more solid ground. It will also take us into the most painful conflicts and challenges of our day. As a person in my sixties, I know that the crucible events in my life, as wracked with pain as they were, drove me, in desperation, deeper into the love of God. Broke my heart open. Humbled me. Made me, perhaps, a tad wiser.

People of faith and those curious about how faith engages challenges have no further to look than difficult conflicts around abortion, peacemaking, climate change, or sexuality. Take same-sex attraction, for example. No other issue has been so divisive for faith-based communities in recent decades. I wonder how, if we remained patiently curious, listening first and loving in ways that are prepared to hold different perspectives together, we might approach the conflict with anticipation rather than fear. We might come to see what appear to be irreconcilable differences *as an opportunity to learn*; a challenging but real gift from our Maker. Am I out of my mind to say this? Maybe. But I believe the necessity to honestly grapple with what has long been a silenced reality in our communities has now become a God-given opportunity to break our hearts open. I believe that a conflict we've allowed to tear us down the middle in families, congregations, and denominations is instead an invitation to show the world our capacity for a love robust enough to hold communities together rather than tear them apart.

Oh, I know we're failing miserably. But the steadfast love of God never ceases. We can still change. We can do the hard work to discover the gifts of God's love *within* our irreconcilable differences. Rather than sowing seeds of division, we can, with active curiosity about how the Spirit may surprise us, meet despite our differences, "at the foot of the cross." We can receive this conflict as God's invitation to learn a new magnitude of love. Only then will the watching world believe that we are followers of Jesus.

Mary Schertz writes that taking the cross of Jesus seriously means that suffering love is required for listening to each other when talking through difficult issues. There can be no holier, compassionate work than to engage patiently in the difficult conversations people of faith will undertake if we desire to find our way together with integrity. Being transparent with each other is hard work, yet that is when we come to know how gracious is the love of Christ, "who for the sake of the joy that was set before him endured the cross" (Hebrews 12:2).[12]

Jesus taught us that the fulfillment of the law is all about loving God with heart, soul, mind, and strength, and our neighbors as ourselves. The fulfillment of the law is all about the integrity of life—where internal affections and external actions harmonize. The fulfillment of the law is about putting our desire for God above all other desires and judging all human desire in light of our desire for God. So yes, we can open our hearts with curiosity about how conflict may be an invitation from God to grow in wisdom and maturity together. With the illuminating Spirit as guide, we can teach each other about the diverse ways we fulfill the law by *putting our desire for God above all other desires; our love for God above all loves.*

SPEAK FROM STORIED, HOLY GROUND

Many of us hunger for spaces where we can freely speak our minds, ask questions without fear, follow where our confusion and curiosity lead us.

In 2008 or so, my husband and I, with two colleagues, chose for a season to host what we called "Soup & a Question" evenings for our theological school students. The invitation read, in part:

> Gather for savory soup and salty table conversation about the Bible, church, money and sex (for mature Christians, with no questions off limits) Friday evenings at 6 p.m. at . . .
>
> The question for this week: What do we really believe about the Bible—its power (or lack thereof) in postmodernity? You are welcome. Sign up at the posted list . . .

Our practice was, over the dinner table, to state only questions. No commentary. Simply questions—that probed deeper and deeper into a topic. I kept a list of the questions that arose. We would then gather in another space with a facilitator who organized the questions and guided the flow of the conversation. Everyone was invited to provide their perspectives. These were freeing evenings, with opportunity to explore wherever a topic took us—with shared respect, and discovery. We always tried to have persons present who could provide context or history on a given topic for when it became clear that background information on a question at hand would be helpful.

Genuine curiosity that is willing to acknowledge all that one doesn't know about a given word or topic frees us to break it open for sincere exploration. When we work the soil, rather than defaulting to code language or assumed meanings of words like *atonement*, *salvation*, *Bible*, or *God*, interest is quickened. When we can play with words or phrases we normally avoid or never heard of, like "at the foot of the cross," or "fulfillment of the law," or *omnipresence*, or *transcendence*, we can tell stories or swap impressions about what they mean or what the tradition has taught. There is no more fertile ground to grow new learning than genuine, playful curiosity about what words mean. Take transcendence, for example. Someone said to me "Oh, that's one of those code words." Well, yes it is, until you break it open and fill it with story. Do you know anyone who doesn't stop whatever they're doing to gape, point, and exclaim on spotting a rainbow, for example? I don't. I don't believe a rainbow ever appears without someone exclaiming, "Oh, my God. A rainbow! Come. Look!" Transcendence is like that.

Chapter 12

The Verve of Scripture Emancipated

SCRIPTURE REIMAGINED FOR LIFE RATHER THAN BATTLES

My parents seemed to have a verse or a proverb for every situation that not only shed light on but ennobled whatever was happening—whether a tantrum, a rainy day, money worries, teamwork, or table manners. My daughter recently reminded me that when she was little, and very scared of the dark, I wrote verses about God's protection and sheltering care on index cards that she kept by her bed for years. What a wonder it is to have scriptural wisdom, poetic flourishes, or a story to illuminate any given moment. Our ability to dignify and honor each other would increase overnight if we made it a community priority to "learn by heart" a rich substratum of poetry, prayers, and wise sayings—many of which cram the pages of Scripture.

As communities of faith, it is urgent that we jettison the literalist, fundamentalist views of the Bible. These deceptive notions about the Bible as a righteous harangue, straitjacket, and dictator of dogma are like deadweights on a drowning person. When we cut loose from them, we learn to trust that the Spirit's illuminating presence will reveal the Word of God throbbing through the text. Rather than mere black-and-white words on the page, the Scriptures will vibrate with life, inviting us to listen, talk about what we hear, and take to heart what we discern. It will be as if we were splashed with cold spring water on a hot summer day—reinvigorated to explore the Bible on a treasure hunt. This can be done in the quiet of our own private spaces, with family members or friends, or with skilled, wise guides—for a groundswell of awakening intrigue.

While president at AMBS, I was often asked about where the seminary stands on this or that controversial issue. The question was reaching for a declaration about conviction. What ethical ground have we staked out on a matter in dispute? Is where we stand "biblical"? Are we on the right side of the battle line? When theological convictions are threatened, can we be trusted to hold firm?

My response was, "We stand on the Word of God," which might sound like a nod back toward the Protestant Reformation and Martin Luther, who is reported to have declared some five hundred years ago: "Unless I am convinced by the testimony of the Holy Scriptures or by evident reason—for I can believe neither pope nor councils alone, as it is clear that they have erred repeatedly and contradicted themselves—I consider myself convicted by the testimony of Holy Scripture, which is my basis; my conscience is captive to the Word of God. . . . Here I stand. I can do no other." Case closed!

Except it isn't. In a face-off with a corrupt pope, appealing to individual conscience was a powerful corrective—particularly a conscience "captive to the Word of God." But as we all know, individual conscience and how one interprets the "Word of God" can be corrupted by fear, pride, and blind self-interest and, in Luther's case, can be used to persecute and kill other Christians called Anabaptists.

I grew up among a people who knew how to take a stand on Scripture and who shared deep convictions about standing strong in the face of persecution, loving enemies, conscientiously objecting to war, witnessing boldly about Jesus' reconciling love, and choosing to die rather than deny our faith—exemplary qualities so needed in this day of corrupt politicians, hate-filled racism, and fear. Yet that revolutionary faith got coded into our cultural DNA in sometimes aberrant forms. Taking a stand, at least for many of the Swiss Germans among us, came to mean, in recent generations, enforcing strict dress codes, excluding the wrong kind of people from communion, writing guidelines to control who's in and who's out, and using proof texts to make sure we're all crystal clear on what the Bible says. Standing strong has often come to mean dividing into smaller and smaller fractions in order to stay away from others who read the Bible differently than we do. A speaker at a memorial service I recently attended said, "The world is not impressed by a people who talk a lot about reconciliation and keep splitting off from one another."

But what if that deeply ingrained cultural DNA to stand strong was held captive by the living Word of God revealed in the Scriptures—Jesus Christ? What if rather than using a litmus test to judge whether other people are Bible-believing

Christians, we gave up our idolatrous certainties about what the Bible says and experienced humility and a little trembling before the Lord God, who asks: "Is not my word like fire . . . and like a hammer that breaks a rock in pieces? See, therefore, I am against the prophets . . . who steal my words from one another. See, I am against the prophets . . . who use their own tongues and say, 'Says the LORD.' See, I am against those . . . who lead my people astray by their lies and their recklessness, when I did not send them or appoint them, so they do not profit this people at all, says the LORD" (Jeremiah 23:29-32).

When persons would ask me, Where does the seminary stand on human sexuality, the authority of Scripture, women in leadership, peace and justice, immigration, climate change, white supremacy, the president—you name it—my response was: This is where we stand on the issue at hand, but come, learn to read the Scriptures with us, prayerfully, skillfully, with humility and awe, and find out why. Learn to sing, play, and dance the Scriptures. Learn to listen to the Scriptures' many voices, from varied contexts, times, languages, genres, and perspectives. Learn to listen to the Scriptures in a community of people who, despite our differences and *because of our differences*, hear the deep verve of the Spirit throbbing throughout this multivalent, many-voiced trove of wisdom.

I offer a story to illustrate how this worked in a seminary class on the synoptic gospels, as told by Mary Schertz, AMBS professor emerita of New Testament: "Class this morning was very fruitful. We were discussing the transfiguration of Jesus. We had just about every opinion laid on the table at one point or another. There was goodwill; everyone was taken seriously by everyone. And we had a very good time and came to some interesting and important conclusions, namely that Scripture is the stabilizing bar as we walk the tightrope of life.

We were talking about falling back on faith as a safety net and then worked our way around to the metaphor that seemed more satisfying—Scripture as the balancing bar. It moves. It has flexibility. It has an allowable range that takes into account variables in body weight, skill, air flow, circumstances, et cetera, but there are also givens and fundamentals that simply have to be taken seriously in order not to fall."

For those of us eager to learn how to move and speak with the verve of Scripture, the door is open wherever there are other persons, including sages (of any age, gender, profession) who are unafraid of the questions and keen for a journey of shared discovery. The door is open to

- grow in awe and a little trembling before the Lord, who asks: "Is not my word like fire . . . and like a hammer that breaks a rock in pieces?";
- acknowledge that our own reading of Scripture is often skewed by our limited perspective, requiring a rich multicultural diversity of voices from a variety of races, genders, and social statuses to provide a fuller picture;
- kneel before God, confessing our prejudice and blindness even as we do our best to name convictions on sexual practice, biblical authority, peacemaking, justice;
- listen long enough to be captivated by the wonder, vibrancy, and power of the Word of God revealed in the Scriptures, in nature, in worship, and above all, in Jesus Christ; and
- learn to speak with winsome, bold, humble conviction in personal, congregational, and public spaces—while constantly seeking to grow in empathy and wisdom.

FIRST LISTEN!

Wendell Berry, American writer, environmental activist, and farmer, said in an interview for the *New Yorker* that the church he grew up in "is full of ghosts for me. I can look at those pews and see my grandfather, and his friends, and others who are dear and close to me still. I'm sitting there very often with my children or my grandchildren or my great-grandchildren. But the gospels, for me, were not a church discovery. I had finally to carry them into the woods and read them there in order to see my need for them."[1]

Where and how we discover what the heart of the gospel is will vary for us as individuals, but what matters most is that we first listen. Listen well. Listen alone in nature. Listen with others who know how to get inside the ancient text and break it open. Listen by asking honest, hard questions and refusing pat answers. Listen even when no answers are forthcoming, because living patiently with the questions frees one to be buoyed by wonderment in a way that clutching for certain, dogmatic answers never can.

Listening well and with our own context in mind will lead us toward new discoveries in the text unrealized by previous generations. Listening first will require inviting others' questions and insights about what they hear in the text. Listening prayerfully and playfully will make us attentive to the promptings of the Spirit. Listening well will awaken us to a verve that can't be captured by any one interpretation or dogmatic declaration.

SUBMIT TO MYSTERY

The authority of Scriptures is centered on what they reveal about who Jesus is, the Word of God who became human and lived among us—"full of grace and truth" (see John 1:1-18).

The Scriptures remind us how the Word of God is within us and around us—even as it was present to our ancestors millennia ago. Moses, in his farewell discourse to the wilderness wanderers before they crossed the Jordan River into what was to become their homeland, said: "Surely, this commandment that I am commanding you today is not too hard for you, nor is it too far away. . . . No, *the word is very near to you*; it is in your mouth and in your heart for you to observe" (Deuteronomy 30:11, 14, emphasis added).

The Scriptures have a moral power with laws that protect life and human dignity. South African peace activist Oscar Siwali, in his sermon at my local congregation, described what happened when Western colonizers came to Africa. "The Bible came to Africa and we lost land," he said. "So why is the Bible still there?" While colonizers used the Bible to justify apartheid, the Bible became the lifeblood for liberating and restoring dignity to the millions formerly oppressed by powerful white landowners.

The Word of God isn't nailed onto the page in black and white. Nor is it boxed in by statements of church dogma or declarations of a church magistrate. That we have creeds, systematized theologies, and confessions of faith helps us to understand some of what previous generations distilled from the Scriptures—capturing some of the light from a vast, uncontrollable fire. But we must never imagine that we control the fire or domesticate its power to do our bidding. While comforting his disciples as they grieved his upcoming departure, Jesus promised, "When the Spirit of truth comes, he will guide you into all the truth" (John 16:13). And the apostle Paul, in a letter to the Christians at Corinth, wrote: "Now the Lord is the Spirit, and where the Spirit of the Lord is, there is freedom" (2 Corinthians 3:17).

As we find ways to listen for what I'm calling the verve of Scripture, I'm drawn to what theologian Hans Boersma describes as a "sacramental sensibility" in his book *Scripture as Real Presence*. Walter Brueggemann summarizes Boersma as suggesting that if we are to submit to the mystery and power of the Word of God conveyed by Scripture, we need an approach that starkly contrasts from the thin, rationalistic, dissecting approach used to examine biblical texts in the previous century. Boersma asserts that Scripture is richer, more complex, diverse, and open to imaginative reading than historical-critical methods permitted. The key to reading the Scriptures openheartedly, he says, is faith in Christ. Why? Because Christ occupies every part of Scripture as "real presence" shining through every page.[2]

IT'S ALL ABOUT BEING IN LOVE

My mother and father passed on their love for the Bible. They never seemed uptight about getting it just right, or anxious about forcing down a correct way to take it in. Rather, it was more like honey on the tongue, water for the thirsty, bread for the hungry, effervescent joy in the morning, the music of the spheres:

> The heavens are telling the glory of God;
> and the firmament proclaims his handiwork.
> Day to day pours forth speech,
> and night to night declares knowledge.
> There is no speech, nor are there words;
>   their voice is not heard;
> yet their voice goes out through all the earth,
>   and their words to the end of the world. (Psalm 19:1-4)

My parents appreciated good education and the way teachers and professors in love with the music of the Scriptures lit our imaginations. There were plenty of teachers and preachers who made the Bible feel flat and boring, but because my parents knew it could be otherwise, they gave me confidence to keep hunting for treasure. And sure enough, I found teachers, preachers, professors, colleagues, friends, and students for whom the Scriptures lit a passionate flame. I remember the moment a professor was so overcome with the beauty of the text about Jesus breaking down the dividing wall of enmity between Jews and Gentiles that he choked up with tears. I remember how a professor spoke with elation as she traced out the trajectory, hidden to most inattentive readers, of women in leadership throughout the Old and New Testaments. I remember the moment when a student wept because of her seamless devotion to Jesus and to those crushed by injustice. I remember a preacher laughing uproariously out of sheer delight when describing the luxurious flow of so much precious oil poured on Aaron's head that it ran onto his beard, and down over the collar of his robes—an image meant to show "how very good and pleasant it is when kindred live together in unity!" (Psalm 133:1-2).

One of the professors who lit my imagination for the shalom vision of God shining through the Scriptures was biblical scholar Willard Swartley. At his memorial in 2019, his brother-in-law remarked on his warm heart, empathy for overlooked persons, enthusiasm for life, and devotion to God. Swartley was a storyteller and a stimulating Bible teacher. He made the study of New Testament Greek a lively encounter. Not long before Swartley's death, he lamented to his brother-in-law that when he left the private college where he taught forty-five years ago, before becoming a seminary professor, there had been one hundred Bible majors, but that currently at that college, now a university, there were no Bible majors. "No one wants to make a career out of the Bible anymore," he grieved.

What has changed? More factors than we can enumerate here. But I would wager that every single factor revolves around love—or the absence thereof. Writing about the late author Rachel Held Evans, a writer for the *Christian Century* observes that Evans saw that the antidote to the poison of a "world where rich white men are in charge and everybody else is exploited and quiet about it," and (I would add) the antidote to the poison of a legalistic, rationalistic use of the Bible to support that exploitation, "is not distance from scripture but greater proximity to it, intimacy even." As Evans wrote, "The gospel doesn't need a coalition devoted to keeping the wrong people out. It needs a family of sinners, saved by grace, committed to tearing down the walls, throwing open the doors, and shouting, 'Welcome! There's bread and wine. Come eat with us and talk.'"[3]

Those who get what empire-shattering good news it was when the angels proclaimed "Glory to God in the highest heaven, and on earth peace to those on whom his favor rests" also get why knowing Jesus makes *all* the difference in the world. Jesus' birth, life, and death overturned every presumption about how God would enter the world. And Jesus' resurrection upended all the principalities and powers of the prince of darkness. How are we not astonished? How are we not drawn like magnets to the love of God in Christ Jesus—a love that has "vanquished the powers of hell"?[4]

HOLD THE WORLD TOGETHER

A seminary class I took as a young adult on themes of liberation throughout the Bible, particularly for women, included a ritual one day of going through photocopied texts with scissors to cut out verses that have been used to wound, silence, and oppress women. While I participated because there was something starkly satisfying about eliminating verses that have been used as a bludgeon or gag order, I was uneasy. I have long appreciated teachers, authors, and friends who wrestle with the seeming contradictions of Scripture to find what wisdom can be wrested from holding their contested views in provocative tension. Holding the world of the Bible together is no easy feat. The biblical narratives speak of

- a world God declared to be good and then destroyed in a flood;
- a God who is a raging, devouring fire and whose wings shelter us;
- a God whose fierce anger and jealousy threaten to destroy and whose steadfast love and mercy never come to an end;
- instructions to wipe out the Canaanite tribes in conquest of their land and instructions to welcome the alien and stranger;
- calls to be a separate, holy people distinct from the world and calls to go into the world, becoming all things to all people;
- instructions about what makes persons ceremonially unclean and instructions to not call anything unclean that God has made clean; and
- the Son who was not sent into the world to condemn the world and that those who do not believe in him are condemned already.

I am intrigued by the way biblical scholar Pete Enns writes about the tensions embedded in the Scriptures. In a public post from February 8, 2017, titled "Nature of the Bible," he describes how the diversity, contradictions, and internal

debates at the heart of Scripture are lost if we're simply looking for information downloaded from God's computer to ours
as an idealized, problem-free, legal brief. What makes the Bible
so interesting and worthy of deep study is that while the parts
don't cohere in all respects, they reflect the contrasting settings
and experiences of the biblical writers who describe the words
and events through which God was revealed to them. It's the
very complexity of the Bible that draws readers in to ponder,
discern, and even argue with it, observes Enns, not as an act of
rebellion, but as an act of faith that engages God and fellow
travelers in conversation about what the Bible teaches us.

The Bible is not some god to be idolized. Over many hundreds of years, however, the Bible has carried the story of Jesus,
"the image of the invisible God" in whom "all the fullness of
God was pleased to dwell" (Colossians 1:15, 19). And it is
Jesus the Christ who reveals the underlying harmonies that
hold the Scriptures together in their entirety. It is not some
modern theory about the Bible's inerrancy but the "real presence" of the Word who is Jesus in the Scriptures that reveals
the many splendored story of God's righteous judgment and
loving mercy throughout. The warp and woof of Scripture—
the sometimes contradictory, paradoxical tensions—are necessary to hold together the weave of an age-old, magnificently
textured fabric.

SPEAK FROM STORIED, HOLY GROUND

Our seven- and nine-year-old grandsons visit us most every
week. We have delightful times playing chess and croquet,
baking cookies, singing around the piano, making treehouse
furniture, feeding the chickens and goats. Ari and Jacob are
part of a Bible quiz team from their church, so we sometimes
help them rehearse questions from the story of the week. One

week, the story was about Abraham preparing to bind his son Isaac for the altar, at God's command. I groaned inside. This was surely a story to be avoided. Why in the world had the quizmasters chosen to include it? How would Grandpa and Grandma fare as interpreters of such a frightening story?

My husband, after seeing the featured story of the evening, exclaimed out loud, "Oh my! Tonight we have one of the most difficult stories in the whole Bible." As he began to read the story to the boys, the questions began, with incredulity. "He's going to kill his son?" "What's a sacrificial lamb?" "What's an altar?"

As the story unfolded, Jacob (a first grader) sat on the edge of his barstool, visibly quivering and wide-eyed the entire time. When the story concluded with the angel of the Lord calling out, "Abraham! Abraham! Do not lay a hand on the boy," and Abraham found a ram in the thicket to sacrifice instead, Jacob let out a huge sigh of relief. He exclaimed happily: "That story was super scary . . . and then *super* happy." And Ari (a third grader) remarked philosophically, "It was about whether he would obey God no matter what."

After this experience and others like it, I determined that our grownup impulse to sanitize the biblical stories for our children and grandchildren is just another way we sentimentalize our faith, turning hardcore stories into silly VeggieTales and cardboard cutouts. It *is* critically important that we always show how individual stories relate to the Bible's overarching narrative of love, or else they can cause great harm to children, and everyone. But as Krista Tippett remarks, the superficial ways she'd heard the stories as a child contributed to her ignoring the Bible for many years. When she came back to read it years later, she came to fiercely love the stories. Rather than presenting idealized views of the way human beings should behave, the stories of the Old Testament tell life like it is. There are no fairy-tale heroes, only "flawed, flamboyant human beings as prone to confusion as to righteousness."[5]

Walter Brueggemann speaks of how Israel included its children in its narrative imagination by telling them stories that were rooted in the memory and experience of their people. People told their children: "These are the stories that must be embraced to be who we are." The stories that defined the identity of the community were not negotiable, Brueggemann said. But the stories could be reinterpreted in each new generation given the changing needs and circumstances of different times and places. So Israel gave its children both identity and great freedom in interpretation.[6]

Talk about faith that starts with how *our* stories connect with the stories of the Bible would be a great way to put skin on sacred words. Last week, a retired former military officer came to our home to care for our goats and chickens while we left for a few days. It was hard to get to instructions about goat care because she was so eager to talk. At one time in her previous life, she was in charge of some thirty-five thousand prisoners in Iraq, which on her watch, were reduced to five thousand. She made those in her charge be kind to the prisoners, a huge improvement after the acts of torture and other violations at Abu Ghraib. She now has a small business offering substitute care for farm animals. She talked about having been a Buddhist for five years, and that two weeks ago, God "really got through to her" while she sat in a restaurant. Her life had been turned upside down. She'd begun hungrily reading the Bible. Someone told her to start with the gospel of Mark. She was awestruck. "That Jesus guy," she said. "He was really something! A straight talker. Assertive. Unafraid to confront. He meant business." I could see how a former military officer might admire those qualities in Jesus.

Personal stories. Bible stories. The overarching cosmic story of God's love. With a nod to Martin Luther's "my conscience is captive to the Word of God," I think our new friend personifies what it's like to be *captivated* by the verve of the Word of God, wide-eyed on discovering the remarkable life force of Jesus, and irrepressible in her desire to talk about her newfound faith.

Chapter 13

Talking Sin, Repentance, Conversion, Salvation

REPENT, FOR THE KINGDOM OF HEAVEN HAS COME NEAR

Unless we are able to confess our sin, repent, and recognize our personal and collective need for salvation, we have no need of faith or faith language. It's really that simple. Most of us prefer to sugarcoat the ways we mess up and are complicit in larger forces of violence and oppression. While we aren't so callous as to consider ourselves masters of the universe or perfection personified, we don't like to think about personal sin that may lurk within or give much thought to larger societal evils.

My grandson asked me the other day, "Grandma, if you could have a superpower, what would you choose?" It didn't take me long to say, "I'd choose to turn back climate change." He readily exclaimed, "I know!" and went off on his nine-year-old list of all that needs to change to bring our lives in harmony with the earth God lavishly gifted to humankind. It was a playful yet sober moment. On further reflection, I wondered why I didn't say, instead of turning back climate change, that everyone would love God with heart, soul, mind, and strength and love our neighbors as ourselves; or eliminate poverty, or enact justice for all who are oppressed, or that "the earth . . . be filled with the knowledge of the glory of the Lord, as the waters cover the sea" (Habakkuk 2:14). I think I'll bring back that conversation with my grandson for some additional rounds of what we might wish to do with superpowers.

But it doesn't take superpowers to sense our vulnerability to evil and to cosmic, social, and institutional forces beyond our control. When we catch even a hint of forces that threaten to undermine, poison, and destroy what we experience as good, true, and beautiful, we may begin small steps toward faith. If we pay attention, likely because the reality of evil shows up in a personal crisis or community-wide traumatic event, we may reach in desperation for help with sacred words provided by a faith tradition such as "deliver us from evil" or "Lord, have mercy" or "The Lord is my shepherd." At moments of extraordinary vulnerability, it may finally dawn on us how profoundly good it is to be able to anchor our lives in the saving power of One who faced down fear and the ferocity of evil with the superpower of nonviolent love. For the sake of our children and grandchildren, teaching them how to anchor their lives in the love of God amid all manner of vulnerabilities will be the greatest gift we can ever give them. Period.

Sadly, far too many of us barrel through life without stopping to reflect on our vulnerability to evil. Nor do we reflect on our participation in evil, the personal harm we cause to those around us by the sinful choices we make, and the many ways we benefit from the extractive desecration of the earth.

Yet the honest truth is that we can't go through life without disappointing ourselves and those we live with. It we're from North America, it's more than likely we can't live life without participating in systems that ruin other people's lives and rape the earth. When we dare to push through the avoidance and see ourselves as we truly are, and see the crushing ugliness of evil unmasked in the society around us, the only honest response is to fall to our knees, pleading, "Lord, have mercy. Christ, have mercy. Lord, have mercy on us."

FIRST LISTEN!

Nikolai Berdyaev, a Russian Christian religious philosopher writing in the early twentieth century about the existential spiritual significance of human freedom and the human person, observed that a "terrible increase of evil" was coupled with "the denial of its existence" and that we are "powerless to resist evil" if we fail "to recognize it as such."[1]

Failing to recognize evil as evil is a far too common malady for people like me—white, educated, economically comfortable, tamely religious, and privileged in ways to which, for most of my life, like many of my church family, I was oblivious.

Evil in my growing-up years was largely framed as a matter of personal sin, focused on sinful thoughts like jealousy, lust, covetousness, and dishonesty, all of which are hugely important to pay attention to and go to the heart of personal character and integrity. Thankfully I heard that message loud and clear. Personal integrity and upright character have been immensely important to me. I am on the watch for mean-spirited attitudes that cloud my judgment and actions that undermine the health of my relationships with others. I am committed to being transparent about ways my actions may be compromised by selfishness, dishonesty, fear, or hatred. I am alert for signs of the fruits of the Spirit in my life and in the lives of others: love, joy, peace, patience, kindness, generosity, faithfulness, gentleness, and self-control. I am grateful for a strong, formational grounding in the basic character dispositions and virtues that give me some hope of embodying what Jesus meant when he called on his followers to be the salt of the earth and a shining light on a lampstand; persons able to love our enemies and pray even for those who persecute us (see Matthew 5:13-48).

Attention to personal sin goes only so far for contending with the systemic forces of evil, however. I and many of my peers thought if we lived as good people, confessing our sins and shining our lights, we'd be fine. Yet here we are, far from fine—with the existential threat of climate change in addition to pandemics, plastic pollution, obsessive overconsumption of stuff, racialized hatred and violence toward marginalized peoples at a fever pitch. So we must listen—listen with a new intensity to detect where evil masquerades, hiding in plain sight.

Malinda Berry speaks of social evils identified in the 1920s by Frederick Lewis Donaldson, Canon of Westminster Abbey, as "wealth without work, pleasure without conscience, knowledge without character, commerce without morality, science without humanity, worship without sacrifice, and politics without principle." These, she said, are "a variation on the seven deadly sins of Christian tradition: envy, greed, gluttony, lust, pride, sloth, and wrath." The classical poet Dante expanded on these in his *Inferno* to add "heresy, violence, fraud, and treachery as circles of Hell."[2]

Lists of evils, while helpful, rarely take us to the heart of the matter, like an illustration of how greed, violence, and fraud masquerade in plain sight. Take, for example, the unmasking of the Doctrine of Discovery in recent years—a worldview promoted by the church and European monarchies in the fifteenth century and inscribed into U.S. law in the eighteenth and nineteenth centuries. This doctrine, Berry writes, "blessed colonial powers to seize the lands of indigenous peoples and thereby to terrorize and massacre indigenous peoples in the process."[3]

Evil was hiding in plain sight, for example, when many of our immigrant ancestors moved onto land from which Indigenous people had been violently removed. Historian Rich Myers describes how wide swaths of land in Indiana and Michigan, including the land on which the seminary where I served was built, originally belonged to the Potawatomi Nation. In 1838, some eight hundred Potawatomi were marched at gunpoint by U.S. soldiers to Kansas on what became known as the Trail of Death. "It is called the Trail of Death," writes theologian David Cramer, "because, during this forced emigration in the chilly months [between] September and November, an estimated 60 of the 800 Potawatomi—most of them elderly or children—died. Those who survived were left homeless and landless, and many of them moved south to Oklahoma."[4] Pilgrimages from AMBS, guided by faculty and Potawatomi elders, have retraced the Trail of Death three times in recent years, in a spirit of repentance and desire to learn from the wisdom of Native peoples whose resilience shows the way toward a restorative and sustainable future.

Our faith, writes Cramer, without us noticing, has become tangled with "American exceptionalism, nationalism, capitalism, militarism, and patriarchy." So while some call for "decolonizing" as what's needed, there is another name: "what Jesus calls *repentance*—turning away from systems of violence and empire in order to embrace the nonviolent kingdom of heaven as those with pure hearts who seek after the righteousness and justice of God."[5]

Learning to talk about faith must involve uncovering where evil is hiding in plain sight and how we might live into Jesus' command that was meant to kick the legs out from under evil: "Love your enemies, do good to those who hate you, bless those who curse you, pray for those who abuse you. . . . Do to others as you would have them do to you" (Luke 6:27-28, 31).

SUBMIT TO MYSTERY

We also tend to stay away from talk about sin and evil because of the guilt, blame, and shame that often comes with the territory. Accusations or insinuations that one has sinned have often been used by those with religious power to control the lives of others in church communities in ways that are dishonest and manipulative.

Dame Julian of Norwich, a medieval English mystic, provides us with a beautiful reframing of sin and guilt, which Elaine Heath expands on. Julian, who lived during a time of horrible suffering brought on by the Hundred Years' War and the bubonic plague, had a series of visions while she was deathly ill. The wisdom Julian shared with others came from a lifetime of meditating on those life-changing visions, which grounded her in the conviction "that the universe belongs to a God who is love, and that eventually 'all manner of thing shall be well.'"[6]

Julian's brilliant insight about sin, writes Heath, was that sin emerges from "original wounds" and that the fall described in Genesis 3 is about wounds to body, mind, and spirit, including "alienation, blindness, fear, suffering, and humanity's inability to extricate itself from its fallen place." God looks on sin "with pity and not with blame," Heath says of Julian's perspective, and "no matter how dreadful our condition, the 'sweet eye of pity is never turned away from us, and the operation of mercy does not cease.'"[7]

Julian's theology abounds with healing images: "Christ as our clothing, our safe place, our strong and tender Mother. In the midst of suffering and sin, brokenness and alienation, Julian sees that humanity is God's bliss, God's reward, God's honor, and God's crown."[8] It is hard to fathom how life-changing it would be for our faith communities if we fully grasped God's loving solidarity with humanity and experienced God primarily as a strong and tender Mother alongside what we see of Jesus' relationship with his Abba—a strong and tender Father.

Rather than majoring on shaming and accusations, it would tenderize our language if we were to talk about sin as arising from wounds to body, mind, and spirit. We would sense solidarity with each other, and overcome rancorous divisions, if we more readily acknowledged our own woundedness and together submitted to the mystery of God's love freely available to heal all wounds, forgive all sins, and make all manner of things well.

IT'S ALL ABOUT BEING IN LOVE

Recently my husband and I visited the church where our two-year old grandson attends with his family. In the foyer when he spotted us, he shrieked with delight, danced a little jig, flinging his arms wide, and made a dash for his grandpa's arms. We often call him our "beamish boy"—with a nod to Lewis Carroll's "Jabberwocky." He beamed from head to toe. Everyone who watched him glowing in his grandfather's arms saw the radiance of pure love.

Jesus said, "Unless you change and become like children, you will never enter the kingdom of heaven" (Matthew 18:3). And he told Nicodemus, "No one can see the kingdom of God without being born from above. . . . Without being born of water and Spirit" (John 3:3, 5).

Tatiana Goricheva describes what it was like for her to be born of Spirit. "But the wind which is the Holy Spirit 'blows where it wills'. It gives life and raises the dead. So what happened to me? I was born again. Yes, it was a second birth, my real one." Goricheva describes how one day while she was wearily doing her regular yoga exercises, she was using suggested mantras from a yoga book, among which was a Christian prayer, the "Our Father." She had never up to this point said a prayer. She began to say it automatically, without expression. After about the sixth time through, "I was suddenly turned inside out," she writes. "I understood—not with my ridiculous understanding, but with my whole being—that he exists. He, the living, personal God, who loves me and all creatures, who has created the world, who became a human being out of love, the crucified and risen God." She says that in that moment, she grasped the "mystery" of Christianity and experienced genuine deliverance. Everything changed for her. She gave up earlier values and ideals and old habits. She began to love people, understand their suffering and that they're made in the image of God. She felt joy and full of light—and not only within her, but that every stone and shrub was bathed in light. The whole world, she says "became a royal, high-priestly garment of the Lord." She wondered how she hadn't seen this before.[9]

Conversion is a mysterious thing—and the way we come alive to God is different for each of us.

My impression is that few of us have an earthshaking experience like Goricheva, though it's a marvel to hear about them when they occur, as described by authors like Anne Lamott and Sara Miles. Conversion may not include "some dramatic experience of conviction and release that occurs once, after which things have forever been made right," writes theologian of human development James Fowler. Conversion may be more like a "recentering of our passion," like falling in love with God, or becoming attached to Jesus Christ with a "loving, committed, and ready-to-suffer passion for the in-breaking commonwealth of love."[10]

My impression, from the circles I frequent, is that we don't hear many stories or testimonies about conversion events, either the more dramatic or the gradual kind, which is another consequence of our tongue-tiedness, I guess. Does it mean they're not happening or that we're neglecting to watch for and anticipate them or to create opportunities to talk about them when they do happen? Goricheva observes, as do many others, how repentance and conversion come particularly hard for the more educated among us, and for those who are rich.

HOLD THE WORLD TOGETHER

I didn't grow up with the doctrine of "total depravity"—a view of the world associated with the Protestant theological framing called Calvinism. "Total depravity" sounded far too grim for my liking. Why wouldn't one talk instead about an original blessing of fundamental goodness?

I was intrigued, however, by a revisiting of this pillar of Calvinism by Heidi Haverkamp, an Episcopal priest and author. She writes of having grown up believing that because we're created in the image of God, we have the capacity to change the world—which means doing the right things, serving, and loving each other. "We didn't talk about how to deal with the enormous weight of evil and suffering in this world," she says, "or how insufficient human efforts can seem in their shadow." But somehow, no matter how hard she tried to do the right thing, the world spun her to her knees with more evidence of cruelty, catastrophe, and waste.

The stark doctrine of "total depravity," Haverkamp writes, doesn't suggest that we're basically good people who sometimes mess up, but rather suggests that we are "messed-up people" who can, with God's help, do some good things. Haverkamp found this matter-of-fact, unflinching look at evil to offer a surprising grace. "Of course the world is full of evil and suffering," she says. "Of course people are unjust and cruel to one another. Of course I feel like a completely inadequate Christian. Of course it's hard to avoid living as a complicit consumer, pollution enabler, and ineffective activist. Of course I feel paralyzed by despair. It's because of total depravity." When unreasonable, unending sin is something we *expect*, rather than thinking the salvation of the world is a solvable problem, Haverkamp writes, "I can shove my shock and despair at human evil into Calvin's theological Hefty bag and find more room on my soul's kitchen table to work on hope and a plan."[11]

This rethinking of a doctrine that, I'm guessing, a lot of us don't know or care about may seem curious. I use it here as an illustration of how people have wrestled with the question of good and evil over many centuries, and come up with all sorts of questions and answers—none of which is foolproof or completely satisfactory. Why is there evil? Who is responsible for evil? How can evil be uprooted? How do we hold the nastiness of evil together with the goodness of God who made a world that has capacity for both good and evil? I'm intrigued with what Haverkamp does in large part because she brings the inadequacy of the answers she was given into dialogue with an old answer that, for her, released energy for fresh coping. This, my friends, is what conversations about faith are all about—raising questions, thoughtfully revisiting old answers, and shaping new or recombined answers that give us fresh vitality.

SPEAK FROM STORIED, HOLY GROUND

Meghan Good, popular speaker and pastor, said to me over lunch one day that Christians are reluctant to talk about God *acting* in the world. It is confidence that God *acts* that infuses talk about faith with an energetic joy. "The broken world is not out there waiting for you to go and save it," she asserted. "It has been saved and it will be saved by Jesus Christ." We need to get over ourselves and instead focus on "the incredible joy of getting to participate in this story."

I hear that joy in Goricheva's story of conversion: "When I am asked what turning to God meant to me, what I discovered through this conversion and how it has changed my life, I can give a very simple and short answer: everything. Everything has changed in me and around me. Or, to put it more precisely: my life only began when God found me."[12]

I hear that joy in James Fowler's description of the impact that conversion has on people in general: "Conversion means a release . . . at a depth of the heart that is truly liberating, that our worth, our value, our grounding as children of God is *given* as our birthright. . . . We are known, loved, supported, and invited to partnership in being with One, who from all eternity intended us and who desires our love and friendship."[13]

Ongoing conversion will be a process of gradually bringing the story of our lives into congruence with the core story of the Christian faith, Fowler says. Ongoing conversion will mean learning to talk honestly about moments of regret, coming clean with repentance, and experiencing the relief of dignity restored and the exhilarating opportunity to partner in God's shalom work.

We'll discover the power of testimony as we find words to describe how love broke through on a weary day or when deliverance showed up and unexpected provision arrived and we were saved. We will learn the lost art of talking about faith when we encourage each other to wrap the skin of testimony around personal pivotal moments, whether as simple as a bird-call on a lonely evening, tears of apology that create a break-through, or a life-altering encounter with God that changes everything. We will learn the lost art of talking about faith when we encourage each other to wrap the skin of testimony around pivotal moments for the community, whether needed reform of the local police force, cancellation of an oil pipeline that posed a threat to local habitats and residents, or the over-turning of a sentence of execution for someone on death row. In learning to talk freely about the small ways we're saved in any ordinary day—in addition to the world-altering events that change the trajectory of personal lives or our community as a whole—we'll discover what a joy it is to participate every single day in God's saving work in the world.

Chapter 14

Beauty's Voice Saves the World

BEAUTY AND SUFFERING ARE BOUND TOGETHER

I am, on occasion, moved to tears by YouTube videos of flash choirs emerging out of the hoi polloi in a shopping mall or street venue to perform Beethoven's "Ode to Joy" or another musical standout. Suddenly, it's as if we're given a window into another world of transcendent beauty. Music often carries me to a "thin place"—where the veil between earth and heaven seems almost to have lifted. When I'm caught off guard by beauty—the call of a white-throated sparrow on a gloomy day, a bloodred sunset when weighed down by grief, a vast carpet of yellow flowers in a winter-ravaged woods—words fail me. Yet even to say "I have no words" speaks volumes and becomes a shared awareness for those of us left speechless by encounters with beauty.

While on sabbatical several years ago, my husband and I stayed in a cousin's condo on the east coast of Florida. I kept a journal day after day. One day's reflection included this: "I woke after light had begun to fill the horizon. I watched the glow climb—in rainbow hues of indigo, violet, orange, yellow, red and green. It was stupendous. When I had first awakened in the darkened bedroom, with the morning numbness that often weighs down, I wondered—where has the magic gone? Why am I wanting out? Why am I impatient with those closest to me? And then I watch the sunrise for the third morning in a row. And the bright morning star. My spirit quickens. It is beauty that captures my imagination, and beauty that may well be a theme for the next season of my leadership."

The journal continues: "This hunch was reinforced for me with the morning's *New York Times* opinion piece, 'Finding Beauty in the Darkness,' coupled with the audiobook from our trip down here of *All the Light We Cannot See* by Anthony Doerr, and reading *Quantum Shift—Theological and Pastoral Implications of Contemporary Developments in Science*—all of which intoxicated me. This focus can reanimate me for the next laps: beauty of the Scriptures, of community, truth, goodness, justice, peace, creation, diversity, worship, family, God . . . of the salvaging, saving Spirit who takes the stone the builders rejected and fashions it to become the chief cornerstone.

"The psalm reading at the Holy Apostles church, as we walked late into the sanctuary this morning, was Psalm 27, which took me back to what had been my focal psalm as I began as president: 'One thing have I asked of the Lord; one thing I seek; that I may dwell in the house of the Lord all the days of my life; to behold the fair beauty of the Lord and to seek him in his temple.'"

Fyodor Dostoevsky has this riveting statement in his novel *The Idiot*, which hooked my intrigue the first time I read it: "Beauty will save the world." Dostoevsky isn't suggesting that beauty alone can save the world, artist Michael O'Brien says (speaking primarily to fellow artists).[1] What Dostoevsky is talking about is how beauty and suffering are bound together—living within both crucifixion and resurrection.

Dorothy Day's granddaughter Kate Hennessy entitled a 2017 biography about her grandmother *Dorothy Day: The World Will Be Saved by Beauty: An Intimate Portrait of My Grandmother*. Hennessy writes, "In the last years of her life, my grandmother often woke up hearing in her mind the words from her beloved Dostoyevsky: 'The world will be saved by beauty.' Of all the words she wrote, of all the quotes she loved to repeat, of all the advice and comfort she gave to countless people, in all five of her books and fifty years of her column, and in a lifetime of diary- and letter-writing, this is what has come to give me the most hope. For if, after years of struggle, weariness, and a sense of deep and abiding failure, she believed in salvation through beauty, then how can we not listen?"[2]

So how do we open ourselves to beauty—beauty that renders us speechless, that takes us to a thin place between earth and heaven, that shines through suffering, that begs to be spoken, sung, danced, painted, and welcomed with its astonishing power to save?

FIRST LISTEN!

In these times so wracked with anxiety and deep misgivings about what the future may hold, it is high time "to invoke and awaken beauty, which we've disastrously neglected," writes poet John O'Donohue. How much ugliness can we endure? he wonders. It is in welcoming beauty that "a new fluency is set free within us and between us. The heart becomes rekindled and our lives brighten with unexpected courage."[3]

I am heartened by the beautiful depictions of shalom in the Scriptures. When I listen to Isaiah's stunning vision of the wolf, lamb, leopard, calf, lion, and bear lying down in the company of a little child, of a nursing child playing over the hole of an asp, and a weaned child putting her hand on the adder's den, and that there will be no hurting or destruction on the entire holy mountain, because the earth will be as full of the knowledge of the Lord as the sea is full of water, I feel just what O'Donohue describes—a new fluency set free within me. I become animated upon hearing Micah's exhilarating vision of swords being beaten into plowshares, spears into pruning hooks, and everyone sitting unafraid under their own vines and fig trees (Isaiah 11:6-9 and Micah 4:3-4, paraphrased).

In listening for and welcoming beauty, we grow in our desire to guard against harm that threatens what we've experienced as beautiful. Philosopher Elaine Scarry says that an experience of the beautiful is sacred. It is life-saving. "At the moment one comes into the presence of something beautiful, it greets you" and we give up our position as the center of things. When greeted by beauty, we suddenly find that we are standing in a "different relation to the world than we were a moment before," and standing on a "fragment of sturdy ground."

When we encounter beauty, we experience a quickening, an adrenalizing, Scarry writes. A desire wells up to be in league with what is true and beautiful. That desire becomes the source of conviction; conviction that compels us to protect and defend what we've experienced as beautiful by doing all within our power to repair injury and attend to problems of injustice.[4]

Listening for beauty—allowing it to captivate us body, mind, and spirit and rekindle our courage—will move us to protect what is beautiful, repair what is broken, and restore what is injured.

SUBMIT TO MYSTERY

A poem by Denise Levertov called "Primary Wonder" recently stopped me in my tracks. It begins, "Days pass when I forget the mystery."[5] I posted it on Facebook, along with a stunning sunset picture I'd taken from the previous evening. A couple of days later, I received this email from a dear friend who experienced profound trauma as a child:

> Dear Sara. Somehow in recent weeks I have finally reached what I believe is the core of my trauma. I've been finding myself staring into this aching void that I doubt can ever be filled. A deeply broken part of myself that cannot be healed or redeemed. The healing work now feels especially futile. I've stopped engaging with it. I have been closing myself off from support and from beauty and gratitude, convinced that nothing can penetrate this consuming darkness. Then you posted a poem that spoke directly to my void. And your stunning sky photo momentarily drew me back into wonder, into something beyond myself. Unexpected gift. Thank you. Please hold hope for me.

When beauty "greets us," our spirits sense we're in the presence of something more. The beauty of a poem, painting, towering oak tree, or tiny violet isn't simply contained in itself but beckons toward something more expansive. Something holy, perhaps.

"To participate in beauty is to come into the presence of the Holy," writes O'Donohue.[6] It is really that simple. And stupendous. "O worship the Lord in the beauty of holiness" the hymn text sings, drawing from Psalm 96:9.

Francis Collins, renowned scientist and person of faith, illustrated this when he talked about how looking through a telescope or hearing the high descant of a Christmas carol surprised him with a sense of awe before he became a Christian, evoking a longing for something he couldn't name. He spoke of the deep sense of grief he felt while listening to the second movement of Beethoven's Third Symphony (the *Eroica*) and, after a tragedy, another symphonic lament which lifted him out of his "materialist worldview into an indescribable spiritual dimension, an experience," he says, "I found quite astonishing."[7]

A recent Religious News Service feature spoke of how evensong, a "hymn-heavy" traditional Anglican evening service, is seeing a large upswing of participants in houses of worship in Great Britain. Are persons perhaps attracted by the artistic expression of the music-based liturgy, and then also find it spiritually appealing? The article quoted from several participants speaking to why they come: "There is a reverence about it. It is a moment when you can pause in your daily life, when you can stop." "It brought tears to my eyes. . . . I used to go to church more when I was young, but the rules, the judging of people put me off. But the church here, with a service like this, brings people together." The dean of Westminster Cathedral is reported to have said, "I profoundly believe that attending a beautiful act of worship, whether evensong or the Eucharist, has converting power."[8]

Somehow, when we submit to beauty, we are changed, converted, humbled, and renewed. We discover, in Scarry's formulation, a "fragment of sturdy ground to stand on." We get in touch with a longing for God.

IT'S ALL ABOUT BEING IN LOVE

I resonate with writers and movement shapers, like Dorothy Day, who suggest that the real power of the gospel is beauty; the beauty that saves the world through all manner of small and large expressions of God's love like the lilies of the field, broken fresh bread, and Bach's St. Matthew Passion. Unfortunately, in European and North American Christianity, the gospel has often been domesticated, made out to seem predictable and dull. However, "to a generation suspicious of truth claims and unconvinced by moral assertions, beauty has a surprising allure," writes pastor Brian Zahnd. "Getting Jesus right is essential if we are to recover the beauty of Christianity, because Jesus *is* the beauty of Christianity! To see Jesus as he is, is to see the infinite beauty of God expressed in a human life."[9]

Robert Capon, after rhapsodies about food and transcendence in his book *The Supper of the Lamb*, pushes all the way back to the source of love's beauty: "I tell you simply what I believe. Love is the widest, choicest door into the Passion. God saved the world not by sitting up in heaven and issuing antiseptic directives, but by becoming man, and vulnerable, in Jesus. He died, not because He despised the earth, but because He loved it as a man loves it—out of all proportion and sense."[10]

Jesus showed us the beauty of a love that holds together grace and truth, tears and celebrative banquets, suffering and transcendence, death and resurrection. Jesus was a boundary-crossing kind of person—the cosmic Christ, "in whom all things in heaven and on earth were created" and the mortal human being who was flogged and bled and died; the kind of person who, because of how he faced into a horrific death with nonviolent love, transformed a violent instrument of torture into the most widely recognized symbol through which peace is made.

HOLD THE WORLD TOGETHER

Several years ago, my husband and I walked the sixty-mile St. Cuthbert's trail from Melrose to Lindisfarne through the borderlands between Scotland and England—a borderland that centuries ago saw horrific bloodshed between the Scottish Highlanders and the English. The beauty of the natural world we experienced on this pilgrimage was beyond anything I remember. Every day I was reminded of Mary Oliver's poetic acclamation: "It must be a great disappointment / to God if we are not dazzled at least ten / times a day."[11]

I'm intrigued by borders. Borders are not a bad thing, though they can be. They help define space, identity, responsibility. Borders need not be solid walls, but can be permeable, like a living cell's walls. They can be places of encounter and exchange with a world beyond our own small piece of earth. When well designed, borders free us both to form our distinct identities and to transcend them; to experience both a homeland and a vast network of transborder connections.

My intrigue with borders, however, is surpassed by fascination with the beauty one discovers in borderlands. It is in borderlands where we discover that beauty has no border; the sky, sun, moon, and stars sing to us all. It is in borderlands that we encounter the Other and are humbled by our own partial vision; we come to see that the beauty of kingdom-come transcends every border; that the beauty of justice enacted, of kindness shown, of shalom realized, is here *and* there.

But it is also at the borders where the conflicts are most intense, where when fear escalates, higher walls are erected, hatred and suspicion is fomented, families are separated, blood is shed. Many battles are fought over borders. The impulses to build the walls higher, reinforce the separation, shore up the polarities, seem almost out of control in our day. The border disputes are so intense that that's precisely where we need to learn to talk about how beauty saves the world. That's where Jesus was—with arms outstretched—talking to both friend and enemy.

SPEAK FROM STORIED, HOLY GROUND

When I called my parents on their seventy-second wedding anniversary in 2016, Mother told me Dad had brought her a bouquet from his garden. "A thing of beauty is a joy forever," she said, quoting John Keats. Dad, who at ninety-eight was still growing vegetables, grapes, and flowers, had brought Mother, whose mobility was limited after multiple strokes, a gift of beauty that brightened her spirits. Mother often quoted lines of poetry and Scripture that set my spirit dancing.

A thing of beauty is a joy forever. I've seen it over and over—and no doubt, each of us would have stories of how beauty has greeted us, moved us toward God. After a recent move to a rural farmette, my husband, whose daily passion is energy conservation, put up new laundry lines. It had been many years since I'd hung laundry outside. I had forgotten how exquisite the scent of fresh air-dried sheets and pillowcases is. There's really nothing like it—crawling between sheets fragrant with natural perfumes that ride on the wings of the wind. Perhaps lapsing in good judgment, I posted a Facebook picture of flapping laundry, and wrote: "First time in a decade I've had the pleasure. It's the little things. Gloria in excelsis Deo." That's how it is with beauty—even beautiful scents. The happiness beauty evokes prompts a desire to send praise skyward.

Another sighting of beauty happened in our local Virginia congregation amid the shock waves of a pandemic. Waynesboro Area Refuge Ministry, or WARM, provides emergency temporary housing to individuals and families who lack the financial resources to maintain stable housing. When one church scheduled to host "sealed up their building" during the COVID-19 outbreak and another scheduled to host was prevented from doing so, since their space didn't allow for beds to be six feet apart (CDC guidelines for homeless shelters), Springdale Mennonite agreed to take on three additional weeks beyond their normal week. A touching moment at dinnertime one evening was when the WARM shelter director officially announced to homeless guests that Springdale would host the shelter for three additional weeks. He was so relieved and overjoyed that the guests had a place to stay that he not only led in a round of thanksgiving applause to the Springdale congregation, but led in a "standing ovation" of thanksgiving to God that a church could offer shelter for four weeks running during a difficult time.

Another sighting of beauty is provided by Elie Wiesel, winner of the Nobel Peace Prize in 1986.

Wiesel's novel *The Gates of the Forest* includes some of the most unresolvable questions about faith and God that I've read anywhere. In one small glimpse of a lengthy exchange between the main character, Gregor, and a rabbi, Gregor asks, "And Auschwitz? What do you make of Auschwitz?" The rabbi responds, "Auschwitz proves that nothing has changed, that the primeval war goes on. Man is capable of love and hate, murder and sacrifice. He is Abraham and Isaac together. God himself hasn't changed." Gregor responds in anger. "After what happened to us, how can you believe in God?"[12]

The extended, fierce exchange between the two takes place within a room filled with dancing and singing: "The *Hasidim* were dancing," writes Wiesel. "They sang; and the song gave them life and caused the sap to well up in them and bind them together. Ten times, fifty times, they repeated the same phrase, taken from the Psalms or some other portion of Scripture, and every time the fire would be renewed again with primordial passion: yes, once God and man were one, then their unity was broken; ever since they have sought each other, pursued each other, and before each other have proclaimed themselves invincible. As long as the song and dance go on, they are."[13]

Toward the end of their exchange, the rabbi says to Gregor: "When you come to our celebrations you'll see how we dance and sing and rejoice. There is joy as well as fury in the *hasid's* dancing. It's his way of proclaiming, 'You don't want me to dance; too bad, I'll dance anyhow. You've taken away every reason for singing, but I shall sing. I shall sing of the deceit that walks by day and the truth that walks by night, yes and of the silence of dusk as well. You didn't expect my joy, but here it is; yes, my joy will rise up; it will submerge you.'"[14]

We encounter beauty in furious and joy-filled song and dance, air-freshened laundry and anniversary bouquets, borderlands and sunrise, hospitality for those who are homeless and Beethoven's "Ode to Joy." No matter in what form beauty greets us, it carries within its embrace the power of salvation—a saving power made real in an ultimate way, with Jesus living, dying, and rising again in beauty. No matter in what form beauty greets us, it cries out with great urgency for us to learn the power of sacred words for repairing what is broken and restoring what is injured—speaking with body, mind, and spirit: *Gloria in excelsis Deo.*

Chapter 15

Earth's Splendor and Suffering Proclaim Faith

PERSONAL SALVATION COMES UP SHORT

"The science is not in doubt. The forecast models are grim. We either rise to the challenge of rescuing the planet or live with irrevocable consequences." So declare the editors of a leading Christian periodical about the threat of climate change. They quote sixteen-year-old climate activist Greta Thunberg declaring at the 2019 United Nations Climate Action Summit: "People are suffering. People are dying. Entire ecosystems are collapsing. We are in the beginning of a mass extinction."[1]

In a "Time to Grow Up" daily meditation, Richard Rohr reflects on how a lot of talk about faith in Christian circles has focused on Jesus as our personal Lord and Savior. When the suffering of the earth is so great, we need to step back and reflect on what difference personal salvation makes in how we live day in and day out, he writes. The early Christians were overjoyed to participate in a community intent on following Jesus in a *way of life* that was "simple, non-violent, shared, and loving." By and large, we've avoided the change in lifestyle that accompanies faith, and instead have decided that one can be "warlike, greedy, racist, selfish and vain" and still believe that Jesus is our "personal Lord and Savior."[2]

Rather than forest, soil, wildlife, and whole classes of people being seen as raw materials for consumption or cheap labor, we must dramatically change our way of living and talking about faith. Faith talk shouldn't be mostly about personal salvation for some sweet by and by. It must be about how we seek shalom for all God's creation. Inner peace and security are hugely important, said theologian Drew Hart in a Facebook post. But the Creator's vision for peace on earth, for shalom, is about so much more. "It means wholeness and harmony, right relations between us and God, within the human family, and between us and the rest of creation."[3]

God declared the vastness of creation—sun, moon, stars, growing things, animals, humankind—to be good. Everything that we see in nature's bounteous splendor tells us something about the creativity, generosity, intelligence, loveliness, playfulness, and fearsomeness of the Creator. So much about the natural world astonishes, leading us to wonder and worship. Yet, as Thunberg and countless others tell us, ecosystems are threatened as never before.

As the reality of the climate crisis inflicts trauma on people groups and entire species, we must find faith-oriented ways to talk about what we can do to stop the destruction of our precious earth home. And we also must find the courage to talk about how to develop the inner and community resilience needed to cope with dire climate events, loss of wildlife on a massive scale, and increasing scarcity of the resources and conditions needed for human life. To do so well, we must first listen to and learn to love the plants, animals, air, soil, and water that sustain our lives as human beings.

FIRST LISTEN!

My parents created a childhood that brought us as a family close to nature and its many gifts. We learned to pay attention to birds, weather, trees, and gardens through their guidance. We often camped out, went fishing or swimming in all manner of lake, river, hot spring, or ocean. We exclaimed at the monkeys, baboons, crocodiles, pythons, and hippos while fishing in the Awash River in Ethiopia. We learned swimming in Rift Valley lakes and body surfing on Atlantic Ocean waves. We planted, picked, canned, froze, and supped on garden vegetables, orchard fruits, and sweet grapes from my father's garden, orchard, and vineyard. We marveled at bouquets of snapdragon, sunflower, larkspur, zinnia, coxcomb, baby's breath, and gladiolas grown in his garden, arranged by my mother.

From my parents' love, I learned to enjoy hiking mountain trails and nearly falling backward gawking at the tops of towering trees. I learned to love birds, and to lure birds in close with bird feeders. Some thirty species have shown up by my writing window this spring alone. On a walk through the back field, I identified more than a dozen tiny wildflower species one afternoon in late March—some with the help of a new plant identifying app. I love that our untreated "lawn" is awash in rivers of white, purple, and blue wild violets. I associate these loves with God's generous profligacy. God's goodness infuses them all. It's as if I see the face of God in every lime green willow leaf, shining dew droplet, mating mourning dove—and find myself on holy ground. Reverence is always just below the surface, with tears of thanks not far behind.

During the early days of the COVID-19 pandemic, various family members from town and city sheltered in place with us, including five grandchildren. I rediscovered the fun of baking bread and soft pretzels with little arms up to their elbows in flour, finding jar lids with sharp edges for cutting donut rings, rolling out cheese sticks with the giant rolling pin my husband made in high school shop class, teaching grandsons to crack eggs into cake batter, and watching their irrepressible desire to stroke the glossy yolks.

We learned again to enjoy family breakfasts of peach and blueberry pancakes (from local orchard and blueberry patch). When I cook, it is often vegetarian. Because my husband and family enjoy meat, we've agreed to buy locally raised meats— beef, chicken, and pork from neighbors. My husband built a chicken pen on wheels to raise our own chickens. After living in cities as academics most of our adult life, this venture into rural sustainable living is a new one for us. Watching grand-children literally leap for joy on discovering a freshly laid egg and frolicking with frisky goat kids provides no end of delight.

Much of my food prep used to be about finding prefabbed shortcuts for putting a meal on the table, excuses for fast foods, and frequent use of mass-produced animal products. I can no longer countenance the factory production of ani-mals for slaughter. When I traveled a lot through the Mid-west, the *horrible* stench of the feedlots in South Dakota and Kansas reached for miles around, turning my stomach. And there were the dismaying experiences of turkeys crammed into truck cages with feathers littering the grassy median past our home, pigs hanging from a conveyor belt with tails uncurling after electrocution (during a short-term college vacation job), chickens jammed so tight into warehouses they could barely move. I have chosen instead to notice and thank the creatures whose lives sustain my life—whether plant or animal. I used to look with an inner smirk on people who did this. Now I can no longer take plant and animal lives for granted or treat all that has given life to fill up our grocery shelves as collateral damage.

The whole story of the Hebrew Bible is about land, the "milk and honey" abundance that the land offers, and how when humans become greedy, selfish, or violent, we lose touch with how dependent we are on the generous gifts of the land—and ultimately, on God. Mistreatment of the land is directly related to mistreatment of other persons and alienation from God. When we begin to comprehend how respect for the land, for our neighbors, and for God are related, we also discover that the language we use to talk about the relationship between land, neighbor, and God must change. The language we use must be devoted to thanksgiving for gifts freely given for the enjoyment of all, and to the restoration of equilibrium and shalom.

Potawatomi botanist Robin Wall Kimmerer echoes the sense of the land's abundance when she writes about her sheer delight as a child on discovering patches of wild strawberries: "Strawberries first shaped my view of the world full of gifts simply scattered at your feet. A gift comes to you through no action of your own, free, having moved toward you without your beckoning. It is not a reward; you cannot earn it, or call it to you, or even deserve it. And yet it appears. Your only role is to be open-eyed and present. Gifts exist in a realm of humility and mystery." And she wondered, "What would it be like to consider the tree in the Kleenex, the algae in the toothpaste, the oaks in the floor, the grapes in the wine; to follow back the thread of life in everything and pay it respect? Once you start, it's hard to stop, and you begin to feel yourself awash in gifts."[4]

SUBMIT TO MYSTERY

On a bright day during a stay-at-home season, we learned that a neighbor had bushhogged a new trail through the back woods on their neighboring farm and set up a picnic table in a clearing in the woods. My husband and I, along with our son's family, eagerly explored the new trail. We took a picnic lunch, marveled at a woods newly opened for enjoyment and the picnic table under a gigantic black oak tree overlooking vineyards, with a view of the Blue Ridge Mountains. Several of us teared up with gratitude. We sang, "All things bright and beautiful, all creatures great and small. All things wise and wonderful. The Lord God made them all."

At the time, we had family members on the front lines of providing care to persons sick with COVID-19, others severely affected by the crisis who were reinventing how they did their jobs and managed their family life, and those whose lives were at significant risk should the virus come close. As we gazed in wonder, I looked up at the black oak towering over our heads—still without leaves after its winter rest. I thanked the black oak for standing strong against wind and storm over many, many years, providing shelter to countless birds and insects. My two-year-old granddaughter, hearing my thanks, thanked the black oak tree as well. It's not as if I believe the tree can hear or receive thanksgiving—though I don't actually know that it can't. The thanks I give is all caught up in thanksgiving to the tree's Creator. But giving thanks is my way of noticing, naming, and honoring the lives on which my life depends, including the small and large trees that fill my neighborhood.

On our walk, I put my newly acquired plant identification app to good use, exclaiming with joy after each discovery of a tree or flower's name. In her poem "Something," Mary Oliver wonders about "this sharpest desire / to discover a name" and why it is that on learning a name, we experience a "singular" happiness in our spirits.[5]

"It is an animate earth that we hear calling to us to feed the martens and kiss the rice," writes Kimmerer. "Most people don't know the names of these relatives; in fact, they hardly even see them. Names are the way we humans build relationship, not only with each other but with the living world. I'm trying to imagine what it would be like going through life not knowing the names of the plants and animals around you."[6]

We share life on this planet with six million other species, most of whom we know nothing about and take utterly for granted. And then there's the overwhelming scope of things that simply refuse to be stuffed into manageable containers, like the fact that there are some two hundred billion stars in our galaxy and the earth is like "a small speck of dust orbiting a star on the outer edges or boondocks of the Milky Way," which is only one of hundreds of billions of galaxies.[7] I'm humbled by the unfathomable mystery of it all.

IT'S ALL ABOUT BEING IN LOVE

Because of my love for birds, the *Science News* September 2019 report that since 1970 we've lost some three billion birds in North America, nearly one in three, or 29 percent, was like a gut punch. Many birds are experiencing a loss of habitat, fall prey to domestic cats, or die from collisions with buildings. The loss is widespread, reports Peter Marra, a conservation biologist from Georgetown University, and affects rare and common birds alike. The study is "a wake-up call," he writes. "We're experiencing an ecological crisis."[8]

Many Christians have used faith language to justify the treatment of animals in ways that undermine the well-being of entire ecosystems, with an attitude toward the natural world that it's ours to use for our own enjoyment, consumption, and, yes, exploitation. There are ways the Bible has been read to suggest that the "superiority" of human beings gives us a mandate to subdue and dominate all living creatures to serve our own selfish desires. A former colleague of mine, on returning from a gathering of animal rights groups, reported that Christians are regarded as the worst among religious groups for our treatment of animals.

Professor of religion Debra Dean Murphy explains how the ways Christians have used words like *dominion* in Genesis 1:26-28 doesn't communicate the nuances of the original Hebrew word, which has "connotations of shepherding, kinship, and communal power." The misuse of words has "underwritten the ruinous relationship with the earth that much of Christianity has permitted of its followers. . . . We need to call out religion's complicity in the orchestrated undoing of the world," she says. "We are facing the undoing of all of us—as a civilization and likely as a species" because we abandoned our "vocation to be caretakers in kinship with all that exists."

Murphy continues with stark frankness: What does it mean to prepare for a good death, she asks, even if several generations out? How do we live "in the end times"? We must learn to practice something like palliative care given to patients who know that death is imminent, she says. With an end-of-the-world catastrophe looming, we are called to cultivate the virtues necessary for living well in any time, and especially in these perilous times: courage, humility, justice, and compassion.[9]

Climate scientist Katharine Hayhoe said in an interview that her favorite Bible verse is from 2 Timothy 1:7: "God has not given us a spirit of fear" (NLT). This is a "litmus test for Christians," she said. "If something is inducing fear in us, it is not from God. What God has given us is a spirit of love, power, and a sound mind." She continued, "We are not to sit on our hands waiting for [Christ] to return, and we are certainly not to tremble in fear. We are to do good works, which includes loving and caring for others. And today that includes addressing global issues like climate change that disproportionately affect the most vulnerable of us." We don't have to change who we are as people of faith to exercise responsible care for the planet and "love others as Christ loved us," she said. We simply need "to connect the dots between the things we already care about, how they are affected by a changing climate, and what we can do that is consistent with who we are."[10]

In life and death, love endures. When we love birds, trees, and wild strawberries, we grieve with the devastating depletion of their numbers. We resolve to talk and act in ways that arise out of love, to restore health to local ecosystems. And we learn how critical it is that we learn the art of talking about a faith that will prepare us to live and to die—a faith that believes love shown for creatures, fellow human beings, and our Creator is never in vain.

HOLD THE WORLD TOGETHER

Talk about God and what it means to be spiritual beings is most intriguing when embodied; rooted in earthy soil, as Jesus frequently demonstrated in his teaching. "The kingdom of heaven is like a mustard seed that someone took and sowed in his field; it is the smallest of all the seeds, but when it has grown it is the greatest of shrubs and becomes a tree, so that the birds of the air come and make nests in its branches" (Matthew 13:31-32). "See, I am sending you out like sheep into the midst of wolves; so be wise as serpents and innocent as doves" (Matthew 10:16). "No one after lighting a lamp puts it in a cellar, but on the lampstand so that those who enter may see the light. Your eye is the lamp of your body. If your eye is healthy, your whole body is full of light; but if it is not healthy, your body is full of darkness" (Luke 11:33-34).

Bonaventure, a medieval Franciscan theologian and philosopher, spoke of there being no divide between sacred and secular, material and spiritual. "Every creature, because it speaks God, is a divine word," Bonaventure said. "From seagulls to stars, from a grain of sand to a snow-capped peak, each created thing contains a unique 'footprint' of God."[11]

This notion that there is no divide between matter and spirit, and that things we touch and see show us God, is often referred to as a *sacramental* understanding of the world. James Smith speaks of how the physical stuff of creation is a way God meets us and captures our attention. God reveals Godself through created things. The created world offers "a sacramental window into transcendent reality," an epiphany of God.[12] The psalmist proclaims:

> You stretch out the heavens like a tent,
>   you set the beams of your chambers on the waters,
> you make the clouds your chariot,
>   you ride on the wings of the wind,
> you make the winds your messengers,
>   fire and flame your ministers. (Psalm 104:2-4)

Many of us who grew up as Christians have a kind of uneasiness about blurring what was emphasized as an important distinction between Creator and creature. Consequently, without necessarily intending to do so, we drain the enchantment of the world of its God-given magnificence. In the name of avoiding paganism, we end up flattening nature into "only a symbol or pointer" to God rather than experiencing nature as "charged with the Spirit's presence which makes it *more* than material." That is the worry of those "who lack imagination," Smith writes, and who think that truth is only about what can be captured in propositions and doctrines. It is the poets who better intuit and express what we see with our sacramental imagination, he writes.[13]

Kimmerer's paradigm-shifting book *Braiding Sweetgrass: Indigenous Wisdom, Scientific Knowledge, and the Teachings of Plants* challenges the grammar and thought forms that have structured Christian faith. An old prejudice against pagan animism has distorted how many of us understand God's world and God's action in it, writes theologian Norman Wirzba about Kimmerer's book. "I wonder how Christian life would change if we believed God to be present to every creature as the divine power and love animating them from within. I wonder how the body of Christ would need to change if we believed the community of life to extend beyond people to include all the life that God loves," he writes.[14]

Surely God didn't create the world out of some sense of necessity. The melodic bird ecstasies that fill the air on an April morning, the clouds that boil and throb with flame and blackness, the neon colors and frills of all manner of marine life flashing iridescence through the blue green waters of a reef, the speckled, laced, ballooning fungi of every conceivable texture—on and on and on. I imagine that God made this all out of pure joy—and anticipated that all these bejeweled constellations of molecules and chemicals would be windows into transcendence—stained glass windows radiating the beauty of holiness.

SPEAK FROM STORIED, HOLY GROUND

Early in the onset of the coronavirus pandemic, I got a sense that a lot of people were in shock—disoriented and staggering to find their footing. I heard hints that I wasn't the only one looking with anxiety-laden intensity for evidence of God fingerprints; for signals of transcendence. One morning, this is what I penned:

> When unrelenting stress bears down, freighting every
>   moment with worry
> When it dawns on you that this isn't going to end anytime
>   soon
> When fear that the world you knew has ended clutches
>   your chest
> When overnight you have to reinvent your job, family life,
>   and everyday routines
> When you don't know which public officials or news
>   reports you can trust
> When each day brings ominous new tidings and
>   government orders
> When what seemed like a manageable time-out turns into
>   an unrelenting slog
> When it's not clear whether everything will be okay ever
>   again
> When low-grade desperation turns into panic that life
>   may spin out of control
> When "all you unknowingly leaned on has fallen"
> Remember.
> Remember that balance comes with slowing down, taking
>   stock, repositioning one's feet.

Remember there are ways to recover one's footing, on
    more solid ground.
Remember that it is possible to find a new normal.
Remember there are deep wells you'd forgotten existed.
Remember there are tried and true ways to draw water
    from those wells.
Remember that all of life is gift: air to breathe, sunlight,
    daily bread, sleep, water.
Remember what is ultimate: The steadfast love of the
    Lord never ceases.
So breathe. Deeply. *Slowly*. Over and over.
Focus on a point of light (candle) or something beautiful
    (flower, sky, tree, icon).
Breathe thanks for what is given: greening trees, cup of
    coffee, bed for sleep, roof over your head . . .
Open your hands. Receive what *is* given
    with thanksgiving.
Remember how Jesus, on receiving five small loaves and
    two small fish, gave thanks.
Remember how by sharing what was given, all were fed.
Learn how thanksgiving for what *is* given shifts your
    focus away from loss—toward possibility.
Discover the new normal that grows from small things—
    received with thanksgiving.
Rediscover that God's mercies never come to an end. They
    are new every morning (Lamentations 3:23).[15]

An intense desire to learn the lost art of talking faith is
sparked when life is upended—when those we love and the
world around us are suffering. We pay attention like never
before to the gifts in our own backyards and families. Confronted with our human vulnerability and limitations, we
search in desperation for windows into transcendence. We tell
stories of those who, in the midst of hard times, learned how
to survive with gifts already in hand.

"Mourning and celebration, as well as lamenting and joy, are not mutually exclusive," wrote Drew Hart in a Facebook post. "I can just hear the ancestors saying, 'Don't let anybody steal your joy.' Joy, thankfully, isn't a possession hoarded or distributed by the powerful."

Neither is the sacred language needed to name earth's splendor and suffering a possession hoarded or distributed by the powerful. Nor is it simply available for talking about one's private spirituality or personal Lord and Savior. The times in which we live give new meaning to biblical phrases such as these:

- creation groaning in labor pains
- the wages of sin is death
- a time to be born, and a time to die
- the valley of the shadow of death
- the trees of the field clap their hands
- where can I go from your spirit—or flee from your presence
- the steadfast love of the Lord never ceases

The art of talking about faith will come alive when we expand the scope of what sacred language describes to include stories about the splendor and suffering of the whole world—the entire cosmos.

Chapter 16

Science and Faith Sing in Harmony

SCIENCE AND FAITH ANSWER DIFFERENT KINDS OF QUESTIONS

Science and faith are intimately related, believe it or not. Why we've seen it otherwise or thought they needed to be seen as competitors is a tragic, misguided way of thinking. Scientists keep showing how fearfully and wonderfully made the world is. Why are we not astonished with every new scientific discovery that reveals what had been unknown and leads the way into larger mysteries of what is not yet known? Why are we not endlessly intrigued to ask theological questions about why everything came to be in the first place—which science, for all its wonderful discoveries, can't answer? When science and God are brought into proper relationship with each other, there is no end to the bright sparks of animated conversation to be had.

And then there's quantum physics, which blows up any notion we might have had about matter and spirit being altogether different substances. Suddenly, there's a whole new intrigue about what biblical and traditional wisdom have been saying for years about the interconnection of physical and spiritual aspects of being. And I, for one, can't stop thinking about all manner of ways that spirit energizes everything—and what John meant, for example, when he said "the Word became flesh and lived among us, and we have seen his glory" (John 1:14). While I'm not a scientist and venture timidly into a discussion where I'm quickly out of my depth, I am captivated by the quantum notion that at the subatomic level, particles have no mass and are pure energy.

Francis Collins, director of the National Institutes of Health and founder of BioLogos, an organization that works to integrate science and faith, is one of the most widely respected physician-geneticists in the world—and an outspoken Christian. After a reporter quizzed Collins for scientifically based answers during the pandemic crisis, he also asked about what Collins hopes more Christians would understand about science and more scientists would understand about faith. Collins answered: "To Christians I would say, think of science as a gift from the Creator. The curiosity that we have been instilled with to understand how the universe works can inspire even greater awe of the Creator. This gift could hardly be a threat to God, the author of it all. Celebrate what science can teach us. Think of science as a form of worship."

And about scientists Collins said: "Scientists, by their nature, are trying to understand how nature works. And I think the message to scientists has to be there are really important questions that fall outside of what science is able to address meaningfully, such as 'Why is there something instead of nothing? What is the meaning of love? Is there a God? What happens after you die?' Those are not questions for which science or scientific methods can be applied."[1]

The persistent notion among some Christian believers that science is in conflict with faith is like a horrible head cold that won't go away. What is it about viruses that seem to defy all manner of efforts to contain them? The perceived conflict between science and faith has taken many forms over the centuries, and seems particularly virulent during this time of polarization in the United States in particular, where some of the leading politicians, evangelical leaders, and their loyalists ignore, denigrate, or outright deny scientific evidence.

We sent our three children to a private, Christian high school around the turn of the century. While the school, in most respects, was a wonderful experience for them, the science teacher our two sons had was stuck in what is sometimes called "young earth creationism." He taught science, but it was distorted by his assumption that any science that didn't affirm that the creation stories in Genesis were seven literal days, happened six thousand years ago, and involved no evolution, was suspect. Thankfully, he was replaced by a much more theologically and scientifically attuned teacher, but it was too late for our sons as high schoolers to get to see how good science and good theology can happily coexist.

The creation stories in Genesis were never meant to provide a scientific explanation, nor to be used to refute science. Our sons' teacher, along with so many others, missed the beauty of these awe-filled texts about God as Creator by reducing them to literalist formulas—and then trying to jury-rig all scientific discovery about the age of the earth and evolutionary processes into that formula. It would be rather like trying to capture the sky in a blue bottle in order to sell folks on the notion that the blue bottle *is* the sky rather than the blue expanse stretching from horizon to horizon—and infinitely beyond.

In a comparable way, many scientists disdain religion and are suspicious of any religious explanation for the way things are, or of any knowledge that can't be verified without concrete evidence, data tables, and replication of experimental outcomes. Like religious fundamentalists, some scientists denigrate other ways of knowing, insisting that scientific methods are the only way to verify what is true.

"Science without religion is lame," Einstein is reported to have said. "Religion without science is blind."[2]

FIRST LISTEN!

I remember an aha moment driving with my family to an Atlantic Ocean beach one day. I have no idea why it struck me when it did—as there were no majestic mountains or stupendous sunsets in view. Maybe it was just dreamy boredom— mile on mile of staring out the window at storefronts and light poles. The question that suddenly riveted my attention was this: Why is there anything at all? I mean, really! Why?

The question was memorable because I soon realized that no real answer was possible—that the longer I reflected on it, the more my mind expanded into a kind of euphoric, wide-eyed ether. Puzzlement about the origins of the universe, and all that is unknowable about why and how things began, reminded me of when I tried to imagine eternity. Time that would never, never end. I didn't like it at all, and quickly put an end to imagining everlasting life, because it made me queasy.

I like questions with clear answers, as we all do. But when it comes to the origins of the universe, why there is anything at all, and where it's all headed, definitive answers are hard to come by. And that's why listening first is all-important—listening for questions that come out of nowhere, or from our children, or those skeptical of dogmatic answers that religious leaders and scientists provide about the nature of things. We need honest questions that push us to pursue multiple ways of knowing in order to get closer to the truth about the nature of things.

Beliefs that God made the earth in six twenty-four-hour days six thousand years ago make God out to be a "cosmic trickster," writes Collins, a view that is intellectually bankrupt, both in its science and its theology. Why people persist in such bankruptcy is one of the "great tragedies of our time," he writes, because it widens "the chasm" between scientific and spiritual worldviews right when a way of working together is so desperately needed. The power of both scientific and spiritual perspectives is urgently needed to better understand what is seen and unseen. Collins describes how immensely satisfying it is to find the harmony between a scientific and a spiritual worldview. He has found that there's really no conflict between being a rigorous scientist and being someone who believes God takes a personal interest in every one of us.[3]

Because Collins listens so carefully to answers that both science and faith provide, he's able to offer a mesmerizing account of "evidence for belief" in his book *The Language of God*. A core illustration of how he holds faith and science together is all about the origins of the universe: "There is at least one singular, exceedingly improbable, and profound event in history that scientists of nearly all disciplines agree is not understood and will never be understood," he asserts, "and for which the laws of nature fall completely short of providing an explanation." The vast majority of physicists and cosmologists have concluded over the last seventy years that the universe began at a single moment, commonly referred to as the Big Bang, approximately fourteen billion years ago. "The Big Bang begs the question of what came before that, and who or what was responsible," he writes. That no one has a clue about all of that clearly shows the limits of science as nothing else has. The consequences of the Big Bang theory for theology, he writes, are profound. "For faith traditions that describe the universe as having been created by God from nothingness (ex nihilo), this is an electrifying outcome. . . . The awe created by these realizations has caused more than a few agnostic scientists to sound downright theological."[4]

Collins continues, "The Big Bang cries out for a divine explanation. It forces the conclusion that nature had a defined beginning. I cannot see how nature could have created itself. Only a supernatural force that is outside of space and time could have done that."[5] This is where we submit to mystery.

SUBMIT TO MYSTERY

"I don't trust a theologian who dismisses the beauty of science, or a scientist who doesn't believe in the power of mystery," popular author and speaker Brené Brown writes.[6]

Pierre Teilhard de Chardin is described as "a master synthesizer of theological and scientific insight, . . . a paleontologist with a flair for mystical prose."[7] He wrote to a friend shortly before his death: "Less and less do I see any difference now between research and adoration." Rather than "dry academic dissertations of abstract principles," Teilhard's writings are "intensely personal hymns of the way in which 'the World gradually caught fire for me, burst into flame.'"[8]

Collins agrees that science can be a form of worship, though it's not easy for scientists to admit their spiritual views.

And unfortunately, church leaders are often out of step with new scientific findings—or attack them outright. The God we read of in the Bible is also the God of the genome, Collins asserts. God can be worshiped both in the cathedral and in the laboratory.[9]

IT'S ALL ABOUT BEING IN LOVE

Robin Wall Kimmerer talks about how when she first applied to a PhD program in botany, her questions arising from indigenous wisdom regarding plant interactions were dismissed as not valid scientific questions. She wished that at the time she had been told that her questions were bigger than science can answer.[10] Over time, she came increasingly to see how science and traditional knowledge, when held together, help us see the world more fully.

"I wanted to see the shimmering threads that hold it all together," she says. "And I wanted to know why we love the world, why the most ordinary scrap of meadow can rock us back on our heels in awe." She reflects on how science privileges only one way, or possibly two ways, of knowing—mind and body—and how as a young developing scientist, she didn't question this. But as she matured in her scientific work, she has drawn on indigenous wisdom and the belief that we understand a thing only when all four aspects of our being are engaged: mind, body, emotion, and spirit. "It is a whole human being who finds the beautiful path," she writes.[11]

My doctoral dissertation and subsequently published book *Anabaptist Ways of Knowing: A Conversation about Tradition-Based Critical Education* teased out eight roots of knowing that, when nurtured together, provide rich growth in understanding: traditional, spiritual, communal, bodily/tacit, intuitive/imaginal, rational, ethical, and practical roots.[12] All of these ways of knowing, when held within the all-encompassing love of God, transform how we talk about faith. As Kimmerer says in her beautiful synthesis of indigenous wisdom and scientific knowledge, we need a new story. We need a new way of relating to a world with scientists who value the sacred and faith leaders who value the discoveries of science. What is there not to love when scientists give us a glimpse into a human genome with its three billion DNA "letters" arranged in a double helix, carried in every cell of our bodies? What is there not to love when the most ordinary scrap of meadow we traversed one afternoon evoked in us a chorus of praise on spotting at least twelve different types of wildflowers, even as pandemic panic stalked the world?

HOLD THE WORLD TOGETHER

Fluency in faith language blossoms when we bring faith and science into conversation with each other. It's hard to imagine a more generative fuel for talk about faith than when we explore what it means to hold matter and spirit together as part of an indivisible whole, for example. Or to talk about what evolution has to do with creation. Or to examine traditional assumptions about what the Bible says on sexuality along with scientific evidence about same-sex attraction.

On spirit and matter, for example, many theologians and scientists affirm that what we used to think of as a dualism are really aspects of one indivisible reality. While the way we experience them is distinctly different, matter and spirit are really inseparably interrelated.[13] For twenty years now, I have worn a silver ring sporting an ancient Celtic knot that I bought on a visit to Iona, Scotland, one of the historically acclaimed homes of Celtic Christian spirituality. The interwoven strands symbolize the ancient wisdom of the interconnectedness of the spirit and physical worlds; indigenous or traditional wisdom from long before scientists affirmed it.

Heidi Russell, a theologian who teaches at Loyola University, does a remarkable job of exploring the theological and pastoral implications of some of the key principles of modern physics. While many persons, both Christian believers and scientists, see science and religion in conflict, Russell argues that science offers us new ways to think about God and our faith traditions. At nature's most fundamental, atomic level, she argues, things are interconnected, which gives nature a "social" character.[14]

It's not clear that anyone understands quantum mechanics, Russell quotes another scientist famously acknowledging, and what's going on when electrons behave like a wave under some circumstances and like a particle under other others. Scientists have long thought particles and waves are two separate realities, and Christians have tended to think of the body and spirit as two separate realities. All recent developments in physics and cosmology, however, seem to indicate that reality in its most fundamental form isn't about individual objects but about relationships and interactions. Russell suggests that even though we can't have certainty about who we are individually or who another person is or who God is, we can be certain that we are in relationship with one another. We can be certain that we affect each other, and that who we are depends on our relationship with one another.[15]

I love the way Kimmerer describes this relationship: "I dream of a world guided by a lens of stories rooted in the revelations of science and framed with an indigenous worldview—stories in which matter and spirit are both given voice." As humans, she says, we may not have wings or leaves like other species but we do have words. Language is both a gift and our responsibility. With words we remember old stories and tell new ones; new stories that bring science and spirit together.[16]

SPEAK FROM STORIED, HOLY GROUND

Learning the art of talking about faith will receive an infusion of energy when we share stories that bring science and spirit together. In doing so, we find ways to make new judgments based on new data that don't "subvert old Torah" or the law of God, as we discussed earlier, but give it vitality for fresh coping.[17] I illustrate with two stories, one on evolution and creation and the other from a friend who's experienced an astonishing personal transformation.

Collins speaks about a Christian group who invited him to talk about being both a scientist who studied the genome and a follower of Christ. He received a wonderful reception from his listeners until he mentioned that the scientific evidence for evolution is overwhelming. He talked about how, in his view, evolution may have been the elegant way God created humankind. As soon as he mentioned this, he says, "the warmth left the room." Why, he wondered, is there such a fear that accepting evolution in biology requires accepting atheism in theology? No serious biologist has doubts about the theory of evolution to explain the complexity and diversity of life, he writes. Because of the evidence of how all species are related, it's hard to imagine how anyone could study life and do serious science without it.[18]

Over time, Collins settled into a synthesis generally referred to as "theistic evolution," which he finds satisfying as a way for scientific and spiritual worldviews to happily coexist, as do many other scientists. It's possible to be fulfilled intellectually and alive spiritually, both worshiping God and using scientific tools to probe into some of the mysteries of God's creation, he writes.[19] Collins's entire book is a plea for people of faith not to settle for a bankrupt biblical or theological foundation, but to see how wholly and beautifully satisfying it is to hold science and faith in a mutually enriching embrace.

Another story comes at the interface of spirit and science from a very different angle. A friend's husband had a major mental health crisis, involving prolonged, profound depression and suicidal impulses. Through the intervention of grief experts, electroconvulsive therapy, and talk therapy that was attentive to the activity of the Spirit of God, he experienced profound healing. This man, whom I'll call Dale, is now a fearless witness to the power and presence of the Holy Spirit in his life. His experience of complete loss, followed by mental health therapies and eventually by wise spiritual guidance, brought him to complete surrender to the Spirit. For twenty-two months (at the time of this writing), Dale has enjoyed the continuous, daily joy of Presence that has not gone away, reports his wife. He's become an unusually vocal fan of the Spirit. Given what he's experienced of the Spirit's intervention, he's also critical of much of church life (in his case, Mennonite) for our reticence to talk about the Spirit's activity in our lives. Dale has sought out opportunities to visit prisoners in jail and to join a largely African American gospel choir. In marked contrast to the people in his predominantly white congregation, the people at the jail and in the choir talk about their experience of the Spirit and about their walk with Jesus all the time. But in the choir context, Dale has been told that all you need for good mental health is Jesus, and that you can't trust mental health therapists.

As this story illustrates, and from my own observation, it seems that to achieve a healthy respect both for open talk about real experiences of the Spirit's presence and for the contribution of scientifically based therapies is rare. Yet Collins's and Dale's testimonies show how wholly satisfying it can be to hold faith and science, Spirit and empirical evidence, in a mutually enlightening embrace.

Theologian Russell asserts that science offers theology no threat but instead "offers the possibility of further revelation."[20] Scientist Collins says he finds it difficult "to imagine that there can be a real conflict between scientific truth and spiritual truth. Truth is truth. Truth cannot disprove truth."[21]

Tracing out some of the many intimate connections between science and faith will not only reinvigorate conversations about faith, ethics, spirit, and matter. The powerful synergy between science and faith will animate Christian public witness as well—providing sturdy spiritual moral ground to stand on, coupled with the authority of the latest scientific evidence.

Chapter 17

Worship and Prayer Unleash Tongues

WORSHIP AND PRAYER ARE WHAT IT MEANS TO BE(COME) HUMAN

I often awake early, light a candle, and sink into prayer. I have learned to anticipate this time of quiet before the household stirs. I begin with several breath prayers that focus my mind, spirit, and body. My heart cry over and over is as simple as "Lord God, Lamb of God who takes away the sins of the world, have mercy on us." Or, from the Northumbria Community: "Christ, as a light illumine and guide me. Christ as a shield, overshadow me. Christ under me. Christ over me. Christ beside me on my left and on my right. This day, be within and without me. Lowly and meek, yet all powerful. Christ as a light. Christ as a shield. Christ on my left and on my right."

A candle or sunrise or icon provides a visual focus. I notice fears, regrets, worries that crowd in. I offer them to God with gratitude that I am not alone in whatever I'm carrying. I pray for immediate family members—and other persons that come to mind. I often turn to a prayer book, Scripture, or a collection of poetry for inspiration. *Take Our Moments and Our Days: An Anabaptist Prayer Book*,[1] which I use as an app on my phone, is a frequent source of inspiration for me.

This morning as I write this chapter, the psalm reading was from Psalm 27, one of my favorites: "There is one thing I ask of the Lord, for this I long, to live in the house of the Lord, all the days of my life, to savor the sweetness of the Lord, to behold his temple." I have often preached on this text, noting how "the house of the Lord" can be a specific temple, or the whole world—and is seen as such throughout the Scriptures— both as a particular place and the entire sweet, splendiferous creation.

The prophet Jeremiah, speaking for God, laments Israel's evils: "For my people have committed two evils: they have forsaken me, the fountain of living water, and dug out cisterns for themselves, cracked cisterns that can hold no water" (Jeremiah 2:13). Over and over again, prophets, in some fashion, implore people who have lost their way to hearken again to God's invitation: "Obey my voice, and I will be your God, and you shall be my people; and walk only in the way that I command you, so that it may be well with you" (Jeremiah 7:23). These words come after an earlier promise. "For if you truly amend your ways and your doings, if you truly act justly one with another, if you do not oppress the alien, the orphan, and the widow, or shed innocent blood in this place, and if you do not go after other gods to your own hurt, then I will dwell with you in this place" (vv. 5-7).

I'm intrigued by the image Jeremiah captures, of God as the fountain of living water in contrast to cracked cisterns of our own making. The image of living water shows up again in Jesus' amazing conversation with the Samaritan woman at the well. He offers her "living water." When she wonders where he gets this living water because he had no bucket and the well was deep, Jesus responds, "Everyone who drinks of this water will be thirsty again, but those who drink of the water that I will give them will never be thirsty. The water that I will give will become in them a spring of water gushing up to eternal life" (John 4:13-14).

Over many years, I have cultivated habits of prayerfulness and receptivity to the Spirit—practices that anticipate illumination, encouragement, owning of what I regret, forgiveness, fresh courage, new insights, new ideas for a way forward. Prayers often connect me with the "fountain of living water." My prayer practices are attentive not only to my own personal needs, but to what it means for my family, church, and community to worship God and "savor the sweetness of the Lord" and to "obey God" by amending our ways so as to act justly with one another.

Without worship and prayer, faith talk is like an amputated body part. There is no life in it, and it deserves to die. At their heart, worship and prayer aren't about doing something extra to be more religious. Rather, worship and prayer are inseparably intertwined with what it means to be(come) human, to be renewed in our "creational vocation" as those who bear the image of God in the world, writes James Smith. We won't flourish as human beings unless we have a dynamic relation with the One who made us, on whom, ultimately, we are utterly dependent. In fact, the flourishing of all creation—what the Scriptures describe as shalom—requires a "right harmonious relationship" with God, and what follows from that: a harmonious relationship with fellow human beings and with nature.[2]

If we aren't finding life-giving ways to pray, writes Sarah Coakley, there are insights and distinctive ways of knowing that simply aren't accessible to us. It's that basic.[3] We may determine to be the most justice-oriented, righteously active persons we know—zealous about making the world right—but unless we cultivate mindful practices of prayer, there is much we simply will not comprehend about who we are, what it means to be human, who God is, and what we are called to do in concert with God. Practices of worship and prayer hold together the zeal we bring to tasks *and* the sustaining power of the Creator of the universe on whom ultimately we rely for life, breath, and the Spirit who enlightens us.

Clearly, we all need food and water to sustain life. Our bodies remind us many times a day to eat and drink. What we tend to forget amid all manner of worries, distractions, and busyness is the water that sustains body, mind, and spirit over the long haul—in good times and bad, in sickness and health, in life and death. When we join with other God seekers in worship, we learn how to talk with God and talk about God as the One who sustains life and renews our moral resolve to do justice, love mercy, and walk humbly with God.

FIRST LISTEN!

Listening over and over again in worship to the powerful shalom vision of God in evidence throughout the Scriptures will free us to lean forward into the future that God envisions for the world. Listening thoughtfully will transform how we relate to the political platforms of various parties and candidates—and how we engage the very real problems of our neighborhoods and earth. When we love God with heart, soul, and mind, first and always, we will be more fully prepared to love our neighbors no matter what.

Smith calls Christian prayer and worship *counter*-formation. The wider culture offers a barrage of "powerful rituals and icons of nationalism" through the sports and entertainment industries, he writes. Much of what we see in "the liturgies" of the mall, football stadium, and political, military, and popular culture are "visions of human flourishing that are antithetical to the biblical vision of shalom."[4] As people who want to talk about God with integrity, we must listen first to the biblical vision of shalom for all creation.

The final book written by Willard Swartley, author or editor of some forty books, is called *Jesus, Deliver Us: Evil, Exorcism, and Exousiai*. He reflects on the Revelation to John, the final book of the New Testament and one that focuses extensively on ultimate allegiance, expressed in worship, as resistance to the Roman Empire. Swartley observes that it is through worship that Christian believers "resist the idolatry of the emperor cult." Revelation is filled with praise anthems proclaiming "God's shalom-triumph" with singing saints from every tribe and nation joining in praise to God and the Lamb on the throne.[5]

Two former seminary colleagues, June Alliman Yoder and J. Nelson Kraybill, wrote "A Christian Pledge of Allegiance" that reads: "I pledge allegiance to Jesus Christ, and to God's kingdom for which he died—one Spirit-led people the world over, indivisible, with love and justice for all." When we pledge allegiance to Jesus as our Lord, rather than to our country, the president, or Wall Street as "lord," it is a political act, a pledge that declares our citizenship is with God's kingdom, not the kingdom of the United States or any other nation-state.

Christians in the early church, surrounded by an oppressive empire, were empowered by prayer and worship to endure persecution and live in peace. The Christian movement grew exponentially, in large part because believers were "energized by the power of God that they experienced in worship." Rumors got out that Christian worship was a place of empowerment, so much so that "outsiders wanted access to the power center of prayer." Swartley encouraged people of faith today to "make worship services a time of rehearsing God's goodness and salvation from sin, evil, and Satan as well as instruction for living the new life in Christ."[6] I love the idea of worship gatherings as a power center of prayer—a place to sing, dance, pray, testify, and proclaim the Word of God as an act of resistance to evil. And I love thinking of worship as a rehearsal of God's goodness and salvation in ways that form us in the way of Jesus.

SUBMIT TO MYSTERY

Each of our three children participated in choirs over the years, either in a children's choir, a high school select choir, a college select choir, or all three. There are standout moments that come quickly to mind. One of the more poignant memories is from a time of personal crisis when our eldest son's college choir sang the traditional African American spiritual which goes, "Somebody prayed for me, had me on their mind, took the time to pray for me. I'm so glad they prayed, I'm so glad they prayed, I'm so glad they prayed for me." It was a new song for me. I felt suddenly on holy ground. Tears welled up, along with overwhelming gratitude for the praying persons in my life who help carry our family through hard times. That was a couple of decades ago.

On Father's Day this year, we received a text from our middle son with a video link. It read: "Happy Father's Day! Here's a song from us." The video showed our son playing the piano as our three-year-old granddaughter, Madeleine, and her mother sang, "Somebody prayed for me . . . My father prayed for me . . . My mother prayed for me . . . My Jesus prayed for me, had me on his mind, took the time to pray for me. I'm so glad he prayed, I'm so glad he prayed, I'm so glad he prayed for me." Their four-month-old daughter watched in rapt attention from a blanket on the floor. Madeleine sang her heart out, body and legs swaying slightly with the beat, completely at ease and unselfconscious. Seeing the joy of this family, even amid COVID-19 restrictions in Harlem, New York, and the ways prayer holds us together in solidarity across the miles, brought me onto holy ground—with tears of gratitude again.

On the recent death of a much loved African American bishop in Harlem, a friend, Steve Kriss, now a prominent church leader, posted this poignant memory: "[The bishop] invited me to join a conga line at the gathering of NYC Mennonite Churches at Camp Deerpark 20 years ago when I first came to serve as a pastoral intern in the city. He said 'You have to get into the dance early so that the other white folks will come along.' I awkwardly joined the line that day as it snaked through the gathering. I swayed/marched/moved along and laughed and felt uncomfortable to a song that repetitively said 'Don't you want to be a part of the kingdom?' to a calypso beat. It was an important life-shaping symbolic moment for my life, work and leadership."

I wonder sometimes why it's hard for a lot of us from the dominant white culture to give ourselves permission to be vulnerable in worship. For me it's usually fear that my behavior will distract someone, make them think I'm foolish, immature, or seeking attention. I wish more of us felt free to wholeheart-edly enter into the mystery of worship and prayer—freely crying out with laments, pleading with God, confessing our deep regrets, praising God bodily and unreservedly; genuine worship and prayer that bring us into the presence of the Holy One.

The Psalms were compiled as the prayer book of the ancient Israelites. They guide us into a sort of "conversa-tional life with God," writes Christopher Smith. "For the psalmists, no emotion is off-limits in their talking with God—joy, thanksgiving, fear, rage, confusion, and many more." Our frequent reluctance to be transparent with God grows out of our resistance to God's transforming work in our lives. Fundamentally, transparency is connected to trust, he writes, so the real question is whether we can trust God. Often we simply can't or don't—for all kinds of reasons, many of which grow out of the "bad theology" we inherited, along with our worst fears about God. This reluctance and fear will dissolve as we learn to be present with God. Trust will be built when we have our own direct knowledge *of* God, not simply knowledge *about* God. And we will grow in our knowledge of God when we encounter God in worship, in the stories of Scripture, and in our lived experience—with the guidance of the Holy Spirit.[7]

Knowledge *of* God acquired through prayer "must involve the stuff of learned bodily enactment," writes Sarah Coakley, "over months and years, in duress, in discomfort, in bewilder-ment, as well as in joy and dawning recognition." She observes that "it is the Holy Spirit who 'interrupts' my human mono-logue to God, it is the Holy Spirit who finally thereby causes me to see God no longer as patriarchal threat but as infinite tenderness . . . who first painfully darkens my prior certainties, enflames and checks my own desires, and so invites me ever more deeply into the life of redemption in Christ."[8]

It is in submitting even in our discomfort to prayer and worship as people who are willing to practice freedom, vulnerability, and listening for the nudging of the Holy Spirit that we grasp for words to talk about what we're sensing and seeing. The Holy Spirit unleashed tongues during the Jewish Pentecost celebration not long after Jesus ascended to heaven, described in Acts 2. Miroslav Volf and Willie James Jennings, in a conversation about a theology of joy, talked about Pentecost, when people from at least twelve different nations were swept up in astonished joy on hearing the disciples of Jesus speaking to them in their own respective foreign languages. Those doing the speaking, observed Jennings, never imagined this would be the sign of the Spirit's coming. They had dreams of power. They didn't have dreams of speaking others' languages in ways that transcended their own particular group's vision of joy. Jesus, through the Holy Spirit, was reconfiguring the family of God, bringing each particular group's vision of joy together into a far more expansive and beautiful shared joy.[9]

IT'S ALL ABOUT BEING IN LOVE

Worship involves many "speech acts," Rebecca Slough said in an email exchange with me. The speech acts we use in gathered worship can also be natural parts of everyday speech, even if we haven't always recognized them as such. Take invoking or calling on God to be present, for example, which happens at the beginning of many worship services. While God is always present, to invoke God or call on the Holy Spirit to come is like a wake-up call for *us* to realize that God is with us in the present moment. Speech acts of worship include praising and thanking God or lamenting loss and evil, whether at home or at church. Confessing sin and releasing burdens of anxiety are speech acts of worship. So are encountering the Word of God and affirming our faith. These are powerful corporate speech acts at church, but they can happen around our tables when we read Scripture to each other or talk about what we believe, naming highlights and low points of our days. Petitioning God for help in times of need and praying for those we care about can be done both at church and around our tables or alone in our prayer corner. Offering ourselves and our resources in service to God, testifying to the ways we've seen God at work, and blessing each other as we go our separate ways to serve God can happen every day as we part for school and work, or corporately among other people of faith.

When we gather to worship and pray together as communities of faith, these speech acts orient our love, desires, commitments, allegiances, and hope as Christians toward our North Star—the God made known to us in Jesus Christ. When we practice calling on God, thanking and praising God, lamenting evil and confessing the wrongs we commit, praying for others, offering ourselves in service and blessing each other in the course of our everyday lives, these speech acts begin to wear grooves of familiarity into our consciousness.

For these speech acts to ring true, they must be rooted and grounded in love. "It's not what I think that shapes my life from the bottom up," asserts James Smith, "it's what I desire, what I love." Or, to put it another way, "our ultimate love is what we *worship*."[10] When we acknowledge a desire to orient our ultimate love toward God, we must learn to attune ourselves to God by practicing the language of prayer as the entryway into full-orbed worship.

"When we come home to the love of God, everything changes, beginning with how we pray," writes Elaine Heath.

At its foundation, prayer is "a contemplative soaking in the infinite love of God." This kind of prayer becomes the vital breath and heartbeat of divine energy. Within this kind of prayer, we sense the deep security of being safely held, the comfort of being safely anchored, and the assurance of guidance for a way forward.[11]

Heath spoke at a public conference I participated in, in fall of 2019. She made an intriguing assertion about the difference between good and bad theology. Good theology (in contrast to bad) helps us gaze into the face of Christ, she said, who gazes back with love. Building time into our normal rhythms to "soak in the love of God" and "gaze into the face of Christ" will directly affect the quality of our prayers—how we talk with God and about God.

God invites us to pray using God's intimate name, writes Andrew Root, which reveals that God is personal and wanting to engage in discourse with us. This is what personal beings do: share with one another through discourse and communication events. It is because God is a "speaking God" that we're invited to pray, he says. Through the Scriptures we see over and over how God announces Godself by speaking to us.[12] And we see how prayer figured large for Jesus, both for grounding his own ministry in love and as a ministry to those around him when his disciples, who often saw him pray, said: "Lord, teach us to pray" (Luke 11:1).

HOLD THE WORLD TOGETHER

Many of us hear public officials say "Our prayers are with you" to communities affected by one disaster or another, sometimes inviting the question of whether any tangible help will be forthcoming. Assuring someone we'll pray for them can sound wonderfully supportive. Or it may sound like a cop-out.

As I reflect on how to hold together prayer with action and worship with service, I like the image of a bowstring. How does one get the tension just right for making the best music?

The bowstring connectivity, for those who work to get the tension right, is powerful. Prayer and action, worship and service draw energy from each other. Those who learn to make music often emerge as leaders who minister healing to others—no matter where they work—at home, in the office, factory, or farm. What they receive from the sustaining love of God experienced in prayer and worship they generously offer to others.

There are many forms of prayer that when held together with action and service become a source of power and vision. And given that any one of us may not pray like the next person, it's important to talk with each other about how to experiment with ways to pray, and to search out a way to pray that may be more congenial than others, depending on one's lifestyle, patterns, and preferences.

Prayer is a specific kind of conversation, writes Christopher Smith; an ongoing dialogue between us and God. Prayer often starts in silence as we prepare for conversation—which is mostly not about our personal agendas but about an encounter. Drawing on practices of listening prayer like the Quaker tradition of silence and the Ignatian tradition of *examen*, people of faith discover that God speaks in different ways to different persons.[13]

There is *lectio divina*, or sacred reading. As a form of prayer, this slow, thoughtful reading and rereading of story, verse, or chapter of Scripture involves listening for a word or phrase that catches our attention, staying with that word or phrase for an extended time, and listening for insight, encouragement, or conviction prompted by the Spirit.

There is the prayer of *examen*, a review at the conclusion of the day, recalling moments when God seemed to come near and moments when God seemed distant; offering thanks for highlights, confessing wrongs done to others, releasing what lingers as regret or disappointment, resting in God's forgiving, reassuring love.

There is a centering prayer, like what I described in my morning ritual above, where a particular phrase, verse, or breath prayer is used to quiet and focus one's body, spirit, and mind: "Be still and know that I am God."

There are prayers of thanksgiving evoked throughout the day by all manner of undeserved gifts; a mindfulness alerted to frequently say thank you for all that is given—even the hard things that prompt us to more fully trust that the Spirit will sustain us.

There is the active prayer of walking the labyrinth, learning to pray with our bodies as we journey into and back out from the center. Such a prayer frees us to be present to what we carry—whether worry, fear, or pain—offering it with each step to the Holy One, anticipating an encounter with grace at the center of the inward journey, and words of assurance to carry us outward again.

There are communion prayers for approaching the Lord's table, where grace is both offered in the broken bread and cup of wine and makes its claim on our lives. Christ's body was broken. Christ's blood was spilled. Christ, who gave life rather than take life, invites us to his table—where, on receiving the "gifts of God for the people of God," we are made whole.

There are prayers of thanksgiving at the beginning of every meal, inviting our great God, the giver of all good, to accept our thanks and bless the food. Such prayers can seem perfunctory. I grieve when I see how even persons who grew up saying table prayers often seem too busy or distracted to say thank you. Out of embarrassment, there was a season that I chose not to pause for giving thanks in a restaurant. Now it is with joy that I pause, delighting in the gifts given and thankful for the many who worked hard so that we can enjoy tasty food.

There is the Lord's Prayer, one that wears deeper and deeper grooves into my own spirit over the years, often evoking tears of longing: "Thy kingdom come. Thy will be done on earth, as it is in heaven."

There is the prayer embedded in the Lord's Prayer, "Deliver us from evil," which is a prayer for freedom and shalom.[14] "Deliver us from evil" has become one of my more frequent breath prayers, and a prayer I offer nearly every day for those most dear to me, and for the whole world.

There are prayers of blessing for our children and grand-children as they leave for school, or at bedtime, or on starting a new job . . . "May the Lord bless you and keep you, may the Lord make his face to shine upon you, be gracious to you, and give you peace."

There is a prayer of rest—Sabbath rest—when we luxuriate in the freedom of time off; a gift so frequently emphasized throughout the Scriptures that unless one is being particularly dense, you can't help but wonder why the Creator made such a big deal about providing a day off, a day that at its root is an act of defiance against the notion that what we're created for is work, work, work—slaves of productivity and consumption that drive the economic machine of whatever political order we belong to.

Some prayer and worship happens around our kitchen and dining room tables. Some happens in chapels and church sanctuaries. Some happens as we walk wooded trails or sit on the deck by the lake. Some in soup kitchens and prison cells, dormitory rooms and offices.

Some prayer and worship happens in structured, regular patterns and some is more spontaneous, when the desire arises to be mindful, to cry out for help or sing hallelujahs. Prayer and worship are all about coming home to the love of God, and returning with fresh courage, renewed energy, refined passion to the daily tasks that fill our waking hours. Finding ways to encourage each other to hold prayer and action together with a fine-tuning of bowstrings will make a world of difference in the quality of music we make.

SPEAK FROM STORIED, HOLY GROUND

Friend and theologian Richard Kauffman acknowledged to me that he's come to the conclusion that testimony and prayer are the primary languages of faith. Testimony, he said, is what we say to others *about* God, and prayer is conversation *with* God. Testimony is telling what I've experienced in my own personal story of faith. Testimony is also talking to each other about the community's story of faith; the stories of those who've gone before us, including the saints. And the stories of Scripture: "A wandering Aramean was my ancestor" (Deuteronomy 26:5); and "Were not our hearts burning within us while he was talking to us on the road, while he was opening the scriptures to us?" (Luke 24:32).

When we dare to learn how to pray and how to talk about the ways in which God has shown up in our lives, there's a kind of grace that infuses the most ordinary moments of our lives—both personal and familial, and in our circle of friends or church. We don't get there quickly—without a lot of stumbles, awkward moments, and regrets—but that's what learning the art of talking about faith requires. Practice. It takes practice to learn to be genuine and natural; to speak about when we've sensed the Spirit's prompting, or felt convicted of dishonesty, or encouraged to be more courageous, or experienced something that defied explanation—something miraculous. We can learn to be truth-tellers—testifying in honest, authentic ways about what we've observed of God's activity in the mundane and in the more spectacular events of our lives.

I grew up in a subculture where following Christ meant practicing every day to be like Jesus. That may sound presumptuous, but it usually seemed worth trying; practicing to be like Jesus. At the breakfast table, we read Scripture, bowed our heads, and gave thanks. On Sundays we regularly worshiped together with those we called brothers and sisters in Christ. We committed to care for each other, and to be accountable to each other, and we meant it. We practiced confessing our sins, receiving and offering forgiveness. We sang hymns of praise and washed each other's feet. We prayed aloud and learned to talk about what we sensed God was wanting us to pay attention to. We made peace with God and neighbor before sharing in communion. We gave generously from our bounty to those in need. We traveled around the corner and sometimes great distances to tell the good news of Jesus to others, to bind up wounds, and to rebuild destroyed homes.

We were fairly simple, straightforward folk who said without batting an eye that Jesus meant it when he said, "Swear not at all; neither by heaven; for it is God's throne: Nor by the earth; for it is his footstool. . . . But let your communication be, Yea, yea; Nay, nay: for whatsoever is more than these cometh of evil" (Matthew 5:34-37 KJV). Yes, back in the day, we heard and memorized the Bible in King James English.

I remember hearing (with humble pride) that our Mennonite forebears had asked for and received special provision from the government to simply "affirm" when asked to swear an oath that we would tell the truth in a court of law. Telling the truth was a matter of integrity. An unadorned yes or no was sturdier than all the oaths in the world because it was spoken by a man or a woman whose word you could trust. That's what my forebears aspired to be, I was told: trustworthy people whose word rang true.

And such I felt called to be: a truth-teller. When invited early in my seminary career to name my calling, my vocation, I struggled to identify any particular career or profession. Instead, what I named to my conversation partner was that I am called to *integrity*. It matters to the core of my being that I ring true in body, mind, and spirit.

I remember memorizing Psalm 1 as a child. I loved the contrast it set out between the way of the wicked and those who delight in the law of the Lord. Its vivid images still make me happy: the fruit-filled tree planted by streams of water whose leaves don't wither. For some reason, I especially liked the image of the wicked being blown away like chaff—a powerful word to a child that basic life choices have life-and-death consequences.

Which brings us into the present frame. When it comes down to basic truthfulness, I'm a fairly simple person. I thank my Anabaptist forebears for the revulsion I feel to the mean-spirited distortions that are spewing forth in public discourse today. Though far from perfect and with plenty to regret, my Mennonite subculture daily schooled us to be honest citizens of God's kingdom on earth. This commitment to truthfulness was inseparably connected with prayer and worship—with assembling together in the presence of God in whom we individually and corporately live and move and have our being. This commitment to truthfulness daily reinforced for us the importance of learning the language of faith so that we were always prepared, as Peter, the close friend of Jesus, said, "to give an answer to everyone who asks you to give the reason for the hope that you have," and to do this "with gentleness and respect" (1 Peter 3:15 NIV).

It's times like these that bring us back to basics. One of Jesus' most devoted disciples described a daily workout this way: "Bless those who persecute you; bless and do not curse them. . . . Live in harmony with one another; do not be haughty, but associate with the lowly; do not claim to be wiser than you are. Do not repay anyone evil for evil, but take thought for what is noble in the sight of all. If it is possible, so far as it depends on you, live peaceably with all. . . . Do not be overcome by evil, but overcome evil with good" (Romans 12:14-21).

Learning the language of faith requires corporate worship where we can be truth-tellers, bringing our genuine selves, with our questions and God sightings, into a space that melds real life seamlessly with the beauty of ancient liturgy, Scripture, and song. Learning the language of faith requires prayers that bring us into the presence of God, where we can honestly name our thankfulness, fears, failures, and longings. In the company of other God seekers and seers who worship and pray together, we will learn a fluency inspired by the Holy Spirit that unleashes our tongues. We will learn to talk about what we've seen and heard of God's activity in the world. We will learn to express praises as broad as the sky and laments as deep as the ocean of God's love. We will discover how honest worship and prayer frees us to speak vulnerably with our children, colleagues, and friends about what it means to trust God and joyfully walk in the way of Jesus.

Conclusion

Talk about a confounding love story!

We talk about what we love. Learning the art of talking about faith will be like hiking the trails of what we love, further and further inward, toward the beating heart of those loves. And then outward with words that name what we've seen and heard. Talking faith isn't mostly about a set of doctrines or heady beliefs or a moral code—though it certainly benefits from wisdom in creeds and confessions of faith distilled over many generations of conversation about God. The warm full-blooded pulse that surges through our bodies, that animates our spirits and fires our imagination, is a mysterious love that "surpasses knowledge," that speaks our name, releases surprising power, and fills us full and running over.

There are many who tell stories, sing, write, paint, and dance rhapsodies about the love pulse they discover. The apostle Paul, who had been hell-bent on attacking anyone who didn't follow his version of God's moral code, doctrines, and heady beliefs, encountered Jesus in a blinding vision on the road to yet another city where he intended to dish out more hate. After that life-changing encounter, he couldn't keep quiet about the love story that upended his version of what faith was all about. He wrote often about love, as in his letter to his friends in Ephesus:

> For this reason I bow my knees before the Father, from whom every family in heaven and on earth takes its name. I pray that, according to the riches of his glory, he may grant that you may be strengthened in your inner being with power through his Spirit, and that Christ may dwell in your hearts through faith, as you are being rooted and grounded in love. I pray that you may have the power to comprehend, with all the saints, what is the breadth and length and height and depth, and to know the love of Christ that surpasses knowledge, so that you may be filled with all the fullness of God. (Ephesians 3:14-19)

As I wrote in the introduction, "When one is swept up into a love story, it's hard to keep quiet. Love, more than any state of being, compels us to find words, brings us to stammering speech; even on occasion to poetic eloquence. When we're in love, we grow animated. We take risks and say foolish things in the hope that love will carry the day."

As with so many things, it is that simple—giving voice to a story of love—and yet it's not simple at all. In *All about Love*, bell hooks describes how we're taught to believe that to talk about love is to be perceived as weak, even irrational. It's especially hard to talk about love "when what we have to say calls attention to the fact that lovelessness is more common than love, that many of us are not sure what we mean when we talk of love or how to express love." While we all learn that love is important, we're "bombarded by its failure." This bleak picture, however, doesn't diminish our longing. We constantly hope that love will prevail and we continue to believe in love's promise.[1]

I spoke in part 1 of what has contributed to the loss of our ability to talk about faith—the discrepancy we feel between the magnetic pull of our deepest longings toward a God of beauty, truth, and goodness and the contrived, false God that we find distasteful, dishonest, and untrustworthy. The anger, disappointment, or embarrassment that tied up our tongues can be honestly named—preparing the way to recover fluency in the language of faith.

Ruby Sales spoke in an interview about how love is not antithetical to being outraged and angry. There are two kinds of anger, she said—redemptive anger and non-redemptive anger. Redemptive anger is the anger that moves us to transformation and human up-building. Non-redemptive anger, on the other hand, is the anger that hate groups like white supremacists root themselves in. Anger itself isn't a bad emotion, but we have to be clear about the distinction.

Sales talked about getting involved in the Southern Freedom Movement not merely because she was angry about injustice, but because she loved the idea of justice. Many people talk about what we hate, but rarely about what it is we love. We need to begin the conversation, Sales said, by incorporating a vision of love with outrage about suffering and injustice. Love and outrage aren't over against each other. The reason we want to have justice is because we love—everybody.[2]

We will learn the lost art of talking faith when we name the anger we feel toward evil—all that destroys, denigrates, and undermines a life that is good. We'll learn the art of talking faith when we name evil for what it is—and rediscover the power of sacred words. We will learn the art of talking faith when we talk honestly about our bodies and how to cultivate resilience in hard times, and listen for wisdom's voice on the street corners and in the Scriptures. We'll learn more freedom in talking faith when we welcome what science reveals and activate a healthy curiosity about the world and God. We'll learn the art of talking faith when we revel in beauty and cultivate love for the wild, stupendous earth. We'll learn the art of talking faith when we root and ground ourselves in love animated by worship and prayer—in community. The confounding story of love is that we are most empowered to resist all manner of life-sapping evil by loving God and discovering that we are loved by God, who also loves every other creature the whole world round.

"'Weep! Weep!' calls a toad from the water's edge, writes Robin Wall Kimmerer. If grief—the twin sister to anger—can be "a doorway to love, then let us all weep for the world we are breaking apart so we can love it back to wholeness again."[3] We pursue faith, and the art of talking about faith, because our lives depend on it. Faith, however we think of it or name it, provides a space we all have in common—a shared space to talk about evil and good, lies and truth, ugliness and beauty, outrage and love.

"There is only one thing to live for: love," declared Thomas Merton. "There is only one unhappiness: not to love God."[4] Love in fact *is* the spiritual life, and without it all the other exercises of the spirit, however lofty, are emptied of content and become mere illusions.[5]

Discovering the countless ways all that is true, good, and beautiful emanates from God who is Love—who "fillest all things and is in all places"—is what the art of talking about faith is all about. *The more we feel the heartbeat of love*, the more we will join with others to repair injury, do justice, and protect what is true, good, and beautiful. The more we comprehend God as the "treasury of good things" and "giver of life," the more we will reach for words to describe what we love as the gifts of God whose *magnificent love is extended to us* in delectable food, a just law, a bird's song, a rowdy game of soccer, a trustworthy leader, a restored prairie, a team of peacemakers, a compassionate community of Jesus followers. People of faith—on saying thank you—find our tongues freed to tell the wonder.

Notes

INTRODUCTION

1 J. K. A. Smith, *Desiring the Kingdom: Worship, Worldview, and Cultural Formation* (Grand Rapids, MI: Baker Academic, 2009), 216; S. Coakley, *God, Sexuality, and the Self: An Essay "On the Trinity"* (Cambridge: Cambridge University Press, 2013), xv–xvi.

2 W. Brueggemann, *The Creative Word: Canon as a Model for Biblical Education* (Philadelphia: Fortress Press, 1982), 8ff.

3 Woman Wisdom is more commonly known by the name of Sophia from Greek translations of the Old Testament and in the New Testament. Others have used Lady Wisdom to name the female persona that is Wisdom in the biblical tradition.

4 G. P. Pemberton, *A Life That Is Good: The Message of Proverbs in a World Wanting Wisdom* (Grand Rapids, MI: Eerdmans, 2018), 125.

5 W. Brueggemann, "Jesus Acted Out the Alternative to Empire" (speech, Sojourners Summit for Change, Washington, D.C., June 15, 2018).

PART 1

1 N. Casey, "Thousands Once Spoke His Language in the Amazon. Now, He's the Only One," *New York Times*, December 26, 2017, https://www.nytimes.com/2017/12/26/world/americas/peru-amazon-the-end.html.

2 J. Merritt, *Learning to Speak God from Scratch: Why Sacred Words Are Vanishing—and How We Can Revive Them* (New York: Convergent, 2018), 52.

3 D. Thompson, "Three Decades Ago America Lost Its Religion. Why?" *The Atlantic*, September 26, 2019.

4 Merritt, *Learning to Speak God*, 17.

5 Merritt, 41–42.

6 M. S. Roth, "When Faith Comes Up, Students Avert Their Eyes," *The Atlantic*, September 1, 2019.

7 Quoted in "Sociologist Wade Clark Roof Dies at Age 80, " *Christian Century*, September 25, 2019, 17.

CHAPTER 1

1 A. Root, *The Pastor in a Secular Age: Ministry to People Who No Longer Need a God* (Grand Rapids, MI: Baker Academic, 2019), xxi.

2 A. Noble, *Disruptive Witness: Speaking Truth in a Distracted Age* (Downers Grove, IL: InterVarsity Press, 2018), 57–60.

3 K. Andersen, "How America Lost Its Mind," *The Atlantic*, September 2017.

4 S. Coakley, *God, Sexuality, and the Self: An Essay "On the Trinity"* (Cambridge: Cambridge University Press, 2013), xv–xvi.

5 W. H. Lamar IV, "It's Not Just the Coronavirus—Bad Theology Is Killing Us," *Faith & Leadership*, May 26, 2020.

6 Quoted in J. K. A. Smith, *Desiring the Kingdom: Worship, Worldview, and Cultural Formation* (Grand Rapids, MI: Baker Academic, 2009), 216.

7 Root, *Pastor in a Secular Age*, 226.

8 L. Daniel, *Tell It Like It Is: Reclaiming the Practice of Testimony* (Herndon, VA: Alban Institute, 2006), xv.

9 Daniel, 90.

10 Root, *Pastor in a Secular Age*, 189, 209.

CHAPTER 2

1 J. B. Grace, "American Delusions," *Christian Century*, March 14, 2018, 37.

2 E. K. Hackett, "Why I Stopped Talking about Racial Reconciliation and Started Talking about White Supremacy," March 25, 2020, https://www.inheritancemag.com/stories/why-i-stopped-talking-about-racial-reconciliation-and-started-talking-about-white-supremacy.

3 J. K. A. Smith, *Desiring the Kingdom: Worship, Worldview, and Cultural Formation* (Grand Rapids, MI: Baker Academic, 2009), 103.

4 T. Goricheva, *Talking about God Is Dangerous: The Diary of a Russian Dissident* (New York: Crossroad, 1987), 91, emphasis added.

5 T. Egan, "Why People Hate Religion," *New York Times*, August 30, 2019.

6 "In U.S., Decline of Christianity Continues at Rapid Pace," Pew Research Center, October 17, 2019, https://www.pewforum.org/2019/10/17/in-u-s-decline-of-christianity-continues-at-rapid-pace/.

7 A. Frykholm, "How to Talk to Climate Skeptics," *Christian Century*, March 14, 2018, 25.

8 A. Noble, *Disruptive Witness: Speaking Truth in a Distracted Age* (Downers Grove, IL: InterVarsity Press, 2018), 125–28.

9 Goricheva, *Talking about God*, 93.

10 M. Florer-Bixler, *Fire by Night: Finding God in the Pages of the Old Testament* (Harrisonburg, VA: Herald Press, 2019), 92–94.

CHAPTER 3

1 *Take Our Moments and Our Days: An Anabaptist Prayer Book*, prepared by A. P. Boers et al., 2 vol. (Scottdale, PA: Herald Press; Elkhart, IN: AMBS Institute of Mennonite Studies, 2007, 2010); also a downloadable app.

2 H. A. Russell, *Quantum Shift: Theological and Pastoral Implications of Contemporary Developments in Science* (Collegeville, MN: Liturgical Press, 2015), 182–85, 135.

3 R. Rohr, "Utterly Humbled by Mystery," NPR, *This I Believe* special series, December 18, 2006, available at https://www.npr.org/templates/story/story.php?storyId=6631954?storyId=6631954.

4 C. Smith, *The Bible Made Impossible: Why Biblicism Is Not a Truly Evangelical Reading of Scripture* (Grand Rapids, MI: Brazos Press, 2011), 69–70, 75–77, 89, 93.

5 Smith, 128.

6 S. Coakley, *God, Sexuality, and the Self: An Essay "On the Trinity"* (Cambridge: Cambridge University Press, 2013), 51.

7 Coakley, 51–52.

CHAPTER 4

1 J. Kenyon, "Cages," in *From Room to Room* (Farmington, MN: Alice James Books, 1978), quoted in S. Paulsell, *Honoring the Body: Meditations on a Christian Practice* (San Francisco: Jossey-Bass, 2002), xiii.

2 K. Tippett, *Speaking of Faith: Why Religion Matters—and How to Talk about It* (New York: Penguin Books, 2007), 216–19.

3 Paulsell, *Honoring the Body*, xiv, 12–13.

4 W. J. Jennings, *The Christian Imagination: Theology and the Origins of Race* (New Haven: Yale University Press, 2010), 2–4.

5 Jennings, 5.

6 C. L. Wenger and S. J. W. Wenger, as told to and shaped by D. A. Good and B. W. Good-White, *Bearing Fruit: A Collection of Memories* (Newton, KS: Mennonite Press Inc., 2017).

7 N. Gallagher, *Things Seen and Unseen: A Year Lived in Faith* (New York: Vintage Books, 1998), 8–9, 186.

8 R. Rohr, "Diversity and Communion," Center for Action and Contemplation, October 21, 2019, https://cac.org/diversity-and-communion-2019-10-21/.

9 S. Coakley, *God, Sexuality, and the Self: An Essay "On the Trinity"* (Cambridge: Cambridge University Press, 2013), 52.

CHAPTER 5

1 A. Lamott, *Bird by Bird: Some Instructions on Writing and Life* (New York: Knopf Doubleday, 1994), 22.

2 D. B. Bass, *Grounded: Finding God in the World—a Spiritual Revolution* (New York: HarperCollins, 2015), 15–16.

3 C. Smith, *The Bible Made Impossible: Why Biblicism Is Not a Truly Evangelical Reading of Scripture* (Grand Rapids, MI: Brazos Press, 2011), 62–64.

4 Bass, *Grounded*, 16.

5 W. Brueggemann, "Jesus Acted Out the Alternative to Empire" (speech, Sojourners Summit for Change, Washington, D.C., June 15, 2018).

6 K. Tippett, *Speaking of Faith: Why Religion Matters—and How to Talk about It* (New York: Penguin Books, 2007), 152–55.

7 R. Sales, "Where Does It Hurt?," interview by K. Tippett, *On Being*, September 15, 2016.

8 Brueggemann, "Jesus Acted Out."

9 Quoted in "Resurgence of Nationalism Is a 'Setback for Humanity,' Says German Theologian Jürgen Moltmann," *Christian Today*, December 4, 2019.

10 M. L. King Jr., *Where Do We Go from Here? Chaos or Community* (Boston: Beacon Press, 1967), 167, 171.

CHAPTER 6

1 J. Merritt, *Learning to Speak God from Scratch: Why Sacred Words Are Vanishing—and How We Can Revive Them* (New York: Convergent, 2018), 49–50, 56.

2 Books published included *Why Not Celebrate! A Wonderful Collection of Celebrations, Especially Useful for Families, Small Groups and Retreat* (Intercourse, PA: Good Books, 1987); *Coming Home: A Thoughtful Resource for Fathers, Mothers and the Rebirth of the Family* (Intercourse, PA: Good Books, 1992); and with Gerald Shenk, *Meditations for New Parents* (Harrisonburg, VA: Herald Press, 1996, rev. 2014).

3 S. W. Shenk, *And Then There Were Three: An Ode to Parenthood* (Scottdale, PA: Herald Press, 1985).

4 A. Root, *The Pastor in a Secular Age: Ministry to People Who No Longer Need a God* (Grand Rapids, MI: Baker Academic, 2019), xix.

5 Root, 188–89.

6 A. Noble, *Disruptive Witness: Speaking Truth in a Distracted Age* (Downers Grove, IL: InterVarsity Press, 2018), 3–4, 7, 18, 25.

7 Noble, 21–24.

8 "Preventing Suicides," *Christian Century*, August 28, 2019, 7.

9 G. P. Pemberton, *A Life That Is Good: The Message of Proverbs in a World Wanting Wisdom* (Grand Rapids, MI: Eerdmans, 2018), 126, 134.

10 Pemberton, 126–28.

11 M. E. Berry, "Gospel Work: The Need for Nonviolent Communication," *The Mennonite*, February 2018, 20–21, emphasis added.

12 Root, *Pastor in a Secular Age*, 275.

13 E. H. Peterson, *The Pastor: A Memoir* (New York: HarperCollins, 2011), 142, quoted in Root, 281.

14 R. W. Kimmerer, *Braiding Sweetgrass: Indigenous Wisdom, Scientific Knowledge and the Teachings of Plants* (Minneapolis: Milkweed Editions, 2013), 111–12.

PART 2

1 K. Tippett, *Speaking of Faith: Why Religion Matters—and How to Talk about It* (New York: Penguin Books, 2007), 6.

2 M. Florer-Bixler, *Fire by Night: Finding God in the Pages of the Old Testament* (Harrisonburg, VA: Herald Press, 2019), 159.

3 S. Paulsell, "Faith Matters: The Strange Stuff," *Christian Century*, December 18, 2019, 35.

4 S. Coakley, *God, Sexuality, and the Self: An Essay "On the Trinity"* (Cambridge: Cambridge University Press, 2013), 44–45.

5 R. Williams, *Wrestling with Angels: Conversations in Modern Theology* (Grand Rapids, MI: Eerdmans, 2007), 77, xix.

6 J. K. A. Smith, *Desiring the Kingdom: Worship, Worldview, and Cultural Formation* (Grand Rapids, MI: Baker Academic, 2009), 26–27, 176.

7 S. Paulsell, *Honoring the Body: Meditations on a Christian Practice* (San Francisco: Jossey-Bass, 2002), 145–47.

8 L. Daniel, *Tell It Like It Is: Reclaiming the Practice of Testimony* (Herndon, VA: Alban Institute, 2006), xv.

CHAPTER 7

1 J. Merritt, *Learning to Speak God from Scratch: Why Sacred Words Are Vanishing—and How We Can Revive Them* (New York: Convergent, 2018), 57–58.

2 Merritt, 61–72.

3 Merritt, 30–32.

4 M. Lind, *Ezekiel*, Believers Church Bible Commentary (Scottdale, PA: Herald Press, 1996). Insight above from 17–22, 32–37.

5 Lind, 349–53.

6 Merritt, *Learning to Speak*, 8.

7 K. Tippett, *Speaking of Faith: Why Religion Matters—and How to Talk about It* (New York: Penguin Books, 2007), 126.

8 A. Frykholm, "Improvising Freedom: Toni Morrison's Religious Vision," *Christian Century*, October 9, 2019, 30.

9 C. C. Smith, *How the Body of Christ Talks: Recovering the Practice of Conversation in the Church* (Grand Rapids, MI: Brazos Press, 2019), 149.

10 S. W. Shenk, "Repairing the Moral Canopy after Institutional Betrayal," in *Liberating the Politics of Jesus: Renewing Peace Theology through the Wisdom of Women*, ed. E. Soto Albrecht and D. Stevens (London: Bloomsbury, 2020).

11 Amy Gottlieb made these remarks in "A Book That Transformed Me," *Christian Century*, October 11, 2017, about Barbara Myerhoff's book based on anthropological research, titled *Number Our Days: A Triumph of Continuity and Culture among Jewish Old People in an Urban Ghetto* (New York: E. P. Dutton, 1978).

12 The first two stanzas of "The Love of God" hymn lyrics are by Frederick M. Lehman, 1917. The third verse quoted here, is traced back to a translation of an Aramaic poem, "Haddamut," written ca. 1050 by Rabbi Meir of Worms, Germany, and further back to the Qur'an (Sura 31) in the seventh century: "If all the trees on earth were pens, / and the ocean were ink, / replenished by seven more oceans, / the writing of God's wonderful signs and creations / would not be exhausted; / surely God is All-Mighty, All-Wise."

CHAPTER 8

1 T. Yoder Neufeld, *Ephesians*, Believers Church Bible Commentary (Scottdale, PA: Herald Press, 2002), 145, 151–54.

2 R. Rohr, "Universal Dignity in a Debauched Empire," Center for Action and Contemplation, May 15, 2017, https://cac.org/universal-dignity-debauched-empire-2017-05-15/.

3 T. Merton, *New Seeds of Contemplation* (New York: New Directions Books, 1962), 34–36.

4 L. Daniel, *Tell It Like It Is: Reclaiming the Practice of Testimony* (Herndon, VA: Alban Institute, 2006), 153, 156.

5 J. K. A. Smith, *Desiring the Kingdom: Worship, Worldview, and Cultural Formation* (Grand Rapids, MI: Baker Academic, 2009), 169.

6 S. Paulsell, *Honoring the Body: Meditations on a Christian Practice* (San Francisco: Jossey-Bass, 2002), 144.

7 Paulsell, 152–54.

8 R. Sales, "Where Does It Hurt?," interview by K. Tippett, *On Being*, September 15, 2016.

9 Drs. Brenda M. Alton, Roma Benjamin, and Drew Hart, "How the Church Views Racism," Facebook Live discussion, June 9, 2020.

10 C. C. Smith, *How the Body of Christ Talks: Recovering the Practice of Conversation in the Church* (Grand Rapids, MI: Brazos Press, 2019), 18.

11 Yoder Neufeld, *Ephesians*, 152.

12 C. C. Smith, *Body of Christ*, 5.

CHAPTER 9

1 W. Brueggemann, *The Creative Word: Canon as a Model for Biblical Education* (Philadelphia: Fortress Press, 1982), 28–30.

2 T. Goricheva, *Talking about God Is Dangerous: The Diary of a Russian Dissident* (New York: Crossroad, 1987), 96.

3 E. A. Heath, *The Mystic Way of Evangelism: A Contemplative Vision for Christian Outreach*, 2nd ed. (Grand Rapids, MI: Baker Academic, 2017), 17, with some expansion by the author.

4 M. Werntz, "Prayerful Resistance: Howard Thurman's Contemplative Nonviolence," *Christian Century*, August 28, 2019, 26–27.

5 Werntz, 29.

6 J. R. Payton Jr., "Crucified and Triumphant: The Cross Isn't Just about Suffering," *Christian Century*, September 11, 2019, 20–23.

7 K. Hennessy, *Dorothy Day: The World Will Be Saved by Beauty—an Intimate Portrait of My Grandmother* (New York: Scribner, 2017), 344.

8 Hennessy, 279.

9 L. Flowers and J. Bailey, "An Invitation to Brave Space," interview by K. Tippett, *On Being*, October 17, 2019.

10 K. Tippett, *Speaking of Faith: Why Religion Matters—and How to Talk about It* (New York: Penguin Books, 2007), 179.

CHAPTER 10

1 R. Rohr, "Utterly Humbled by Mystery," NPR, *This I Believe* special series, December 18, 2006, available at https://www.npr.org/templates/story/story.php?storyId=6631954?storyId=6631954.

2 G. P. Pemberton, *A Life That Is Good: The Message of Proverbs in a World Wanting Wisdom* (Grand Rapids, MI: Eerdmans, 2018), 93–94.

3 Pemberton, 31.

4 Pemberton, 8–9.

5 W. Brueggemann, *The Creative Word: Canon as a Model for Biblical Education* (Philadelphia: Fortress Press, 1982), 67, 71, 87.

6 Brueggemann, 84, 90.

7 Pemberton, *Life That Is Good*, 32, 90–91, 96.

8 Pemberton, 99, 106.

9 Bethany Tobin is an artist who is passionate about creating works of art that engage the life of discipleship to Christ. She has exhibited work in Virginia and North Carolina and completed several commissions and murals. She received a bachelor of fine arts in painting and drawing from James Madison University in 2006 and a masters of theological studies in theology and the arts from Duke University in 2009. Her website is https://bethanytobin.wordpress.com/2009/12/09/all-things-consist/.

10 D. L. Hayes, "Forged in the Fiery Furnace: African American Spirituality," *Sojourners*, August 2012.

11 D. L. Hayes, *No Crystal Stair: Womanist Spirituality* (Maryknoll, NY: Orbis Books, 2016), 43–44.

12 W. M. Swartley, *Jesus, Deliver Us: Evil, Exorcism, and Exousiai* (Eugene, OR: Cascade Books, 2019), 97. Italic in the original.

CHAPTER 11

1 A. Frykholm, "Improvising Freedom: Toni Morrison's Religious Vision," *Christian Century*, October 9, 2019, 31.

2 R. F. Capon, *The Supper of the Lamb: A Culinary Entertainment* (New York: Doubleday, 1969), 39–40.

3 M. Oliver, "Yes! No!," in *White Pine: Poems and Prose Poems* (Orlando: Harcourt, 1994), 8. First published 1991.

4 F. Foer, "Attention Is the Beginning of Devotion," *The Atlantic*, May 9, 2019.

5 Capon, *Supper of the Lamb*, 19.

6 R. Rohr, "Beholding," Center for Action and Contemplation, August 13, 2019, https://cac.org/beholding-2019-08-13/.

7 D. J. Duncan, *God Laughs and Plays: Churchless Sermons in Response to the Preachments of the Fundamentalist Right* (Great Barrington, MA: Triad Books, 2006), 203.

8 My localized adaptation of Duncan, 204.

9 J. K. A. Smith, *Desiring the Kingdom: Worship, Worldview, and Cultural Formation* (Grand Rapids, MI: Baker Academic, 2009), 19.

10 T. Merton, *The Wisdom of the Desert: Sayings from the Desert Fathers of the Fourth Century* (New York: New Directions Books, 1960), 6, 24, 14, 17–18.

11 Merton, 23.

12 M. Schertz, "A New Testament Reflection: Born in the Image, Redeemed by the Lamb," in *On Being Human: Sexual Orientation and the Image of God* (Eugene, OR: Cascade Books, 2011), 94–96.

CHAPTER 12

1 A. Petrusich, "Going Home with Wendell Berry," *New Yorker*, July 14, 2019.

2 W. Brueggemann, "Fall Books: Scripture as Real Presence: Sacramental Exegesis in the Early Church" (review), *Christian Century*, October 11, 2017, 51.

3 J. Byassee, "Rachel Held Evans, Public Theologian," *Christian Century*, September 11, 2019, 30. R. H. Evans quote from *Searching for Sunday: Loving, Leaving, and Finding the Church* (Nashville: Thomas Nelson, 2015), 149.

4 A phrase from "Alleluia, the Great Storm Is Over," text and music by Bob Franke (Peabody, MA: Telephone Pole Music, 1982).

5 K. Tippett, *Speaking of Faith: Why Religion Matters—and How to Talk about It* (New York: Penguin Books, 2007), 49–50.

6 W. Brueggemann, "Passion and Perspective: Two Dimensions of Education in the Bible," *Theology Today*, July 1985, 173.

CHAPTER 13

1 Quoted in W. M. Swartley, *Jesus, Deliver Us: Evil, Exorcism, and Exousiai* (Eugene, OR: Cascade Books, 2019), 15.

2 M. Berry, "Editorial," *Vision: A Journal for Church and Theology* 20, no. 2 (Fall 2019): 3.

3 Berry, 3.

4 D. Cramer, "An Open Apology to Kaitlin Courtice from a Baylor Alumnus," *Anabaptist Revisions* (blog), Patheos, February 17, 2020, https://www.patheos.com/blogs/anabaptistrevisions/2020/02/open-apology-kaitlin-curtice-from-baylor-alumnus/, summarizing Rich Meyer, "Behind Our Shared Forgetting," *Vision: A Journal for Church and Theology* 20, no. 2 (Fall 2019): 46–54.

5 Cramer.

6 Summarized in E. A. Heath, *The Mystic Way of Evangelism: A Contemplative Vision for Christian Outreach*, 2nd ed. (Grand Rapids, MI: Baker Academic, 2017), 30.

7 Heath, 30–32, 34, 36.

8 Heath, 37.

9 T. Goricheva, *Talking about God Is Dangerous: The Diary of a Russian Dissident* (New York: Crossroad, 1987), 17–18.

10 J. A. Fowler, *Becoming Adult, Becoming Christian: Adult Development and Christian Faith*, rev. ed. (San Francisco: Jossey-Bass, 1999), 140.

11 H. Haverkamp, "Thoroughly Sinful: Learning to Love the Doctrine of Total Depravity," *Christian Century*, October 9, 2019, 28–29.

12 Goricheva, *Talking about God*, 10.

13 Fowler, *Becoming Adult, Becoming Christian*, 140.

CHAPTER 14

1 M. O'Brien, "Will Beauty Save the World?," *Dappled Things: A Quarterly of Ideas, Art and Faith* (blog), accessed October 29, 2020, https://dappledthings.org/4266/will-beauty-save-the-world/.

2 K. Hennessy, *Dorothy Day: The World Will Be Saved by Beauty: An Intimate Portrait of My Grandmother* (New York: Scribner, 2017), ix.

3 J. O'Donohue, *Beauty: The Invisible Embrace. Rediscovering the True Sources of Compassion, Serenity, and Hope* (New York: HarperCollins, 2004), 3, 5–6.

4 E. Scarry, *On Beauty: And Being Just* (Princeton: Princeton University Press, 1999), 23–25, 31, 57, 89–90, 112.

5 D. Levertov, "Primary Wonder," in *Selected Poems* (New York: New Directions, 2002), 192.

6 O'Donohue, *Beauty*, 226.

7 F. S. Collins, *The Language of God: A Scientist Presents Evidence for Belief* (New York: Free Press, 2006), 36. Collins is, to date, the

longest-serving chief of the National Institutes of Health, and the 2020 recipient of the Templeton Prize in Religion and Science.

8 C. Pepinster, RNS reported as "Evensong Services Draw a Crowd in Britain Even as Church Attendance Declines," *Christian Century*, October 11, 2017, 22.

9 B. Zahnd, *Beauty Will Save the World: Rediscovering the Allure and Mystery of Christianity* (Lake Mary, FL: Charisma House, 2012), 208.

10 R. F. Capon, *The Supper of the Lamb: A Culinary Entertainment* (New York: Doubleday, 1969), 190.

11 M. Oliver, "Good Morning," in *Blue Horses: Poems* (New York: Penguin Press, 2014), 22.

12 E. Wiesel, *The Gates of the Forest* (New York: Schocken Books, 1966), 194.

13 Wiesel, 189.

14 Wiesel, 198.

CHAPTER 15

1 "A Prophet's Speech," *Christian Century*, October 23, 2019, 7.

2 R. Rohr, "Time To Grow Up," Center for Action and Contemplation "Daily Meditations," February 4, 2013.

3 M. J. Gorman, *Participating in Christ: Explorations in Paul's Theology and Spirituality* (Grand Rapids, MI: Baker Academic, 2019), 240.

4 R. W. Kimmerer, *Braiding Sweetgrass: Indigenous Wisdom, Scientific Knowledge, and the Teachings of Plants* (Minneapolis: Milkweed Editions, 2013), 24, 154.

5 M. Oliver, "Something," in *Why I Wake Early* (Boston: Beacon Press, 2004), 38.

6 Kimmerer, *Braiding Sweetgrass*, 201, 208.

7 H. A. Russell, *Quantum Shift: Theological and Pastoral Implications of Contemporary Developments in Science* (Collegeville, MN: Liturgical Press, 2015), 120.

8 J. Lambert, "We've Lost 3 Billion Birds Since 1970 in North America," Science News, September 19, 2019, https://www.sciencenews.org/article/3-billion-birds-lost-since-1970-north-america.

9 D. D. Murphy, "Faith Matters: Reading Genesis in a Dying World," *Christian Century*, October 23, 2019, 51.

10 A. Frykholm, "How to Talk to Climate Skeptics," *Christian Century*, March 14, 2018, 25–27.

11 Quoted in E. A. Heath, *The Mystic Way of Evangelism: A Contemplative Vision for Christian Outreach*, 2nd ed. (Grand Rapids, MI: Baker Academic, 2017), 95.

12 J. K. A. Smith, *Desiring the Kingdom: Worship, Worldview, and Cultural Formation* (Grand Rapids, MI: Baker Academic, 2009), 141–42.

13 Smith, 147–48.

14 N. Wirzba, "A Book That Transformed Me," *Christian Century*, October 11, 2017, 34–35.

15 MennoMedia published this meditation titled "When All You Unknowingly Leaned On Has Fallen" as a *Leader* resource, April 7, 2020. The phrase "all you unknowingly leaned on has fallen" is from "For Courage" in J. O'Donohue, *To Bless the Space between Us: A Book of Blessings* (New York: Doubleday, 2008), 107.

CHAPTER 16

1 P. Wehner, "NIH Director: 'We're on an Exponential Curve,'" *The Atlantic*, March 17, 2020.

2 Quoted in K. Tippett, *Speaking of Faith: Why Religion Matters—and How to Talk about It* (New York: Penguin Books, 2007), 100–1.

3 F. S. Collins, *The Language of God: A Scientist Presents Evidence for Belief* (New York: Free Press, 2006), 5–6, 176–78.

4 Collins, 54, 64–66.

5 Collins, 67.

6 B. Brown, *Rising Strong: How the Ability to Reset Transforms the Way We Live, Love, Parent, and Lead* (New York: Random House, 2017), xiii.

7 M. Higgins, *Thomas Merton: Faithful Visionary* (Collegeville, MN: Liturgical Press, 2014), 36.

8 Quoted in P. Piazza, "Chronicles of the Cosmic Christ," *Washington Post*, January 14, 1979.

9 Collins, *Language of God*, 211, 230.

10 R. W. Kimmerer, *Braiding Sweetgrass: Indigenous Wisdom, Scientific Knowledge and the Teachings of Plants* (Minneapolis: Milkweed Editions, 2013), 45.

11 Kimmerer, 46–47.

12 S. W. Shenk, *Anabaptist Ways of Knowing: A Conversation about Tradition-Based Critical Education* (Telford, PA: Cascadia Publishing, 2003).

13 W. M. Swartley, *Jesus, Deliver Us: Evil, Exorcism, and Exousiai* (Eugene, OR: Cascade Books, 2019), 288. Swartley notes that theologian Marva Dawn observes, however, that there are also spiritual forces that exist apart from "material agents" and so, while it is right not to impose a "false dualism of matter and spirit" on biblical texts as has so often been done, it seems important not to eliminate "a different realm of spiritual forces separate from material agents" as players in the cosmic battles between forces of good and evil.

14 H. A. Russell, *Quantum Shift: Theological and Pastoral Implications of Contemporary Developments in Science* (Collegeville, MN: Liturgical Press, 2015), 61.

15 Russell, 30–31, 35, xxv, 64.

16 Kimmerer, *Braiding Sweetgrass*, 346–47.

17 W. Brueggemann, *The Creative Word: Canon as a Model for Biblical Education* (Philadelphia: Fortress Press, 1982), 67, 71, 87.

18 Collins, *Language of God*, 146, 161, 99.

19 Collins, 198–99, 201.

20 Russell, *Quantum Shift*, xxi.

21 Collins, *Language of God*, 198.

CHAPTER 17

1 *Take Our Moments and Our Days: An Anabaptist Prayer Book*, prepared by A. P. Boers et al., 2 vol. (Scottdale, PA: Herald Press; Elkhart, IN: AMBS Institute of Mennonite Studies, 2007, 2010); also a downloadable app.

2 J. K. A. Smith, *Desiring the Kingdom: Worship, Worldview, and Cultural Formation* (Grand Rapids, MI: Baker Academic, 2009), 162–66.

3 S. Coakley, *God, Sexuality, and the Self: An Essay "On the Trinity"* (Cambridge: Cambridge University Press, 2013), 19, 48.

4 J. K. A. Smith, *Desiring the Kingdom*, 11, 121–22.

5 W. M. Swartley, *Jesus, Deliver Us: Evil, Exorcism, and Exousiai* (Eugene, OR: Cascade Books, 2019), 196–97.

6 Swartley, quoting Alan Kreider and Origen, 232–33, 235.

7   C. C. Smith, *How the Body of Christ Talks: Recovering the
     Practice of Conversation in the Church* (Grand Rapids, MI: Brazos
     Press, 2019), 93.

8   Coakley, *God, Sexuality, and the Self*, 45–6, 55–56.

9   "Theology of Joy: Willie James Jennings with Miroslav Volf,"
     Yale Center for Faith and Culture Theology of Joy consultation,
     September 19, 2014, YouTube video, 20:28, https://www.youtube.
     com/watch?v=1fKD4Msh3rE.

10 J. K. A. Smith, *Desiring the Kingdom*, 51.

11 E. A. Heath, *The Mystic Way of Evangelism: A Contemplative
     Vision for Christian Outreach*, 2nd ed. (Grand Rapids, MI: Baker
     Academic, 2017), 72.

12 A. Root, *The Pastor in a Secular Age: Ministry to People Who No
     Longer Need a God* (Grand Rapids, MI: Baker Academic, 2019),
     274–75.

13 C. C. Smith, *Body of Christ*, 83, 85, 87.

14 Swartley, *Jesus, Deliver Us*, 1.

CONCLUSION

1   b. hooks, *All about Love: New Visions* (New York: Harper,
     2000), xxvii.

2   R. Sales, "Where Does It Hurt?," interview by K. Tippett, *On
     Being*, September 15, 2016.

3   R. W. Kimmerer, *Braiding Sweetgrass: Indigenous Wisdom,
     Scientific Knowledge and the Teachings of Plants* (Minneapolis:
     Milkweed Editions, 2013), 359.

4   T. P McDonnell, ed., *A Thomas Merton Reader* (New York: Image,
     1974 reissue), 185.

5   T. Merton, *The Wisdom of the Desert: Sayings from the Desert
     Fathers of the Fourth Century* (New York: New Directions Books,
     1960), 17.

The Author

Sara Wenger Shenk is a theologian, preacher, and the author of six books. She is President Emerita of Anabaptist Mennonite Biblical Seminary (AMBS) where she served for nine years. Her blog, *Practicing Reconciliation*, was lauded as a steady and deeply theological resource in anxious and polarized times. Shenk earned degrees from Eastern Mennonite University,  Garrett-Evangelical Theological Seminary, and Union Presbyterian Seminary in Richmond, Virginia. For nine years, she and her husband, Gerald Shenk, served as students and teachers in the former Yugoslavia, and she has served on the faculty and administration of Eastern Mennonite Seminary.